The Long Game

The Long Game

Inside Sinn Féin

AOIFE MOORE

SANDYCOVE

an imprint of

PENGUIN BOOKS

SANDYCOVE

UK | USA | Canada | Ireland | Australia
India | New Zealand | South Africa

Sandycove is part of the Penguin Random House group of companies
whose addresses can be found at global.penguinrandomhouse.com.

First published 2023
002

Copyright © Aoife Moore, 2023

The moral right of the author has been asserted

Set in 13.5/16pt Garamond MT Std
Typeset by Jouve (UK), Milton Keynes
Printed and bound in Great Britain by Clays Ltd, Elcograf S.p.A.

The authorized representative in the EEA is Penguin Random House Ireland,
Morrison Chambers, 32 Nassau Street, Dublin D02 YH68

A CIP catalogue record for this book is available from the British Library

Trade paperback ISBN: 978–1–844–88579–4

www.greenpenguin.co.uk

For me daddy, who loves this type of book,
and for me mammy, who really doesn't.

Contents

'An nathair nimhe': A Note on Sources

In April 2021, upon signing the contract to write this book, the first person I told was the president of Sinn Féin, Mary Lou McDonald. We stood alone in the car park of Leinster House. I told her what I wanted to do: write a fair and accurate account of the recent history of the most popular political party on the island, without fear or favour.

I told McDonald first because I felt that, as the leader of the party, she should hear about it directly from me. 'No better woman,' she said, when I told her my news.

She enquired about my parents, who 'must be so proud'. I asked for her cooperation. I was aware that Sinn Féin tended to view the media as hostile, and were sometimes quick to sue. But I had a good working relationship with McDonald, and I knew that Sinn Féin played favourites when it came to media. I told her that I felt she knew me, and knew my background, coming from a working-class nationalist area of Derry and a family touched by British state violence.

McDonald asked if she could tell 'Michelle and Pearse'. I said yes, but I asked her not to write it down in an email until I had a research plan and an interview schedule. She agreed, and wished me well.

In the early days, I spoke with people in the Sinn Féin press office in Belfast, many of whom I have known for years through my work as a journalist. They wanted a written proposal for the interview requests, specifying who I wished to speak to, what I wanted from them and what the book was about. The first email was sent on 20 May 2021 and re-sent three days later, noting McDonald's approval.

In a follow-up phone call, the press officer said to me: 'They want this published before the next election to try and damage us.' I had no idea who 'they' were supposed to be, and I said as much to the press officer.

I contacted a number of TDs and MPs in the early days, all of whom agreed to an interview. One date was set for a chat in Fermanagh, and the friendly representative offered to make me lunch while I was there. But then this interview was cancelled, as were all of the others.

I received a call from one press officer who accused me of misleading the representatives and of previously lying about a former Sinn Féin MP. When I refuted the allegation, he said: 'Don't worry, we remember things like that.'

At the end of the summer of 2021, I approached McDonald again for an interview in Leinster House. We stood in the sunshine while I pleaded for an answer either way on cooperation. I told her the press office had been difficult and obstructive. She sympathized, and said she would get back to me. But she didn't.

I decided to email weekly, repeating the request, until I received an email from a Belfast solicitor representing Sinn Féin, Pádraig Ó Muirigh, on 8 March 2022.

Dear Aoife,

Re: My client Sinn Féin

I refer to the above, whom I represent, and your request for a 'formal interview' with Sinn Féin elected representatives and staff in relation to your forthcoming book.

I would be obliged if you could confirm those Sinn Féin elected representatives and staff whom you are referring to and provide a summary of the allegations alleged and/or a copy of the relevant extracts of your book. On receipt of same I will consult with my client before reverting to you in relation to any right of reply.

My client has instructed that any further queries in relation to this matter are forwarded to our office, and not directly to Sinn Féin.

Politicians who I dealt with on a daily basis refused my requests for interviews. Staff were told to ignore me and refuse interviews.

McDonald, who had often stopped and chatted, ignored me in the corridor, refused to meet my eye.

The Sinn Féin politicians and officials who spoke to me for this book did so in secret, without party approval. As I worked, I heard that the party had become nervous about reports that people had been speaking to me. The press officer who told me that the party 'remember things' maligned me to other Sinn Féin members and representatives. The moniker he gave me was 'an nathair nimhe': 'the poisonous snake'.

Then Shane Ross came along.

In October 2022, journalist and former government minister Shane Ross published a biography of Mary Lou McDonald. The book documented the life of the Sinn Féin leader whose middle-class upbringing made her an anomaly. The book attracted much attention and sold well, but it was not especially explosive. The biggest story to emerge from it related to Ross's questioning of where McDonald and her husband got the money to buy and extend their impressive house.

Two weeks after the book's publication, Joe Lynch called. The Cork man is Sinn Féin's head of press for 'the twenty-six counties' and he wanted to talk about my book. We met in Buswell's Hotel, opposite Dáil Éireann, along with Siobhán Fenton, a former BBC journalist and author who is now a senior communications operative in the party.

Lynch said that the party might be willing to cooperate now. 'It's nothing personal,' he said. 'We don't cooperate with anyone, but we might make an exception.'

When I queried whether this newfound friendliness was related to the negative press surrounding the Ross debacle, he replied: 'No comment.'

In the aftermath, an absent-minded TD mentioned that a list of people who were allowed to speak to me had been compiled. If you weren't on the list, you were not to reply. 'I don't know if I'm on the list yet,' he said.

When I told him that he had given away the existence of a list, he replied: 'Ah fuck.'

On 6 November 2022, Mary Lou McDonald said on the Newstalk radio show *On the Record with Gavan Reilly* that 'to the best of [her] knowledge' I had never asked for an interview with her. This is false. Even if she knew nothing of my dealings with the press office, I spoke to McDonald three times in person seeking an interview.

Later that month, I drove for two hours from Dublin to Stormont to interview Michelle O'Neill and Conor Murphy. When I arrived I was told that both had been called away on last-minute business. I was given twenty minutes with Gerry Kelly. In the end, I conducted interviews with four current Sinn Féin representatives through official party channels. They didn't tell me much.

None of this was especially surprising, given Sinn Féin's deep-seated instinct for secrecy and mistrust of the media.

If I had felt that a book about Sinn Féin depended on the co-operation of McDonald and other top figures in the party, I would never have taken the project on. I believed that there would be Sinn Féin members and elected representatives, past and present, who would be willing to speak to me even without the blessing of the party, and that they would be my best sources. So it has proved. The stories and documents they shared have given me remarkable insight into the workings of the strange, secretive party that stands on the brink of taking power in Ireland.

In researching this book, I conducted interviews in every corner of the island of Ireland, as well as internationally, with present and former members of Sinn Féin. Former members of the Provisional IRA, and current and former elected representatives from other political parties, also spoke to me, as did former and current members of the British and Irish security services. Books about Irish history and politics tend to be dominated by male voices, and so I made a particular effort to speak to as many women as possible.

Some of the people I interviewed swore an oath, when they joined the Provisional IRA, to follow the precepts of the IRA's 'Green Book', including: 'Your prime duty is to remain unknown to the enemy forces and the public at large.' Although the IRA's campaign is long over, many former volunteers still feel the force of that oath. Accordingly, such people spoke to me on the condition that I would not use their names. Similarly, many Sinn Féin members without a paramilitary past are acutely aware of the party's culture of secrecy, and they too spoke to me on this condition (and without the knowledge of their party leadership). I was willing to agree to the condition on the basis that it was necessary for the protection of people's careers and, in some cases, their personal welfare; and because few members of the republican movement would have spoken on any other basis. It is thanks to these people that this book was possible.

Prologue

Two Bombs in Derry, 1990

On the last Sunday of January 1990, a crowd of some 5,000 people gathered in Derry to mark the eighteenth anniversary of Bloody Sunday. They followed the route of the civil rights march that had ended in the massacre of fourteen marchers by British paratroopers in 1972: one of the defining atrocities of the Troubles, and a huge recruiting tool for the IRA.

The Troubles were far from over, and British soldiers took up positions behind the turrets of the city's medieval walls, which afforded a clear vantage of the Bogside, the overwhelmingly Catholic area west of the river Foyle.

Some of the people who turned out for the demonstration were family members, friends and neighbours of those who had been killed and injured on Bloody Sunday. Others were republican activists who had travelled to Derry for the occasion. Among the latter was Charles 'Cha' Love, a sixteen-year-old from Strabane, Co. Tyrone, about a half-hour's drive from Derry. In his spare time, Cha sold copies of *An Phoblacht*, the Sinn Féin newspaper, and collected money for the Prisoners' Dependants Fund. He was also a fan of Def Leppard, Bon Jovi and Whitesnake. In the autumn of that year, he was due to travel to New York to spend a year living with a host family and attending a local high school. He had met the family as part of one of the many 'peace projects' that brought Catholic and Protestant youths together in ways that were often impossible in Northern Ireland. The theory was that those children who lived alongside each other would be less likely to throw bombs at each other in the future.

Cha had travelled to Derry on the bus with two friends. He was near Free Derry Corner, awaiting the speeches, when there was an explosion from the direction of the city walls.

Chunks of stone and masonry shot into the air and flew towards the marchers. One of them struck Cha on the head. He fell to the ground. Debris rained down after the explosion as women and children screamed while running for cover from the hail of rock. Someone ran from a house in Glenfada Park and wrapped Charles in a pink blanket. There was a plume of black smoke and a hole had been blasted into the wall where the bomb had been set. Sinn Féin president Gerry Adams was among the people present who watched on in horror.

The *Irish Times* journalist Mary Holland described what happened next:

> There were sharp light showers in the city that afternoon, and when the ambulance had taken the dying boy to Altnagelvin hospital, those who had crowded round him stood looking at his blood mixing with the falling rain on the ground.
>
> At about a quarter to five, two middle-aged men came from one of the houses nearby, carrying a bucket of warm water and a stiff garden broom. They swept the pavement clean, Charles Love's life-blood lapping with the water in the gutter and slipping gently down a drain in the road.

Mitchel McLaughlin, a former general secretary of Sinn Féin, had helped set up the Bloody Sunday Initiative to campaign for justice for the victims of the massacre and their families. The group was non-political, but was backed by both Sinn Féin and the SDLP. The annual march was part of the group's campaign to pressure the British state into conducting a full inquiry into the massacre.

McLaughlin lived in a two-up, two-down house in Blucher Street in the heart of the Bogside, a short walk from Free Derry Corner. It was in that house that a group of activists – march organizers, Sinn Féin members, IRA members, and some people who were all three – gathered that evening in the aftermath of the killing of Cha Love. The atmosphere was one of dread as McLaughlin's wife, Mary Lou, made tea and the room filled with cigarette smoke. Senior Sinn Féin figures Gerry O'Hara and Jim Gibney were among a number of men who stood with their backs to the wall in the cramped living room as condensation fogged the windows.

One of those present, who had planted bombs in the name of Irish freedom, told me that the death of Charles Love caused him to question the efficacy of armed struggle, and that he never returned to it.

While the six o'clock news blared on the living room TV, Paul Hill stood in the hall having an argument with his solicitor on the house phone. Hill, one of the Guildford Four, had come to Derry to give a speech at the demonstration. Despite the killing of Charles Love, the speeches had gone ahead, and Paul Hill had told the crowd that he abhorred violence. He and the other members of the Guildford Four had been falsely convicted of perpetrating two bombings in Surrey in 1974, and spent fourteen years in prison before being exonerated and released three months before the Derry march. The subsequent exoneration of Hill and the other three young people was among the biggest embarrassments the British justice system had ever endured. Though he was a free man, Hill's movements were being closely monitored. Now, his solicitor was begging him to leave Derry immediately: the solicitor felt he should not be linked to anything to do with the conflict. Hill refused.

Martin McGuinness wasn't there in McLaughlin's living room: he had other things to do.

He was the IRA's Officer Commanding in Derry, and a member of the Army Council. He had also been involved in electoral politics for Sinn Féin for a number of years. He had won a seat in the Ulster Assembly elections in 1982, and unsuccessfully contested the Westminster seat to represent his home town in 1983 and 1987. By 1986, the Assembly had dissolved with McGuinness never having taken his seat, owing to Sinn Féin's abstention from the government institutions on the island of Ireland and in Britain.

McGuinness knew that the bomb that had rained death on a young republican activist preparing to march in the Bogside had been the work of the IRA. He also knew that everyone in the community was aware that the IRA would never place a bomb in Derry without him knowing about it.

The bomb had been placed in the city walls with the intention that it would explode inward, towards the soldiers who would be monitoring the march from on high. Instead, the force went outwards, towards the Bogside and Cha Love, blasting debris at full force at the crowd gathered below. Where McGuinness went that night is unknown, but his comrades assume that he visited those involved with the bombing to find out what had happened.

By the following day, the IRA had claimed responsibility for the bombing and said it regretted the death of the young bystander, which it called a 'freak accident'.

On Monday, it was time for damage control. McGuinness

spoke to the press, calling Cha's death 'a tragedy'. He went on: 'There will be those who will compound his family's grief by their political exploitation of his death . . . I do not imagine for one second that the IRA sought to deliberately kill civilians.'

McGuinness visited the march organizers next, because their judgement on what had happened would set the tone for the rest of the city and the republican movement beyond. He leaned on the organizers not to condemn the IRA's actions too strongly.

The media had already called the Bloody Sunday Initiative and a statement was expected. McGuinness got sight of the draft statement and cajoled the group into a softer line. He took issue with certain words, asked for sentences to be removed, and reminded those present that the real enemy was the British Army. Not the people who had planted a bomb in a crowded urban setting, on a hallowed day, and killed a child.

In the end, the statement released by the Bloody Sunday Initiative described the bomb as 'a gross error of judgement by the IRA for which they must be severely criticised'.

Even if the bombing had not gone horribly wrong, it would have been seen in the area as a strange misjudgement by the IRA. A Bloody Sunday commemoration, in memory of peaceful civil rights marchers who had been massacred, with thousands of nationalists gathered nearby, was not the time or the place to try to attack the security forces.

One way of understanding the fiasco is in the context of tension within the republican movement between those who wished to pursue electoral politics and those who felt that armed struggle was the only legitimate pathway. One specific theory, articulated by the journalist and activist Eamonn McCann, holds that the Derry bomb was intended to send a message to those at high levels of the movement who were committed to ending the conflict via peaceful means: 'March all you like, was the message, [but] it's us, the army of the people, who will hand you down freedom.'

In the days following Charles Love's death, around a hundred senior figures in the IRA and Sinn Féin gathered in Conway Mill on Conway Street, off the Falls Road in republican west Belfast. The room was cold. The room was always cold. The abandoned mill had long been out of use and the windows rattled in the February wind.

The mood was tense as people filed into their seats.

The debate was closed down before it even got started. It was clear to those present that the IRA commanders there were not happy to have a discussion on the fatal blunder in Derry. Appeals for discussion on how and why it had happened were dismissed.

The commanders told those present that they had held an investigation into the events that led to Charles Love's death. A view had formed that an informer had been involved, that the British troops had been tipped off and that they had tampered with the bomb so that its force would be aimed towards the crowds in the Bogside below the city walls. Conspiracy theories were often employed during those fraught times, to cover for fatal stupidity.

You didn't have to believe them, but you didn't argue with them. No one has ever been held accountable for the bomb that killed Charles Love – not by the state, nor by the IRA's ruthless internal discipline.

There was a debate a month later at the Sinn Féin Ard Fheis. A report from the party leadership had attributed part of the blame for a decline in the party's vote to 'IRA operations that went wrong'. The *Irish Times*'s report on the 1990 Ard Fheis states: 'However, in spite of the embarrassment caused to the party by the killing of Charles Love during last Sunday's demonstration, it is understood there are no moves to disband the IRA unit responsible or to expel its members.'

Patsy Gillespie was forty-two years old, and father to three children with his wife, Kathleen, when IRA operatives in Derry chained him to the steering wheel and pedals of a van containing explosives and forced him to drive to the Donegal border, while following closely behind in a second vehicle.

The IRA men held Gillespie's family at gunpoint in their home in Shantallow while their husband and father was driven to his death. He had told Kathleen he would be home soon.

This wasn't the first time Gillespie had been targeted in this way by the IRA, who viewed him as a 'legitimate target' because he worked as a civilian cook in a British Army canteen within Fort George. He had previously been forced to drive a bomb into his place of work, but had escaped without injury.

The use of the chains was new. Gillespie must've known he wouldn't get away this time.

It was 4am when the 1,200lb bomb exploded at the Coshquin barracks. Patsy Gillespie and five British soldiers were killed. It's believed that Gillespie's shouts of warning as he slowed the van at the checkpoint helped save other lives.

Kathleen later recalled a policeman telling a subsequent inquest of finding a human heart while investigating the bomb site. 'When I thought about it, I thought, "He is talking about bits of Patsy's body."'

Patsy Gillespie was identified by a piece of flesh attached to a zip belonging to the grey cardigan he was wearing when he was taken from his family. The zip was found on the roof of a bar in Co. Donegal.

The use of a civilian in this way horrified the public, and the Derry brigade of the IRA came under severe criticism both internally and externally. In one private meeting of IRA leadership, a Belfast quartermaster took off his shoe while smoking a cigarette and blew smoke into it. He held the shoe out to McGuinness with the smoke rising from it and said: 'What's this, Martin?'

McGuinness, incredulous, said nothing.

'That's Patsy Gillespie,' the Belfast man said.

'That's sick,' McGuinness replied.

'No, Martin, that was a joke. What's sick is strapping that man to a bomb and blowing him up. And not only is it sick, it's a bit counterproductive.'

In truth, it seems clear that McGuinness had come to the same conclusion about the IRA's campaign.

Numerous former combatants have told me that, by this time, McGuinness had given up on the IRA ever being able to bomb or murder the British out of Ireland, and spent most of his time trying to convince others that the path of violence had to be abandoned.

The tragedy was that, despite the understanding at the top of the republican movement that violence was never going to achieve its aims, the killing continued. Even as civilians continued to die on the streets of Derry, Belfast, London and other cities, towns and villages, the movement was undergoing a murderously slow transformation. By degrees, initiative was shifting away from the bombers and towards the politicians. It happened far too late for Cha Love, Patsy Gillespie, and their families and friends. But a new incarnation of Sinn Féin was being born, setting out on the long road to taking power in Ireland.

1. 'The IRA will decide'

In February 1974, a general election was called in the United Kingdom. In the Belfast West constituency, the sitting MP was Gerry Fitt. The co-founder of the small Republican Labour party in 1963, Fitt had first won the seat in 1966. In 1970, he had defeated the only other candidate, the Unionist Party's Brian McRoberts, by just over 3,000 votes. Now, in 1974, things had changed. Nearly five years into the Troubles, Fitt was standing for re-election as leader of the SDLP. The party had been formed in August 1970 and quickly established itself as the political home for non-sectarian and non-violent nationalist principles at a time when Northern Ireland was gripped by conflict.

For those who supported the Provisional IRA or other armed republican groups, the electoral options were far from obvious. In February 1974, Provisional Sinn Féin, as the party was then known, was forbidden from contesting elections in the UK – a ban that would be lifted in May of that year. The ban made no practical difference at that point, as the party was ideologically committed to a refusal to participate in elections in any jurisdiction: a central issue in the republican split in the winter of 1969–70.

Among the other candidates to stand for Belfast West in 1974 was John Brady, representing the Republican Clubs: the political wing of the Official republican movement.

And then there was Albert Price.

Born in west Belfast, Albert Price had joined the IRA in

the 1930s and played a part in the bombing campaign carried out in England in 1939 and 1940. Two of his comrades were convicted of involvement in a bombing in Coventry in August 1939 and hanged for the murder of five civilians they had killed. Price made his way back to Ireland, where he continued his IRA activities. He was interned by the Irish government at the Curragh Camp during the 1950s border campaign.

He married Chrissie Dolan, who had joined the IRA's female wing, Cumann na mBan, in 1932. The couple settled in west Belfast and had four children: Damien, Clare, Dolours and Marian. Albert would sit at the kitchen table and teach his children how to mix explosives using wooden bowls and utensils. He would tell stories of fighting for Ireland. Marian's favourite was the story of how her father once tunnelled out of jail in Derry with twenty other prisoners while a comrade played bagpipes to cover the noise they made as they dug towards freedom.

Dolours and Marian Price both joined the Provisional IRA in 1971. In March 1973, the sisters travelled to London and helped organize the car bombings of the Old Bailey and Scotland Yard. The bombs, which injured over 200 people, are also believed to have contributed to the death of sixty-year-old Frederick Milton, a caretaker who worked in a building next to the Old Bailey and suffered a fatal heart attack. Another two bombs timed to explode at the same time as the others were found and defused.

The IRA had not bombed England since Albert Price and his comrades, one of whom was Paddy Adams (uncle of Gerry), had done so just before the Second World War.

Dolours Price later claimed the idea for the operation was hers and that it was approved by Gerry Adams, as

Officer Commanding of the Belfast brigade of the IRA at the time.

She said:

I had long been of the opinion that fight as we could, the Brits would let us keep going so long as the death and destruction was kept at a respectable distance from mother England.

I was convinced that a short, sharp shock, an incursion into the heart of the Empire, would be more effective than 20 car bombs in any part of the north of Ireland.

I presented the plan to Gerry Adams and he then had to take it to the whole brigade staff – people such as Ivor Bell. They then had to send it up to the general headquarters staff and then to Sean MacStiofain, then the chief of staff. They had to discuss and sanction it, which they did.

For the meeting, I sat on the arm of Adams' chair. Adams started talking and said it was a big, dangerous operation. He said, 'This could be a hanging job.'

The Price sisters, along with their comrade Hugh Feeney, were arrested when attempting to board a flight back to Ireland. The sisters and eight others were charged with conspiring to cause an explosion likely to endanger life. Their fast-tracked trial could not be held at the normal location of the Old Bailey, because of the extensive damage they had done to the building. One of their comrades pled guilty and another was acquitted.

Following their conviction, Marian and Dolours immediately announced they would go on hunger strike until they were returned to Northern Ireland to serve their sentences closer to home as political prisoners.

Within days, four of the prisoners dropped out of the strike, leaving Hugh Feeney, Gerry Kelly and the Price sisters to continue their political fast.

The prison authorities began force-feeding the four prisoners.

For Marian and Dolours, the force-feeding took place in the same cell in Brixton jail that had held Terence MacSwiney, the Lord Mayor of Cork, who died on hunger strike in October 1920.

It was against this backdrop – of this life lived in the shadow of the fight against British rule, and now a real fear that both his daughters could die in a British prison – that Albert Price ran for election.

As a veteran republican and the father of two Provisional IRA hunger-strikers, Albert Price's natural political home was Provisional Sinn Féin. But the party did not at that time participate in elections.

Sinn Féin presented its abstentionism as an expression of its rejection of the institutions of the UK and Ireland and the partition of the island. But the party had hardly been a major electoral force in the years before it stopped contesting elections.

The provisional republican movement sometimes informally supported candidates standing for election under rubrics such as 'Independent Republican' and 'Unity'. So while there was never any question of Albert Price running as a Sinn Féin candidate in the February 1974 general election, he hoped to secure the backing of the movement.

But the movement did not merely refuse to back Albert Price's campaign. When Price went ahead and put his name on the ballot as an independent republican, Sinn Féin actively shunned him. It didn't matter if you'd devoted your whole life to republicanism, or if your daughters were IRA bombers dying on hunger strike in England. You did not contest an election unless the movement said you could.

Being the 'political wing' of the IRA was not the same thing as being a normal political party. What Sinn Féin did, unflinchingly, was support and sustain the armed campaign of the Provisional IRA: a guerrilla paramilitary force whose aim was to unite Ireland, North and South, into one nation, free from British rule. Through its campaign of bombing, shooting and kidnapping, by the end of the conflict in Northern Ireland the Provisional IRA was responsible for more deaths than any other organization.

The relationship between Sinn Féin and the IRA during the Troubles is often described by those involved as 'two sides of the one house'. Some people were IRA and some people were Sinn Féin and some were both.

'It depended on what people wanted to do or what they thought they were capable of,' a one-time member of both sides of the house told me.

'I would have known people in the army who had no regard at all for Sinn Féin,' he added.

'I remember actually canvassing their houses during election time for Sinn Féin, even in the 1980s, early 1990s, and some of them were looking at you with a degree of disdain, and these were men I was in the IRA with.'

The seven-member IRA army council was at this time responsible for setting the overall strategy of the republican movement, both militarily and politically. The council was appointed by the twelve-member IRA army executive, elected by the membership at a general army convention (GAC).

Sinn Féin was entirely subordinate to the paramilitary leadership structure. In the 1970s, the party's main roles were to produce propaganda, provide support and cover for the IRA, and raise money to support the families of IRA prisoners. According to Jim Gibney, a long-time party activist, its membership was about two-thirds female. In republican heartlands across the north, party members raised money for the Green Cross, a fund to support prisoners' children. This was seen by Sinn Féin as a direct descendant of the Irish Volunteer Dependants Fund, set up in the wake of the Easter Rising of 1916. Party members also sold newspapers such as *Republican News*, *The Volunteer* and *An Phoblacht*, and organized marches protesting against internment and poor conditions for republican prisoners.

'The IRA then had no regard for Sinn Féin, they were [viewed as] Green Cross collectors,' says another person who operated on both sides of the house. 'We used to say it was made up of cowards and women. These are people who do the collections, look after your family when you're inside, but there was no chance that you were sort of taking a political lead from them.'

Sinn Féin had no premises to speak of at the time. The closest thing to a party headquarters was 170A Falls Road, the *Republican News* office, a damp building above a doctor's surgery that was regularly raided by the British Army.

'There was an anathema to elections and constitutional action, which was sort of embedded in our DNA,' a veteran republican told me. 'There was an instinctive feeling that to exclusively adopt an electoral approach or to devote your resources to it, and your personnel, and your time and your energy, meant that that time, energy and personnel wasn't being devoted to the main issue.'

The prevailing belief within the movement, from the rank and file right up to the Army Council of the IRA, was that if you were even considering politics, you were going soft on war. And war was the only show in town.

The 'cowards and women' view of Sinn Féin was unfair. The party was an illegal organization in Northern Ireland until 1974, and membership could result in a criminal conviction.

'We were always aware that the Brits were trying to say that if somebody was a Sinn Féin member, that meant they were a potential IRA supporter,' says a former high-level operative. 'So then it's a case of, if they're an IRA supporter maybe there are IRA men staying in their house who are on the run. Maybe there's gear in their house. Or maybe they'll drive somebody to an IRA meeting.

'So there was still, more so than in the South, a sort of shadowy underground aspect to Sinn Féin.'

At party meetings in Northern Ireland, the operative says, 'There was always a tendency to omit details or leave things out in paperwork. You'd say to each other, "Don't minute that", or that if somebody new joins, maybe, don't put them down as members yet, not because they have a probationary period, [but] because you don't want them exposed.'

In the South, Sinn Féin was less clandestine and more conventionally organized. Minutes of meetings were kept and the normal organizational structures could be maintained. In the North, by contrast, most decisions were taken by the local IRA commander with very little discussion or debate, and most members were at pains to hide the fact that they were in Sinn Féin at all.

Sinn Féin's president at this time was Ruairí Ó Brádaigh, a former IRA Chief of Staff. Ó Brádaigh would use Sinn Féin

Ard Fheiseanna (party conferences) to announce republican policy, which was IRA policy, and the members would take it back to their local group.

One IRA man who had not been a member of Sinn Féin remembers being brought to a party meeting in Coalisland, Co. Tyrone, in 1975. It was a 'six-county' meeting to debate issues of importance to members in Northern Ireland.

Around fifty people had gathered in a local hall. At the top of the room, the key figures in the party leadership sat at a long table.

In the centre was Ruairí Ó Brádaigh, stout and bespectacled. At his side was Máire Drumm, the vice-president of the party.

Máire Drumm, née McAteer, a native of Newry, was a member of the IRA's female wing, Cumann na mBan. She joined Sinn Féin aged twenty-one.

She became the Chairperson of the Ulster Council of the Camogie Association, going on to become All-Ireland Vice-Chair. When she went to visit her former camogie coach in Crumlin Road Gaol, she met IRA volunteer Jimmy Drumm. They were engaged while Jimmy served his prison term, got married upon his release, and settled in Andersonstown, west Belfast.

Jimmy went on to found the Provisional IRA with Joe Cahill, Seamus Twomey, Billy McKee, Leo Martin, Billy Kelly and John Kelly, and spent much of his life in prison.

Diarmaid Ferriter's article on Máire Drumm in the *Dictionary of Irish Biography* refers to 'her comment that she had never really had to face the quandary of birth control as both a devout Catholic and a feminist, because her husband was locked up for most of her child-rearing years'. It was a good joke, but it wasn't entirely accurate: in spite of everything,

Jimmy and Máire had five children, and Jimmy's periods of incarceration meant that Máire, like many republican wives, raised the children largely alone.

In 1970, she was one of some 3,000 women who broke the Falls Road Curfew and marched past the British Army with prams loaded up with food and supplies for residents who had been corralled into their homes. The British had called the curfew in the republican area after a raid on civilian homes searching for weapons led to riots. The residents were given only one hour to leave their homes per day, until the band of women, led by Drumm, broke the army barricade.

People who knew her well described her as affable and funny, and she was often photographed dressed in florals and knitted cardigans, with her hair in pin curls, and wearing thick-rimmed glasses. Her motherly image was at odds with her abrasive rhetoric and unwavering support for the IRA.

In July 1971, she was arrested for 'seditious speech' when she told an audience in Belfast: 'You should not shout "Up the IRA", you should join the IRA.'

On 28 October 1976, while she was recovering from an eye operation in Belfast's Mater hospital, loyalist gunmen disguised as doctors burst into her room and shot her. She was fifty-seven. Twenty thousand people, including the actress Vanessa Redgrave, attended her funeral.

On the night of the Coalisland debate, discussion turned to the upcoming UK referendum on EEC membership. After the speakers had summed up their viewpoints, Drumm stood up and told the crowd: 'Well, that was all very good but at the end of the day the IRA will decide.'

Many of those present were disgusted, according to the former IRA member who described the meeting to me, at 'the idea that these people would sit and talk about this for an hour and a half and then she would say, "Fuck it, it doesn't matter."'

Ó Brádaigh tried to row back on Drumm's blunt remark, telling the attendees that he would bring their very important feedback 'to the party'. But it was clear that Drumm was right. The president and vice-president of 'the party' were right there at the table. Everyone knew that Ó Brádaigh would be consulting with the Army Council of the IRA, which decided on all Sinn Féin's policies.

On 28 February 1974, Albert Price received 5,662 votes, 11.88 per cent of the overall share in Belfast West, which left him a distant third. The SDLP's Gerry Fitt held the seat.

Three months later, in May 1974, British Home Secretary Roy Jenkins announced that the forced feeding of the Price sisters would end. Their father travelled to see them on their hospital ward and told the press afterwards that his daughters were 'happy about dying'.

Two weeks after the forced feeding of the Price sisters ended, a Co. Mayo member of the IRA, Michael Gaughan, who had been on hunger strike after being imprisoned for robbing a bank in London, died. The authorities claimed he had succumbed to pneumonia, while his family suspected the cause was a result of intestinal injuries caused by the feeding tube. Gaughan's death led Jenkins to agree to the transfer of Dolours and Marian Price to Armagh Women's Prison, and Hugh Feeney and Gerry Kelly to Long Kesh. On 8 June, the Price sisters, Feeney and Kelly called off their strike.

Sinn Féin in May 1974 was a party of sparse membership, with members using fake names, no headquarters, no voters and no real policies. A party that would expel a dedicated supporter – and father of two active hunger-strikers – for the crime of running for election. The same party now holds the aim of holding power in both the North and South.

So, what changed?

The legalization of the party in May 1974 had a significant effect on normalizing politics for the republican movement. The party retained its policy of abstentionism, but the ability to operate more openly would prove to be transformative. A Belfast Executive was set up within Sinn Féin to boycott that year's Assembly elections, and this select committee would remain the beating heart of the party's organizing for decades.

Sinn Féin also opened advice centres and formed the Relatives Action Committees (RACs) in response to a change in the status of paramilitary prisoners in 1976. Four years earlier, under a Conservative government, paramilitaries in Northern Irish prisons had been granted 'Special Category Status'.

The status had no basis in law: it was purely administrative. It fell to the prison governor to designate who had such status and who didn't, but almost every application for Special Category Status was successful. The paramilitary prisoners were not required to work, could wear their own clothing, and were allowed weekly letters and visits, as well as food and tobacco parcels.

A report on prisons at the time noted that:

Special category is regarded as a badge of respectability particularly amongst young prisoners. No matter what efforts are made to explain to a young prisoner or his parents that it is very much in his own interests to accept work or training as an ordinary prisoner rather than spend his time in idleness under the evil influence of adult criminals in the special category compound the family attitude is almost invariably that they can hold up their heads in the local community if their son is with his para-military colleagues; but they would be ashamed to regard him as an ordinary criminal. Finally, special category status encourages prisoners, their organisations and their families to hold firmly to the mistaken belief that one day they will be the subject of an amnesty.

By 1976, there were over 3,000 prisoners in Northern Ireland, of whom around half were special category. The 'special category' was becoming the main category, and this was seen as a 'political and disciplinary disaster'. Merlyn Rees, Secretary of State for Northern Ireland in Wilson's Labour government, announced that, from 1 March, newly arriving paramilitary prisoners would be treated like everyone else.

The stated purpose of the RAC was 'to defend the political status of Republican and Republican Socialist P.O.W's'. This focus on prisoners' rights was popular, and broadened the republican movement's support base.

Jim Gibney, a former internee and Sinn Féin operative who at the time was a key link between the prisoners, the RAC and Sinn Féin, suggested that the RAC distance itself from the party, and forge links with trade unions and tenant associations.

In September 1976, nineteen-year-old Kieran Nugent was the first republican to be sentenced for paramilitary offences under the new prison regime. He refused to wear a prison uniform and was thrown naked into a cell. Each IRA prisoner who followed Nugent into prison would refuse a convict's uniform and would remain naked, with only a blanket for comfort and cover.

Prison rules stated that the prison uniform must be worn when leaving the cell. Thus, men who were 'on the blanket' could be confined to their cells twenty-four hours a day, and could not receive their monthly visit.

The protest escalated in March 1978. Prisoners had been complaining of the violent tactics used against them by prison officers when emptying their slop buckets. Now they refused to slop out. Instead they would smear faeces on the walls of the cell and live there with it.

In 1980, the women in Armagh women's prison would join the 'dirty protest' after an altercation with male prison authorities that left many of them injured. Nell McCafferty wrote about the conditions in which the women lived for the *Irish Times*:

> There is menstrual blood on the walls of Armagh Prison in Northern Ireland. The 32 women on dirt strike there have not washed their bodies since February 8th, 1980; they use their cells as toilets; for over 200 days now they have lived amid their own excreta, urine and blood.
>
> The windows and spy holes are boarded up. Flies and slugs grow fat as they grow thin.
>
> They eat and sleep, and sit in this dim, electrically-lit filth, without reading materials.
>
> They are allowed out for one hour per day, hopefully to stand in the rain. The consequences for these women, under these conditions, will be, at the least, urinary, pelvic and skin infections. At worst they face sterility and possible death. They are guarded by male wardens, presided over by a male governor, and attended by a male doctor.

Reports from the women, headed by Mairéad Farrell, some-times filtered out of the prison. One prisoner recalled:

> they [the prison officers] took your clothing off and when you were completely naked you were then bent over and they would do an internal search of your anus and vagina, and all the while you're struggling and struggling and then you'd end up getting punched and stuff like that.
> *It's sexual assault.*

The campaign to secure political status for republican paramilitary prisoners settled on what would become known as the 'five demands':

1. The right not to wear a prison uniform
2. The right not to do prison work
3. The right of free association with other prisoners, and to organize educational and recreational pursuits
4. The right to one visit, one letter and one parcel per week
5. Full restoration of remission lost through the protest

In October 1980, seven republican prisoners in the Maze and three in Armagh women's prison launched an ill-executed hunger strike in pursuit of the five demands.

By December 1980, with one of the prisoners near death, Brendan Hughes, O/C of the IRA's Belfast Brigade and the leader of the hunger strike, called it off.

Thus it was that the next – and transformative – phase of the prison protest and of Sinn Féin's evolution was triggered not by the death of one or more republican hunger-strikers, but by the death from natural causes of a democratically elected republican MP.

Frank Maguire, a 51-year-old pub landlord, was originally from Gort, Co. Galway. He had been interned for IRA membership in his youth.

Following in the footsteps of his uncle John Carron, who was elected to Stormont for Fermanagh South in 1965, Maguire was elected to Westminster as a 'Unity' MP for Fermanagh–South Tyrone in October 1974. The 'Unity' designation was used by candidates acceptable to both nationalists and republicans, and allowed for the representation of republican voters while Sinn Féin continued to abstain from elections. Maguire polled 32,795 votes, 2,510 more than the unionist incumbent, Harry West.

Maguire spent much of his time as an MP defending the interests of republican prisoners, and was close to Sinn Féin both ideologically and in his approach to Parliament. While he did not formally refuse to take his seat, he never made a speech and attended the House of Commons only once. On that occasion, in November 1976, he flew to Westminster to cast the deciding vote which kept James Callaghan's Labour government in power, after a Conservative Party attempt to bring it down.

When a similar situation arose three years later, in March 1979, Maguire refused to support a vote of confidence in the Labour government, on the grounds that he had not received adequate assurances about the treatment of republican prisoners in English jails.

As a result, the government fell, and at the ensuing general election the Conservatives, led by Margaret Thatcher, took power. If the government's approach to republican prisoners under Callaghan had been unsatisfactory to Maguire and other republicans, it was about to become much worse. Maguire, for his part, increased his majority at the 1979 general election. Maguire was a key voice on the National H-Block Committee and used his position as a democratically elected parliamentarian to demand action on the campaign for political status.

On 5 March 1981, Maguire died of a heart attack at his home in the border town of Lisnaskea, Co. Fermanagh.

Four days earlier, Bobby Sands had launched a new republican hunger strike in the Maze prison. This hunger strike was bigger and better conceived than the previous one. Each man who was participating in the strike would begin refusing food at two-week intervals. It was planned that if their demands were not met, the men would die one after another, with new men continuing to join, for as long as it took.

Sands was a popular and handsome 27-year-old. Sands wasn't from a typical republican background: his father was a Protestant, and he spent most of his time as a child in the mixed area of Rathcoole playing football with Protestant friends. He had joined the IRA in 1972 and was in the H-block prison on his second conviction. He had been captured in 1976 after bombing a furniture warehouse and getting into a shoot-out with RUC members while trying to escape arrest.

Upon his arrest, Sands spent much of his time in prison writing poetry, had written for *An Phoblacht* under the pen name Marcella, after his sister, and had once, before his second stint in prison, attempted to set up a community newspaper in Twinbrook.

The hunger strikes quickly became the central drama of life in Northern Ireland. People who hadn't gone on marches since Bloody Sunday in 1972 now turned out on the streets again, protesting against British policy on prisoners. Rioting was a regular occurrence in cities and towns during the 1981 hunger strike, and 30,000 plastic bullets were fired by the British Army in north and west Belfast alone. In 1981, there were 118 deaths in the Northern Ireland conflict, seventy of which were directly caused by the IRA. One of these was the murder of Joanne Mathers.

A 29-year-old town planner, Mathers was collecting completed census forms in Derry and had already been threatened by republicans. The IRA had called a boycott of the census in support of the hunger strike, and threatened census workers who did not observe the boycott.

A masked IRA gunman accosted her in a residential street and attempted to rip her clipboard from her hand. When she would not let go, he shot her in the head. The injuries were not immediately fatal and she rushed into a nearby house, where the gunman followed her and shot her several times as she lay on the living-room floor. Her killer then ripped the census forms from her clasped hand.

Joanne Mathers's son Shane was two years old when his mother was killed. No one has ever been charged with her murder.

The death of an MP who advocated for republican prisoners, coming just days after the launching of a major new hunger strike, presented Sinn Féin with a big question. The party's policy of refusing to participate in elections was very much intact, the idea of entering electoral politics had been discussed at length within the movement for years, both inside and outside prison walls. The first serious discussions began in 1979. A view had taken hold among some prisoners that Sinn Féin should contest the council elections in Northern Ireland. In 1977, the Irish Republican Socialist Party, founded by former members of the Workers' Party of Ireland (aka Official Sinn Féin), had stood a candidate in the general election in the Republic. Although the candidate was not elected, the publicity the party managed to generate impressed some within the IRA.

At the 1980 Ard Fheis, party member Francie Molloy proposed that Sinn Féin should contest the local council elections in May 1981. But the leadership opposed the motion, so naturally it was defeated.

Some prisoners – including Jake Jackson, Tommy McKearney, Pat McGeown and Bobby Sands – were strongly advocating that Sinn Féin enter the local elections. Introducing a republican voice on local councils was the obvious next step for many who wanted to advocate for their communities and show the level of support the IRA had to the world. These men were arguing that the IRA, fronted by Sinn Féin, needed to build a popular platform for the struggle, and that participating in electoral politics was a way of doing that. However, the republican movement had a tendency to allow tactics to become sacred writ, and this had been the case with abstentionism.

One former prisoner recalls querying why republicans did not eat Christmas dinner in prison. His O/C responded that it was a protest.

'A protest against what? Christmas?'

It was what they had always done, so it wouldn't be changing. That mindset was hard to shake, whether it was turkey or elections.

Today, some Sinn Féin veterans say they were always in favour of entering politics – even some who argued against it at Ard Fheiseanna.

'I actually thought that was a good idea that had merit,' one party veteran told me. 'But I didn't think the time was right. You know, we were in the middle of a hunger strike, and the prison protest, which by the way, was totally draining. The H-blocks, Armagh, it was a picket, it was protests, leaflets, pamphlets, dealing with press. I mean, for five years, the prison protest dominated every single Republican meeting every single week. To the extent that you wished it would end or go away.'

The idea to have Bobby Sands stand in the Fermanagh–South Tyrone by-election was Jim Gibney's. Gibney saw a Sands candidacy as carrying great propaganda potential in the Republic – where representatives of Sinn Féin and the IRA were barred from the RTÉ airwaves – and across the North. An Irishman starving to death while running for election would be an effective way to build support for the H-Block campaign. Initially, Gibney had not even considered the possibility that Sands could win.

It was understood that Sands would need to be the sole candidate seeking the republican–nationalist vote if he was to have a chance of winning the by-election. And even if he did get a clear run, victory against a single unionist candidate was far from assured.

A member of Sands's campaign recalls: 'If we got Bobby running alone against one Unionist, Harry West, who was the [former] leader of the Ulster Unionist party, we'd still have the danger of losing and Thatcher saying: "There's no support, even your own people rejected you. Why should I give you your five demands?"'

At a meeting of the Sinn Féin Ard Comhairle in Dublin, party vice-president Gerry Adams was the first to formally propose the idea of running Sands. Adams was backed by the other vice-president, Dáithí Ó Conaill. There was some debate over the risks, but it was agreed in principle that Sands should run if they could convince other potential nationalist or republican candidates to drop out.

A meeting for Fermanagh republicans was held in the Swan Hotel in Monaghan. The bulk of the attendees were against standing a prisoner, despite the leadership's support for Sands.

According to Danny Morrison, some Fermanagh republicans argued that Noel Maguire, the late MP's brother, should receive republican backing.

Another potential candidate was Bernadette Devlin. A founding member of the college-based civil rights movement People's Democracy, Devlin had been elected as a republican–nationalist 'Unity' candidate for Mid Ulster in a by-election in 1969, aged twenty-one.

Having promised voters to 'take my seat and fight for your rights', Devlin swore the Oath of Allegiance and then made a combative and prescient maiden speech in the House of Commons. She warned that if British troops were brought into Northern Ireland to deal with rising civil unrest – a possibility that was being debated at the time – 'I should not like to be either the mother or sister of an unfortunate soldier stationed there . . . it has to be recognised that the one point in common among Ulstermen is that they are not very fond of Englishmen who tell them what to do.'

Devlin lost her Westminster seat in 1974, but continued to campaign for the rights of prisoners and the working class in Northern Ireland. In January 1981, just weeks before the death of Frank Maguire, Devlin was shot nine times in front of her children by loyalists. Her husband Michael was also shot and seriously injured.

Devlin was not a member of Sinn Féin, but her stature among republicans was such that the party released a statement saying: 'We regard it as a direct attack on us and on our struggle. But they should know that it will not deter us.'

She survived the attack and appeared publicly for the first time in the aftermath of the shooting to attend Frank Maguire's funeral while still on crutches. Sinn Féin took this as a signal that she might have been considering running for the seat. As a close ally of Maguire, she would have been a popular candidate to replace him. Having survived an assassination attempt as a mother of two young children, and with the experience of the Commons already behind her, she would be a hard candidate to beat.

The Sinn Féin leadership held a private meeting afterwards and decided to press ahead with Sands. They spoke to Bernadette Devlin, who agreed not to stand. They also spoke to Noel Maguire. That was a more difficult conversation, but he too agreed.

On 26 March 1981, Sinn Féin announced that Sands would stand – though this would be no Sinn Féin candidate or campaign. Sands would run as an 'Anti H-Block' candidate. Any deviation from the party's abstentionism policy would have to be voted on at an Ard Fheis.

The 'Anti H-Block' banner also had the advantage of allowing other republicans who were not Sinn Féin supporters, like Devlin and Frank Maguire's family, to campaign for the hunger-striker on humanitarian grounds rather than support for the IRA.

However, the field still hadn't been cleared of other nationalist candidates. Sinn Féin did not know what the SDLP would do. Fitt's party was in a tricky situation. If they chose not to contest the by-election, they feared they would appear to endorse the hunger strike and, by extension, the IRA. If they did run a candidate, they would split the nationalist–republican vote. The unionist would win, Sands would likely die, and the SDLP would be blamed. After a four-hour meeting, they decided to stand aside.

Sands was supported by the Irish Republican Socialist Party, People's Democracy – Bernadette Devlin's organization in Mid Ulster – and a number of other small groups. Devlin was listed as the proposer on Sands's election papers. Noel Maguire, who had had second thoughts, deposited papers to stand in the election, then withdrew at the last moment, stating: 'I have been told that the only way of saving Bobby Sands's life is by letting him go forward in the elections. I just cannot have the life of another man on my hands.' Outside the returning office, Adams and Owen Carron were the first to shake his hand. Maguire called on his supporters to back Sands.

Jim Gibney had been hiding behind a wall near the Electoral Office in anxious anticipation. He was told that if by 3.50pm Noel Maguire had not withdrawn his nomination papers, he was to withdraw Bobby Sands's name from the contest. Four o'clock was the final deadline to withdraw papers. Maguire eventually appeared and withdrew his name. Sands was on the ballot.

The 1979 general election suggested that the constituency had a majority for nationalists of about 5,000 votes. In theory, that meant if only one nationalist ran, they could expect to win. But Sands was no normal nationalist candidate. It was one thing to be a prisoners' advocate, as Maguire had been. It was another to be an actual IRA prisoner. The movement worried that many nationalists would see a vote for Sands as a vote for the IRA, and refrain from turning out.

The support of Devlin and other activists not associated with the IRA was a help for Sands. Those who were uneasy with the armed struggle might feel better about voting for a convicted IRA man if a civil rights leader and former MP was behind him.

The hunger strike, too, had altered the political climate. Even those who abhorred violence and the IRA were struck not only by the sacrifices of the hunger-strikers but by the coldness of Thatcher and her government. Many nationalist parents, who couldn't say for sure whether or not their teenage son was in the IRA, saw their boys in the smiling photographs of the prisoners and were moved.

Campaigners for Sands descended in their hundreds from all over the country to the little villages of Fermanagh and south Tyrone. Those canvassing for Sands recall being harassed by the RUC and the British Army.

'We actually found the harassment probably was counterproductive, because then the local people sympathized with us,' recalls one canvasser.

'Trying to give out 500 leaflets on an evening and getting followed or your leaflets taken away or what have you – the people didn't like that.'

Very few current Sinn Féin members in the North had ever run an electoral campaign before, and many of the party's campaigners knew little or nothing about the constituency. One group of Belfast women reported a very frosty reception from parishioners leaving a local church service in the area, which seemed worrying until they worked out that they had canvassed the local Church of Ireland.

The republican heartland of west Belfast was a world away from rural Fermanagh and the problems the nationalist community faced there were different. But the seat had been fought for by republican candidates for decades, and the republican people of the constituency were prepared. This wasn't even their first jailed candidate: in the 1920s, Cahir

Healy had won the seat twice while interned, and Sinn Féin had last won the seat in 1955 with Phil Clarke, serving time for an IRA raid on an army barracks.

'Us city slickers thought we were gonna go down to Fermanagh and show them how it was done,' the canvasser recalls. 'When we got down there, it was fascinating, because it was obvious they had been planning something like this for years. They had registration committees, as they had already run elections in the 1950s campaign. They kept registers of when kids went away for work and then came back and made sure they were added back on the register.'

The by-election was held on 9 April. Bobby Sands received 30,493 votes, to 29,046 for the Ulster Unionist Party leader Harry West.

Jim Gibney recalls that one IRA man described the election of their comrade at the time as 'worth twenty bombs in England'. Gibney went on to say Sands's election result 'changed the world' for some of his comrades. The idea that there might be something beyond the gun was something that many people in the movement had not considered. But others took great heart in what they viewed as a statement of support for the armed campaign. The British had claimed for years that the IRA had no backing in their own communities, yet here were thousands of votes that proved they were wrong. If 'twenty bombs in England' were a way to get British attention, here was a much more effective way.

The hope within the movement that a sitting MP would not be allowed to die on hunger strike – that the British would feel they had to grant the demands of the republican prisoner – proved to be unfounded. Bobby Sands died less than a month after the by-election, after sixty-six days without food. As his election and hunger strike had, his death made global headlines. Margaret Thatcher had overseen the death of a member of parliament. Thatcher argued: 'Mr Sands was a convicted criminal. He chose to take his own life. It was a choice that his organisation did not allow to any of their victims.'

The hunger strikes, meanwhile, ground on. Northern Ireland remained a tinderbox. May 1981 alone saw more plastic bullets fired than in the previous eight years: 16,656 of these bullets, with the ability to cripple and maim, were directed at men, women and children.

The grand total used in 1981 was somewhere close to 30,000.

In May 1981, another opportunity arose in the Republic, when the Taoiseach, Charles Haughey, called a general election to take place in June. The H-Block campaign had gone global and the death of Sands had put pressure on Thatcher. The world was watching and if prisoners were elected members of the Irish parliament, it would put pressure on any future Taoiseach to advocate strongly for Britain to negotiate the end of the hunger strike.

Sinn Féin announced that, under the Anti H-Block campaign, they would put forward nine prisoners for election, four of whom were on hunger strike. Two of the nine – Kieran Doherty and Paddy Agnew – were elected to Dáil Éireann. The net effect of the nine Anti H-Block candidacies was to cost Haughey a majority and force Fianna Fáil into opposition. The Anti H-Block candidates took a combined total of 40,000 first-preference votes: not a vast number, but enough to suggest a level of support in the Republic for the IRA and the hunger-strikers.

Sands's death forced another by-election in Fermanagh–South Tyrone, on 20 August 1981. His election agent, Owen

Carron, was elected with a slightly larger majority than Sands.

On 3 October, the hunger strike ended after intervention from some prisoners' families. Ten republican prisoners, beginning with Bobby Sands and ending with Mickey Devine, had starved to death. The prisoners' demands had still not been granted. But republicans' view of the possibilities of electoral politics had been altered for ever.

The Sinn Féin Ard Fheis was to be held in October 1981. Among the motions for consideration by the party was one to abandon the party's policy of refusing to contest elections in the Republic.

This time the republican leadership had agreed this motion had to pass, but it was far from clear that the membership agreed. Some members argued that Sands's election had been a one-off and that electoral politics would distract from the armed struggle.

Danny Morrison, who was Sinn Féin's director of publicity and the editor of *Republican News*, recalls that Gerry Adams called on him to speak in favour of competing in elections. Morrison had made the exact opposite argument the year before.

On the Ard Fheis platform, Morrison says, he spoke off the cuff, and delivered the most infamous speech in Sinn Féin's history. He argued that it was not necessary to choose between elections and violence: 'Who here really believes we can win the war through the ballot box? But will anyone here object if, with a ballot paper in this hand, and an Armalite in this hand, we take power in Ireland?'

Morrison has since claimed he hadn't thought of this formula before he got up to speak. It just came to him.

'My motivation was twofold. First of all, there was an element, when I said "the Armalite", obviously I was playing to the gallery for IRA people, IRA supporters, that politics wouldn't impact on the [armed] campaign itself, wouldn't undermine it, it wouldn't defund it.'

At the same time, he believed that republican success in elections was helping the movement.

'Brits had real problems with the election of Bobby Sands. And the Free Staters had real problems with the election of Kieran and Paddy, and Brits now have a real problem with Owen Carron.'

One man in the audience recalled that Martin McGuinness had turned to him after Morrison's speech and said: 'What the fuck is going on here?' McGuinness was supportive of the motion itself, but was concerned that Morrison had given away the strategy decided by the IRA Army Council, who had not given him permission to make it public.

The motion passed. From then on, there would be no more Anti H-Block candidates, there would only be Sinn Féin candidates. The election offices in Dungannon and Enniskillen were turned into constituency offices for Owen Carron MP.

'We had this attitude that in getting elected and then representing the people, we were giving them something back for a change,' one senior Sinn Féin representative recalls. 'It used to be, "Give us your sons, give us your daughters, buy the paper, go to the march, support the prisoners, lend us your car." Now it was giving them a constituency service.'

Likewise, it had become clear to the Sinn Féin and IRA leadership that abstention from Dáil Éireann was counterproductive. Jim Gibney, Sinn Féin's national organizer in 1982, noted at the time that the vast majority of citizens in the South viewed the Irish state's institutions as 'legitimate'.

'Whatever we might think about them, we have to change our approach if we want to build across the island as a whole.'

In April 1982, the new British Secretary of State for Northern Ireland, Jim Prior, published a White Paper setting out plans for 'rolling devolution'. Elections for a new Northern Ireland Assembly, to be based in Stormont, were scheduled for October.

For the Stormont elections in October, Sinn Féin needed twelve candidates to qualify for TV and radio time. In the end they fielded a total of thirteen in target areas around Northern Ireland, places where they believed they had a fighting chance.

In Mid Ulster, Sinn Féin had three candidates. Morrison was in bed early one morning when a nervous Tom Hartley appeared at his door. He had been sent by Gerry Adams to tell a dazed Morrison that they had to go to Mid Ulster immediately. Two of the candidates had pulled out. Morrison and Hartley were tasked with getting at least one of them back on the ticket – otherwise, the party would lose its TV and radio time.

The problem was rooted in local rows about how to carve up the constituency. Sinn Féin, which had taken an extended break from electoral politics, had immediately fallen into the sort of petty local infighting that chronically afflicts more conventional parties. Neither of the withdrawing candidates was willing to reconsider. It was unthinkable that Sinn Féin would lose its broadcast rights, so Morrison – who was largely based in Dublin, where he edited *Republican News* – was chosen to stand. Two minutes before the deadline, he handed in papers to the electoral office in Omagh and then drove to Dublin to work on that week's newspaper.

Sinn Féin's campaign teams were continually stopped and

harassed by the British Army, the UDR and the RUC. A team putting up posters near Kildress were fired on from a passing car, and others were arrested and held for up to three days.

After the count on 21 October 1982, Gerry Adams topped the poll in Belfast West. Martin McGuinness was elected on the first count in Derry and Owen Carron on the first count in Fermanagh–South Tyrone. Jim McAllister was elected in Armagh and Danny Morrison in Mid Ulster. Overall, Sinn Féin took 5 out of 78 seats in the Assembly, on 35 per cent of the nationalist vote and 10 per cent of the overall vote.

The party now had an electoral foothold in the North. There was no longer any way for the British or Irish governments to claim that the IRA had no support. When Martin McGuinness was elected, his supporters chanted 'IRA! IRA!' in front of the world's press at the election centre. For his part, Gerry Adams, then thirty-four, told the BBC: 'The IRA have said that while the British army is in Ireland they will be there fighting.'

Members of the IRA were now politicians. Men who had left school with very little education, and who had no trade or career due to a life dedicated to violence, were now representing some of the most deprived areas in the UK.

Abstentionism wasn't dead. Sinn Féin was contesting elections, but it wasn't taking seats in Stormont. The five newly elected Assembly members, refusing to recognize the legitimacy of the institution, focused on local constituency work without ever taking their seats.

In the constituencies, one former Assembly member recalls, 'We discovered that the SDLP had been doing fuck-all for years ... We just assumed that they were doing very simple constituency work, [but] it didn't appear they ever did. I was overwhelmed. It's like being a social worker and an agriculture expert in some constituencies. We hadn't a clue in some respects.'

Despite their electoral successes north of the border, the South held no such promise. Sinn Féin – run by Northerners, focused on the future of the North – looked like a single-issue party, and that issue didn't feature too highly on the priority list of people in Cork or Kildare.

By 1985, Sinn Féin had fought elections at local government, regional assembly, Westminster and European levels. The party could claim to represent around a third of northern nationalists, while in the South they struggled to get over 2 per cent of the vote.

In 1986, hoping to make electoral success a reality in the South, Sinn Féin dropped its policy of refusing to recognize the institutions of the Republic. Just three years before, when making his debut speech as Sinn Féin president, Adams had told delegates: 'We are an abstentionist party. It is not my intention to advocate for change in this situation.' He had been planning such a change for around four years.

On 15 October 1986, after a special convention held outside Navan in which they debated the issue, the IRA issued a statement in which it said that it would support Sinn Féin in the decision to end the policy of abstentionism in the South.

On 2 November 1986, 590 delegates attended the Ard Fheis. Those instructed by Adams say they had created almost 200 cumann groups to carry the vote his way. The debate went on for five hours.

McGuinness and Adams were at pains to note that Sinn Féin and the IRA were inextricably linked. 'To leave Sinn Féin is to leave the IRA', Adams was quoted as saying.

'The IRA freedom fighters and the Sinn Féin freedom fighters are one and the same thing,' said McGuinness. He added the armed struggle would continue 'until the last [British] soldier has left our soil'.

According to media reports from the time, the abstentionists were mostly from Dublin, and had argued that if the party entered the Dáil it would be tainted. 'When you lie down with the dog, you get up with the fleas,' one said.

Ruairí Ó Brádaigh warned the delegates that once they entered Leinster House, they would have to abide by its rules. 'In God's name, don't let it come about [. . .] that Haughey, FitzGerald, Spring and those in London and Belfast can [. . .] say, "Ah, it took 65 years but we have them at last,"' he said.

Ó Brádaigh's pleas were falling on mostly deaf ears. The new young leaders had convinced enough of their comrades that theirs was the only way forward.

'We ensured going into that Ard Fheis that there were sufficient numbers who were on board with the strategy, who would guarantee us a two-thirds majority. So it would have been almost impossible for Ruairí [Ó Brádaigh] and them to defeat Motion 162. They just hadn't got the numbers,' one leader at the time told me.

The leaders of the old guard, Ruairí Ó Brádaigh and Dáithí Ó Conaill, had lost. A small group of around thirty older republicans walked out with the two leaders, despite McGuinness's shouted plea: 'We will lead you to the republic.'

2. The Ends of Violence and the Purposes of Peace

Gemma Berezag worked as a cleaner in the headquarters of Midland Bank in the London docklands: the heart of the British financial district. On 9 February 1996, though, Gemma didn't go in to work: she stayed at home in the Isle of Dogs to be with her youngest child, seven-year-old Rajaa, who was feeling ill. Her husband, Zaoui Berezag, went in her place, helped by their son, Farid, and oldest daughter, Layla.

At 7.01pm, Zaoui and the children were sitting in their car outside a small shop when a 500kg IRA truck bomb exploded.

Two shopkeepers, Inan Bashir and John 'JJ' Jeffries, died immediately at the news kiosk they ran at South Quay DLR station. They were blown through two walls, and their bodies were not found until the next day. Jeffries' father spent an entire day checking and rechecking the list of the wounded in the Royal London Hospital in Whitechapel, hoping his son's name would appear.

Zaoui Berezag spent two weeks in a coma and suffered permanent brain damage. He was blinded and paralysed, and lost a leg. His son Farid required surgery to remove metal that was lodged close to his spine. Similarly, metal lodged in Layla's leg.

Gemma's life changed for ever. For twenty years, she would be her husband's primary carer. She changed Zaoui's nappy ten times a day – but struggled to afford the nappies. Gemma developed a deep depression and killed herself in 2016, aged fifty-eight.

The bomb ended a seventeen-month IRA ceasefire. War was on again.

The end of the IRA ceasefire – unanimously decided by the Army Council nine days before the Docklands bombing – was the culmination of a tense period. The ceasefire had brought about concessions from the British: troop withdrawals began, and certain IRA prisoners were transferred to serve their sentences in Northern Ireland. However, there was a widespread view within the IRA that the British were kicking the can down the road, dithering on withdrawal. In the spring of 1995, Gerry Adams warned 'the sound of angry voices and stamping feet' would become overwhelming.

There was discontent, too, over the Sinn Féin leadership's attempts to make the party a democratic force. In 1994, it emerged that Sinn Féin had agreed to receive training in fundraising and electioneering at the National Democratic Institute in Washington, DC. Founded in 1983, the 'non-profit, non-partisan, non-governmental' organization works 'to strengthen and safeguard democratic institutions, processes, norms and values to secure a better quality of life for all', according to its website. Sinn Féin had accused the group of being a CIA front when it offered similar training to the SDLP years before. Presumably remembering this, the membership passed a motion at the 1995 Ard Fheis condemning the move as 'undemocratic'.

Again and again, efforts by the Sinn Féin leadership to change the party's image were undercut by forces within the movement. When the UK's Prime Minister, John Major, visited Derry in May the same year, a handshake was planned between him and Sinn Féin's general secretary, Mitchel

McLaughlin. But after republicans rioted in the city, and seven police officers were hurt, the plan was called off.

Republicans' sensitivity in the mid-1990s to the implications of political training or a handshake may give the impression that the peace process was still in its infancy. The truth is that the republican movement had been engaging with the British government for decades.

On 26 June 1972, the Provisional IRA commenced its first ceasefire. On 7 July, a small group of six IRA men boarded a British military plane in secret and headed for London.

The first meeting between Gerry Adams and Martin McGuinness – who would together lead the republican movement for over thirty years – took place not in an IRA safe house or at an Army Council meeting or in prison, but at a meeting hosted by the British government on Cheyne Walk in the Royal Borough of Kensington and Chelsea.

The British side was led by the Secretary of State for Northern Ireland, Willie Whitelaw. Seán Mac Stíofáin, one of the founders of the Provisional IRA, recalled in his memoirs that the 'military situation' was the preoccupation of the British, and 'they would scarcely be interested in talking to any Republicans just yet apart from representatives of the military wing. Therefore I rejected a suggestion that our team should include a leading member of Sinn Féin.'

Dáithí Ó'Conaill and Mac Stíofáin represented the national leadership, along with Séamus Twomey. Gerry Adams and Ivor Bell were there from Belfast. Martin McGuinness represented Derry.

Whitelaw would later tell the House of Commons he had met with the men in an attempt to preserve the 'fragile' ceasefire and he wanted to 'save lives in any way I could'.

Adams was twenty-three years old at the time, and the leader of the Belfast Brigade of the Provisional IRA. He had been released from prison so that he could participate in the talks. His comrade Ivor Bell had insisted: 'No fucking cease-fire unless Gerry is released.' Adams was already seen as an irreplaceable part of the republican movement. The jumper he wore to the Cheyne Walk talks had a hole in it.

The IRA delegation were novices at political negotiation. They came with a list of what the British deemed outrageous demands. They wanted the British to acknowledge that all Irish people, North and South, had a right to self-determination, and they wanted a complete withdrawal of British forces from Irish soil.

The demands never changed in the following decades, but the republican movement got better at negotiating.

James Martin Pacelli McGuinness was born in Elmwood Street in the Bogside area of Derry on 23 May 1950.

It was a place of abject poverty. Large Catholic families were packed into small houses, with multiple children often forced to share a bed. Employment was scarce for Catholic men, and the local economy was held up largely by women working in the local shirt factories.

McGuinness's mother was from the Inishowen peninsula in Co. Donegal, the natural hinterland of Derry city. Peggy moved to Derry to work in a shirt factory, due to lack of opportunity in her rural homeplace. She lodged four to a bed with three other women before marrying William McGuinness, a foundry worker. The couple went on to have seven children, of whom Martin was the second.

Martin McGuinness was working as an apprentice to a butcher when he joined the IRA as a young teenager in 1970.

He quickly rose through the ranks, and by the start of 1972 he was the Provos' second-in-command in Derry. He had only recently turned twenty-two when he travelled to London for the secret peace talks in the summer of that year.

In 1973, McGuinness was arrested in Co. Donegal in the vicinity of a red Ford Cortina carrying 113kg of explosives and almost 5,000 bullets. He turned up at court with his usual shock of curly fair hair dyed black and a large moustache.

He refused to recognize the Special Criminal Court in Dublin, which sat without a jury, and loudly declared: 'We have fought against the killing of our people ... I am a member of Óglaigh na hÉireann and very, very proud of it.'

When he was released from prison in May 1973, he remained in the Republic under threat of arrest in the North. His father died the same year, and was buried at Cockhill in Donegal, rather than in Derry, so that his son could be present at the burial.

The same year, his girlfriend, Bernie Canning, was being held in Armagh Jail on suspicion of explosives offences. McGuinness bought an engagement ring in Donegal and passed it on to a friend to give to her in jail. Bernie was later cleared, but McGuinness was convicted of IRA membership again in 1974 and briefly imprisoned in Portlaoise Prison. A week after his release, he and Bernie Canning were married in the same church where his father had been buried the previous year. They would have four children: Fiachra, Emmet, Fionnuala and Gráinne.

McGuinness would later claim to have left the IRA in 1974. In reality, he was heavily involved with the IRA throughout the seventies, becoming Chief of Staff in the early eighties and remaining in a leadership role throughout the entirety of the peace process.

According to an account of a conversation between an official of the Irish Department of Foreign Affairs and the Bishop of Derry, Edward Daly, the clergyman said in 1987 that while McGuinness would usually 'keep his own hands clean', he had personally organized the killing of an IRA informer, Frank Hegarty, who was shot in the head in May 1986.

Hegarty was an IRA quartermaster in Derry who fled to England in 1986 under the protection of British intelligence after he gave information to British handlers on three separate dumps of IRA arms smuggled from Libya.

Hegarty's wife and children were held captive by the IRA in Donegal for ten days, in order to dissuade Hegarty from giving the British more information. British intelligence later offered his wife over £100,000 to relocate to England and stay with her husband. She refused.

Bishop Daly and the Hegarty family claim that McGuinness lured Hegarty home with a promise of safety. McGuinness, they say, knelt at the feet of Hegarty's mother, Rose, a woman he knew well, and assured her no harm would come to her son if he returned and spoke with his former comrades.

He did. In the short time Hegarty spent in Ireland, a meeting was organized at An Grianán fort, just across the Donegal border from Derry, so that he could see his son and daughter.

The next day, Hegarty was abducted from a hotel car park in Buncrana, Co. Donegal, and shot in the head four times. His body was dumped on the side of a border road with his eyes taped shut.

His family were given a tape recording of Frank being tortured, and admitting to working for the British. He said: 'I don't know if I'll ever see you again.'

Bishop Daly also told the Department of Foreign Affairs official that he was certain McGuinness was a Provisional

IRA Chief of Staff 'at least for the North-West if not for the entire North'.

A close confidant of McGuinness's in the IRA's Derry brigade told me that there was never an occasion when McGuinness wasn't prepared. At this time, McGuinness was a member of the IRA Army Council too, but it was never discussed, and even his confidant had only an 'inkling' about it.

'He would say to me, "Drive me to Armagh" and I'd do it no questions asked. He knew every wee back road in Ireland. I mean, every feckin road . . .

'I was driving him to South Armagh, I would have no clue where we were. He'd say: "We have to go to this house or that house", he knew everybody there and he'd get out and say: "Stay here."

'Another car would come and they'd go away and I could be left sitting there for five hours, I was twiddling my thumbs and getting tea.

'He'd come back and say, "Let's go."' There would be no conversation between the men as they traversed the dark country roads.

On one occasion in Sligo, McGuinness and a number of other key IRA figures had a meeting in a country hotel with a businessman who claimed to know where a very promin-ent member of the British Army lived. The businessman was prepared to give all the information he had, and carry out a reconnaissance mission of the soldier's house, to assist the IRA in an assassination. He mentioned, too, that he would bring his girlfriend along on the recce.

Bobby Storey asked the businessman what role the woman would play. Before the businessman could answer, McGuin-ness stood up: 'Fucking naw. Everyone up. Let's go.' He pointed at the businessman. 'Fuck him. That boy's a chancer.' The rest of the IRA men dutifully followed their leader out of the hotel.

McGuinness was meticulous and untrusting, with a keen eye for detail. He was also a non-drinker.

'He had a great radar for bullshit,' his former comrade says.

He was deeply religious, and his cellmates recall him wearing religious medals around his neck. As a commander, he did not take kindly to 'dirty jokes or men chasing women when they were supposed to be working'.

Gerry Adams III was born on 6 October 1948, the first son of Annie and Gerry Adams Jr.

His grandfather, the first Gerry Adams, had been a member of the Irish Republican Brotherhood in the early 1920s. Gerry Jr would join the IRA at sixteen and spend eight years in prison in 1942 for an ambush on the RUC which wounded two officers in Belfast.

Upon his release at twenty-one, Gerry Jr married Annie Hannaway, whose father had served as Éamon de Valera's election agent when he ran for election in West Belfast in 1918, and whose brothers were IRA legends in their home city. Annie herself was a member of the IRA's female wing, Cumann na mBan, as well as a mill worker, and would go on to have ten children.

Gerry Adams has always denied being a member of the IRA. Nobody believes the denial, which has been a source of mirth and anger over the decades. A number of people have spoken publicly about being in the Belfast brigade of the IRA with Gerry Adams, about taking commands from Gerry Adams as a leader in the IRA. Some claim they carried out murders which Gerry Adams had a role in planning.

Even as he flew to London on the RAF plane to meet

Whitelaw for truce negotiations, Adams knew the active service units in his home city were being heavily armed. The IRA were ready to show the British that if they were not serious about leaving Ireland, things were going to get worse. Sure enough, the London talks went nowhere and two days later the IRA ceasefire was over.

On the afternoon of 21 July, which came to be known as Bloody Friday, an estimated nineteen IRA bombs exploded in Belfast – from the south of the city in Botanic Avenue to Great Victoria Street in the city centre, the port ferry terminus and Queen Elizabeth Bridge up to Salisbury Avenue in north Belfast – in the space of eighty minutes.

Nine people were killed by the bombs: five civilians, two British soldiers, a Royal Ulster Constabulary (RUC) reservist and an Ulster Defence Association (UDA) member.

Of the 130 people who were injured, seventy-seven were women and children.

Six of the dead were killed by a car bomb at Oxford Street bus station. A police officer who was at the scene told the journalist Peter Taylor:

> The first thing that caught my eye was a torso of a human being lying in the middle of the street. It was recognizable as a torso because the clothes had been blown off and you could actually see parts of the human anatomy. One of the victims was a soldier I knew personally. He'd had his arms and legs blown off and some of his body had been blown through the railings. One of the most horrendous memories for me was seeing a head stuck to a wall. A couple of days later, we found vertebrae and a rib cage on the roof of a nearby building. The reason we found it was because the seagulls were diving onto it.

The carnage of Bloody Friday alienated many moderate nationalists from the IRA. Ed Moloney has argued that 'Bloody Friday and its aftermath marked a watershed in the IRA's fortunes. From then on the organization would be on the defensive both politically and militarily.'

Brendan Hughes, a confidant of Adams's, was centrally involved in the planning of Bloody Friday. Many years later, after falling out with Adams over his own opposition to the Good Friday Agreement, Hughes would give extensive testimony to Anthony McIntyre, a former IRA prisoner, as part of an oral history project on the Troubles sponsored by Boston College.

Hughes told McIntyre that he was filled with deep regret about his actions throughout his IRA career: 'not one death was worth it'. He said that Adams, by denying his involvement in the IRA, was trying to evade his responsibility for massacres like Bloody Friday.

Gerry was always the O/C. Even if he was not the O/C in name, Gerry was the man who made the decisions. [Adams and Ivor Bell] could have stopped everything; they could have stopped every bullet being fired. If they had wanted to they could have stopped 'Bloody Friday' . . . [When Adams denies IRA membership] it means that people like myself and Ivor have to carry the responsibility for all those deaths, for sending men out to die and sending women out to die, and Gerry was sitting there . . . trying to stop us from doing it? . . . I'm disgusted by it because it's so untrue and everybody knows it. The British know it, the people . . . know it, the dogs in the street know it. And yet he's standing there denying it . . .

A writer for *Republican News*, using the pen name 'Brownie', wrote in May 1976: 'Rightly or wrongly, I'm an IRA volunteer and rightly or wrongly, I take a course of action as a means of bringing about a situation in which I believe the people of my country will prosper.'

For a long time it was understood that 'Brownie' was Gerry Adams. Confirmation, if confirmation was needed, came in 2018, when Danny Morrison wrote in the *Irish Times*: 'I have known Gerry Adams 46 years. In 1975, as editor of *Republican News*, I asked him would he write a weekly column from Long Kesh, which he did under the pen man [*sic*] Brownie.' And as the Slugger O'Toole blog has pointed out, the 'Brownie' column was attributed to Adams by *An Phoblacht*'s 'About Us' section until 2004.

In 2018, in an interview with the BBC's Andrew Marr, Adams insisted that his position has been 'consistent, that I was not a member of the IRA, but I've never distanced myself from the IRA'.

In the interview, Adams clasped his hands under his salt-and-pepper beard and looked out from his small round glasses as Marr asks him if he had ever been tempted to join. Adams's face and voice did not change, but he looked away from Marr for a split second and down at the floor: 'No, no, I wasn't, no,' he said, before looking back at Marr's face.

'The thing about Gerry is, he could look his dearest friend in the eye and lie,' one Sinn Féin staffer told me. 'That is, if Gerry had any real friends.'

One former IRA commander told me that he remembers Adams as a lanky teenager when he first joined D-Company, aged eighteen, in 1969. D-Company of the Belfast Brigade of the IRA was the same unit Adams's father had belonged to. Within six years of his joining, the unit became the most ferocious in the city.

Tall, quiet and pensive, Gerry Adams is continually referred to as a 'hard man to know'. One of his family members told me that you 'could know Gerry all his life and never really know him'.

There is no account or evidence published of any volunteer carrying out an IRA operation with Adams, or of Adams ever firing a shot. Adams gave orders and people followed them.

A relative who once went on the run with Adams told me: 'I remember once where we billeted away down south somewhere, and I came in from an operation, and Gerry was sitting writing a letter to the *Irish News*.

'He says to me: "Come look at this" and it was a letter slagging off the republican movement and the IRA operations we had been carrying out, signed with a fake name.

'I said, "Gerry, what the fuck are you doing? This is against everything we stand for", and he explained to me that after the *Irish News* published the letter, he'd write his own letter in reply, in his own name. He'd correct the errors in the first letter and stand up for the movement. It was all about making him look better.'

Almost everyone interviewed for this book who dealt with Adams has noted his patience, ability and foresight. 'Gerry sees everything a hundred miles down the road,' one Sinn Féin staffer told me. 'Gerry's always playing the long game.'

It was such foresight that enabled Adams to lead an armed paramilitary campaign, see off two splits, persuade an entire army and its supporters to trust in politics, and retire on his own terms, complete with a rebrand as an eccentric grandfather type, pottering around his garden, writing cookbooks, making a podcast and spending time with the 'little people' in his life, his grandchildren.

For many years when there was no visible peace process, the British had a secret back channel with both loyalist and republican paramilitaries.

For the IRA, Derry businessman Brendan Duddy and his MI6 handler, Michael Oatley, known to the IRA only by his codename, 'Mountain Climber', as well as a number of other MI5 and MI6 officers, operated a conduit between the British government and the IRA leadership from 1973 to 1993.

Jonathan Powell, who would play a key role in the peace process as an aide to Tony Blair, claims in his memoir that the channel was used on three major occasions: to negotiate the 1974 IRA ceasefire; during the abortive IRA hunger strike in 1980; and in the early stages of the peace process in the 1990s.

He wrote: 'From a British government point of view there were no negotiations. Throughout the series of meetings which now occurred at ever more frequent intervals at a safe-house in Derry to which the Republican participants were on each occasion smuggled from across the border under the eyes of the British Army, Oatley . . . maintained that the purpose of the dialogue was not to negotiate, but to advise the IRA of what action the British government and security forces might take if there were a cessation of violence . . .'

During the 1980s, Adams – who in 1983 was elected MP for Belfast West and became president of Sinn Féin – made his own approaches towards peace.

Father Alec Reid was a Redemptionist priest, raised in Dublin and Co. Tipperary, who worked at Clonard Monastery in west Belfast. Adams joined a Clonard confraternity as a teenager, saying prayers and singing hymns with other boys his age.

In his memoir *Hope and History*, Adams says he first met Reid on Easter Sunday in 1976. Reid was involved in peace-making ministries, and Adams had requested that he intervene in the feud between the Provisional and Official republican movements in Belfast.

In later years, Reid recalled in a BBC documentary that Adams's view was that the 'only way to stop the IRA' was to agree a pan-nationalist strategy for peace between the IRA, the SDLP and the Irish government.

Reid wrote to John Hume on 19 May 1986, stating that the nationalist parties North and South should come together and agree a common approach for ending the conflict. Hume phoned Reid the following day, and the two men met the day after that.

The substance of their conversation was relayed back to Adams, and for a time the priest operated as a messenger between the two party leaders.

When Hume and Adams were ready to meet in person, the encounters took place in secret. Adams recalled being struck by the tense, isolated figure that Hume projected. Adams operated with a team of loyal confidants. Hume, by contrast, had a poor relationship with his deputy leader, Seamus Mallon, and he had kept the meetings confidential even from his own party.

On 11 January 1988, Adams and Hume held a meeting at Clonard Monastery that was announced publicly. Hume came in for criticism from the British Secretary of State, Tom King, and from commentators who worried about the consequences of bringing Sinn Féin into some sort of pan-nationalist front.

At the same time, Fr Reid was lobbying Charles Haughey, who had recently started his third stint as Taoiseach, to meet with Sinn Féin, in order to make the agreed nationalist policy a reality and end the IRA's campaign for good. He asked the journalist Tim Pat Coogan to lobby on his behalf in Dublin.

Department of Foreign Affairs officials were already aware of suggestions that Adams was looking for a way to end the conflict.

Cahal Daly, the Catholic Bishop of Down and Connor, spoke to an Irish diplomat in early 1987. The diplomat's report stated: 'The bishop has picked up a rumour that Gerry Adams is currently trying to put together a set of proposals, which would enable the Provisional IRA to call a halt to their paramilitary campaign.

'He has reached the view that the "armed struggle" is getting nowhere, that it has become a political liability to Sinn Féin, both North and South, and that, as long as it continues, there is little chance that he will be able to realise his own political ambitions. What he is believed to be working on is some form of "declaration of intent" to withdraw, with however long a timescale, on the part of the British government.

'If he managed to negotiate something of this kind, the Provisional IRA would be able to lay down their arms without much loss of face, claiming that they had achieved the breakthrough towards which all their efforts had been directed.'

It is unlikely this rumour reached Daly by accident, as Adams was known to use such leaks to his advantage while managing to keep his darkest secrets watertight. It is likely such a rumour was planted in order to soften the ground for what was to come next.

In April 1987, Sinn Féin released an eight-page paper titled 'A Scenario for Peace'.

The document repeated the old demands: British withdrawal from Northern Ireland, the disbandment of the RUC, the release of IRA prisoners and 'national self-determination'.

But it also included a nod – albeit barbed – to the culture and rights of the unionist population:

Sinn Féin seeks a new constitution for Ireland which would include written guarantees for those presently constituted as 'loyalists'. This would recognize present-day social reality and would include, for example, the provisions for family planning and the right to civil divorce.

The resolution of the conflict would free unionists from their historic laager mentality and would grant them real security instead of tenure based on repression and triumphalism. We do not intend to turn back the pages of history, or to dispossess the loyalists and foolishly attempt to reverse the Plantation. We offer them a settlement based on their throwing in their lot with the rest of the Irish people and ending sectarianism. We offer them peace. We offer them equality.

The paper also proposed a constitutional conference at which all elected officials, unionist and nationalist, could come to a peaceful settlement.

Haughey kept a wide berth at first, but in 1988 eventually agreed to allow a Fianna Fáil delegation to meet with Sinn Féin.

Likewise, on 23 March 1988, Sinn Féin and SDLP delegations met for the first time. The Sinn Féin delegates arrived in an armoured black taxi.

Adams chose Tom Hartley and Mitchel McLaughlin for the talks specifically because the pair had no known link to the IRA. Danny Morrison also attended.

Adams recalls in *Hope and History* that the meeting was awkward. The parties met twice more, with one additional private meeting between the leaders.

At this point Adams said he 'was trying to create an alliance of Irish political parties and opinion, informal or otherwise'. He claimed that this was in order to improve relations with Britain and for the well-being of the nationalist people. It is more likely that Adams knew any public alliance with the SDLP would give Sinn Féin a much-needed air of legitimacy and respectability. It would subtly show the British that the republican movement, bombs and all, was not so repulsive to the nationalist people.

The IRA was meanwhile continuing to cause havoc. In July 1988, an IRA bomb killed Robert James Hanna and Maureen Patricia Hanna, both forty-four, and their son, David, six, who were driving home to Hillsborough after a holiday in the United States.

Three people in nearby cars were injured. The IRA said the bomb was meant for British soldiers.

On 1 August, an IRA bomb killed a British soldier and injured nine more at an army barracks in London.

Three days later, on 4 August, two Protestant builders were shot by the IRA in Belleek, near the border in County Fermanagh. The two workers had been carrying out repairs at the RUC station. Willie Hassard, fifty-nine, and Fred Love, sixty-four, were ambushed at point-blank range by four gunmen as they drove home in their van.

On 20 August, eight British soldiers aged between eighteen and twenty-one were killed and twenty-eight injured while travelling in a bus when a 200lb IRA roadside bomb exploded in Ballygawley, Co. Tyrone.

State documents later revealed that, in the wake of the eight deaths, Prime Minister Margaret Thatcher warned the head of the RUC that she would no longer send 'her boys over in waves to be killed'. This was later described by an official as a 'panic reaction'.

The continued violence only served to make the SDLP's decision to sit with Sinn Féin more damaging to Hume's party.

A memo from the time written by NIO official J. E. McConnell of the political affairs division stated: 'The talks between the SDLP and Sinn Féin have been condemned by the Unionist, Alliance and Workers' parties as giving credibility to supporters of violence and as jeopardizing the prospects of talks between the constitutional parties. Subsequent comments by Seamus Mallon advocating a place for Sinn Féin in inter-party talks have also been condemned amid speculation that the SDLP and Sinn Féin may be planning to form a 'pannationalist front' – on the condition of an end to violence.

'Any role for Sinn Féin in a discussion process would be seen by unionists as that party having successfully "bombed and killed" their way to the conference table.'

In the end, the SDLP rejected Sinn Féin's proposal for the two parties and the Dublin government to try to persuade the British government to end the union.

Private engagements between Hume and Adams, however, continued. Adams was open about the low opinion in which he held Hume's colleagues, but he saw Hume as someone he could reason with.

In February 1992, the Sinn Féin leadership published 'Towards a Lasting Peace', a policy document which offered new concessions. Having previously stressed that unionists were a minority on the island of Ireland, the party now said that unionist cooperation would be sought in any constitutional change: 'Peace requires a settlement between Irish nationalists and Irish unionists.'

The document was written by a close circle among the Sinn Féin leadership, including Jim Gibney (known as 'God's

Little Helper', God being Adams himself), Gerry Kelly, Tom Hartley, Aiden McAteer and Mitchel McLaughlin.

In April, Adams lost his seat at the general election, owing to a significant swing in favour of the SDLP.

The day after the general election, IRA car bombs at the Baltic Exchange in London killed three people, including a fifteen-year-old girl, Danielle Carter.

Danielle and her sister, Christiane, aged eight, were waiting in their father's car outside the exchange when the 100lb Semtex bomb exploded. Danielle, a gifted hockey player, died instantly. Her younger sister was showered with glass from the windscreen and nearby offices. A passing taxi driver took Christiane to hospital, where she had more than 100 stitches, leaving scars on her face and body.

Danielle's body was removed by police, unbeknown to their father, Danny, who had been returning a car he used for business nearby. Danny spent the night searching hospitals across London, convinced that his eldest daughter was still alive. He learned of her death at 5.30am the next day.

In March 1993, an MI5 spy known to the IRA as 'Fred' met Martin McGuinness and Gerry Kelly. Prime Minister John Major had cancelled the pre-planned meeting after an IRA bomb killed two children in Warrington, but the British spy went on a solo run.

The five-hour meeting was held at the home of Brendan Duddy in Derry.

'McGuinness did most of the talking. It was not a friendly interrogation,' the MI5 agent told the journalist Peter Taylor. Gerry Kelly kept minutes of the meeting.

Sinn Féin released a document in 1994, in the aftermath of the meeting, stating the MI5 agent told them that Irish unity was the goal:

The final solution is union. It is going to happen anyway.
The historical train – Europe – determines that. We are
committed to Europe. Unionists will have to change.

This island will be as one.

Peter Taylor, in his book *Operation Chiffon*, says Kelly,
McGuinness and Brendan Duddy all confirmed the spy said
this in their presence. He adds that Sir John Chilcot, Permanent Under-Secretary at the Northern Ireland Office, 'came
pretty close to confirming it' despite there being no British
record of what was said at the meeting.

The idea that this was the British position seems fantasti-
cal. Perhaps it suited the British to give republicans the idea
that it was their position. In any case, Kelly has since credited
the meeting with giving republicans some hope that dialogue
with the British and the other political parties of Northern
Ireland was possible.

The republican leadership was increasingly conscious of
the ineffectiveness of the IRA's campaign. And yet the violence seemed to become ever more reckless and pointless.

When Adams was spotted outside Hume's family home in
April 1993 – the first public evidence of meetings between
the two since 1988 – it led to widespread condemnation of
the SDLP leader. The episode made clear to Adams the
strength of the anti-IRA and therefore anti-Sinn Féin senti-
ment in the media and governments in London and
Dublin – something that would not change while the IRA
continued its violent campaign.

On 10 April, in the aftermath of the meeting being revealed,
Hume and Adams issued a joint statement, saying: 'the Irish
people as a whole have a right to national self-determination'.

The statement strengthened Adams's position, helping

him to convince his comrades on the IRA Army Council that any further violence could harm the alliance with Hume.

In June 1993, the Irish President, Mary Robinson, caused uproar by shaking hands with Adams at a west Belfast community centre.

A memo from Jonathan Stephens to NIO officials stated that the British government had only learned Adams would be there the day before. '[Mayhew] feared the meeting would be seen as the head of state of a country with a territorial claim over NI meeting Sinn Féin which justified violence in support of that territorial claim.'

Despite such hiccups, the two governments were now working in earnest to lay the groundwork for a new dispensation in Northern Ireland. On 15 December 1993, John Major and Taoiseach Albert Reynolds issued the Downing Street Declaration.

The document stated that Britain had 'no selfish strategic or economic interest in Northern Ireland':

Both Governments accept that Irish unity would be achieved only by those who favour this outcome persuading those who do not, peacefully and without coercion or violence, and that, if in the future a majority of the people of Northern Ireland are so persuaded, both Governments will support and give legislative effect to their wish. But, notwithstanding the solemn affirmation by both Governments in the Anglo-Irish Agreement that any change in the status of Northern Ireland would only come about with the consent of a majority of the people of Northern Ireland . . .

In January 1994, Reynolds's government announced that section 31 of the Broadcasting Act would be lifted. This meant that Sinn Féin members could once again appear on the airwaves in the Republic of Ireland, a huge step on the road to political legitimacy.

Another such step soon followed. After Adams was invited to speak at an event hosted by the National Committee on American Foreign Policy, a campaign began to help Adams acquire a visa to travel to the US.

Adams's visa requests up until this point had always been denied by the US, on the grounds that he had links to a terrorist organization. However, John Hume advised Senator Ted Kennedy that he should lobby for Adams to be able to enter the States, because it would advance the cause of peace.

Kennedy and three other senators wrote to President Clinton, saying, 'We believe that granting a visa at this time will enhance, not undermine, the peace process.'

The visa was granted. Adams was allowed into America for forty-eight hours and was barred from travelling more than twenty-five miles from New York.

Meanwhile, a spate of loyalist killings in the summer of 1994 made the republican leadership worried about announcing any ceasefire.

In late August, Adams and McGuinness met with the IRA leadership. It was hoped that Joe Cahill, a veteran republican, would be granted a visa to travel to the US to convince Irish republicans there of the merits of a ceasefire.

In the meantime, Hume and Adams released another joint statement, their fourth:

A just and lasting peace in Ireland will only be achieved if it is based on democratic principles. It is clear that an internal settlement is not a solution. Both governments and all parties have already agreed that all relationships must be settled.

All that has been tried before has failed to satisfactorily resolve the conflict or remove the political conditions which give rise to it. If a lasting settlement is to be found there must be a fundamental and thorough-going change, based on the right of the Irish people as a whole to national self-determination.

The exercise of this right is, of course, a matter for agreement between all the people of Ireland and we reiterate that such a new agreement is only viable if it enjoys the allegiance of the different traditions on this island by accommodating diversity and providing for national reconciliation.

On 29 August, Joe Cahill's visa was approved. On the same day, the Army Council met in Donegal to vote on a ceasefire. Adams, McGuinness, Pat Doherty, Cahill and the South Armagh adjutant of Northern Command voted in favour. Kevin McKenna, chief of staff, voted against. Mickey McKevitt did not have voting rights but made it clear he was against a cessation.

On 31 August 1994, the IRA announced a 'complete cessation of military operations', and called for 'inclusive negotiations'.

Martin McGuinness was dispatched around Ireland to explain the ceasefire to the membership. Members were told that the IRA had the British on the back foot, and that this cessation of violence would focus minds and bring the British to the table in order to discuss withdrawing from Ireland. This was nonsense, but it was part of an emerging pattern whereby the leadership told the rank and file what it thought it wanted to hear, in order to allow politics to prevail.

The British government was sceptical about the republican movement's bona fides. The first talks between Sinn

Féin and the Northern Ireland Office did not take place until December 1994, and at that point there was still no sign that government ministers were in the mood for negotiating.

McGuinness headed up the Sinn Féin side, accompanied by Gerry Kelly, Lucilita Bhreatnach, Seán McManus and Siobhán O'Hanlon. Quentin Thomas, Northern Ireland Office (NIO) Permanent Under-Secretary, led the British contingent.

According to minutes of the meeting, Thomas said: 'The enterprise we begin is to find an accommodation, a reconciliation where those old links become benign . . . We must find a way to bury, with dignity, the sacrifices, mistakes and horrors of the past. We share responsibility . . . to work to end the conflict.'

McGuinness said the British had failed to recognize Sinn Féin's mandate and, remarkably, denied the party had any link to the IRA. 'The IRA is nothing whatever to do with us,' he said.

The key British position was that high-level talks could not begin until the IRA had given up its arsenal of weapons.

The Irish government believed weapons decommissioning should not be a pre-condition to talks but should happen 'during the talks process at the latest'.

The major concern was that any attempt to force the republican leadership into decommissioning could cause a split as it had done previously, with armed groups splintering off and further violence erupting. Keeping the IRA together was essential to avoid more bloodshed.

The British demand for decommissioning, and the republican movement's refusal, brought about a stalemate. Almost eighteen months after they stopped, the bombs resumed – with tragic consequences for the families of Inan Bashir, John Jeffries and Zaoui Berezag.

Adams expressed his 'sympathy' for those injured and his commitment to the peace process. But he declined to condemn the bombing.

One IRA man (and later Sinn Féin negotiator) told me the Docklands bombing was 'macho military bullshit', but said it 'proved to the British government that we're not negotiating from a point of weakness. If they messed with us, they'd know.' The IRA was always at pains to prove it wouldn't be beaten or surrender, and was prepared to exact a huge human cost to make the point.

Within three weeks of the Docklands bombing, the British and Irish prime ministers set a date –10 June 1996 – for the start of 'all-party' talks.

'All-party' did not mean, literally, all parties. It meant all parties that signed up to the 'Mitchell Principles', six criteria for inclusion – including a renunciation of violence and a commitment to disarm.

The stalemate dragged on. In April 1997, on the cusp of a general election, Prime Minister John Major laid out the reasons for the continued exclusion of Sinn Féin from talks in an *Irish Times* op-ed:

> By their words and by their deeds Sinn Féin exclude themselves from the Stormont talks. We would like to see them there. But there can be no question of them entering the talks without the restoration of a credible and verifiable ceasefire. That must include an end to all paramilitary activity – including the targeting of victims – and a commitment to the principles of democracy and non-violence.

Major lost the election in a landslide. The new British Prime Minister, Tony Blair, made it clear Northern Ireland was top of his agenda. His first official visit outside London was to Belfast, where he set out his priorities:

> People often ask me if I am exhilarated by our election victory. Of course I am excited by it. But most of all I feel the most profound humility at the trust put in me; and with it, an equally profound sense of responsibility. I feel it, perhaps especially, about Northern Ireland. This is not a party political game or even a serious debate about serious run-of-the-mill issues. It is about life and death for people here. An end to violence and there are people, young men and women particularly[,] who will live and raise families and die in peace. Without it, they will die prematurely and in bloodshed.

The Sinn Féin leadership operated at all times in fear that the republican movement would split – as it had numerous times in the past. The crunch came not in 1998, when the Good Friday Agreement was signed, but in 1997, when Sinn Féin had to demonstrate its commitment to the Mitchell Principles in order to join the all-party talks.

There was much opposition to another ceasefire, but the leadership's view eventually prevailed. On 19 July 1997, the IRA announced they would be laying down their weapons again.

Mickey McKevitt resigned from his position as IRA quartermaster during an IRA Executive meeting on 23 October 1997, citing his opposition to the Mitchell Principles. Five other headquarters staff followed, along with a number of others from other departments.

McKevitt and other dissidents founded the Real IRA the following month. The new paramilitary group was equipped with explosives from Provisional IRA ammunition caches McKevitt had been in charge of.

The much-feared split was now a reality. It was small enough that the damage could be contained; but if the final peace agreement drove more Provisionals into the McKevitt faction, the consequences could be catastrophic. A break-away movement with access to weapons and no commitment to electoral politics could create more years of misery and death, while jeopardizing the fragile consensus the Sinn Féin leadership had worked to build.

By that point, Sinn Féin had already entered talks, along with nine other parties and the British and Irish governments. Both the DUP and UUP refused to speak with Sinn Féin.

Sinn Féin's negotiating style proved frustrating for the governments and the other parties. They could never make a decision without consulting the IRA. Of course, Sinn Féin's status in the negotiations was linked to the fact that its pos-ition was indistinguishable from that of the paramilitaries. There was a running joke: when Adams and McGuinness went back to 'check with leadership', they went into the gents' toilets and spoke to each other.

The truth, of course, was more complex. The supremacy of Adams and McGuinness in the republican movement was unchallenged, but this status – and the stability of the movement – depended on the fact that they never got too far out ahead of where the IRA rank and file were at. 'We knew that if this was to work . . . we had to convince Gerry and the boys and that Gerry had to convince the real boys,' says one senior Irish official. 'I mean, they didn't make any secret of it, but you could never get a definitive answer on anything because they had to consult the IRA on everything.'

Consulting 'the real boys' often involved conversations in a field around a tractor – with its engine running to thwart listening devices.

Adams enjoyed an informal and friendly relationship with the Taoiseach, Bertie Ahern, during this time, but this didn't seem to matter or mean anything in negotiations, according to sources who took part in the peace process. Adams would lie, knowing that those opposite him knew he was lying. He would bang his hands on the table and lose his temper when things weren't going his way.

'You never bloody well knew, with Gerry, you never knew,' says one Irish government negotiator. 'I was used to it, but you never knew where the line was with Gerry.'

One negotiator recalls telling Bertie Ahern that they had found Adams intimidating, to which Ahern replied: 'I know *you* can't, but if it were me, I'd just tell him to fuck off.'

Michael Collins, a senior Irish official, dealt with Adams directly. Collins was a gifted and experienced negotiator. Colleagues say that one day he returned to Ahern's office 'visibly shaken'.

According to one witness, 'Adams had been really rough. Collins was really taken aback and you know, he's not a man to be messed around, and that wasn't the only time it happened.'

High-level Irish officials, and Ahern himself, began to approach McGuinness alone, away from Adams, in order to get a better read of the situation.

'Martin was actually great,' one senior official says. 'If Martin said it, I knew that was true. So he'd say; "I can't sell that. I'm not sure how I can sell that", or "I'm not sure if I want to sell that."'

Irish officials recall that Ahern became closer to McGuinness over the course of the talks and they would often have private conversations outside of official channels.

'It was obvious Bertie had a better relationship with Martin,' one says. 'The thing with Martin was that he'd never tell you that he pulled the trigger on anyone but you were left to the conclusion that he did from the things he'd say. He left you in no doubt that he had been, what he considered, an experienced soldier.'

According to this official, whereas Adams was prone to getting upset for no good reason, McGuinness was different.

'If Martin was shouting at Ahern and maybe they had argued over something, you kind of felt . . . it was usually about something that was fair enough to be shouting about.'

One Sinn Féin negotiator believes that Adams used displays of anger tactically.

'There are times where I think Gerry deliberately talked nonsense in order to delay things, because he did have this capacity to upset the balance of a meeting,' the negotiator says. 'He'd give off this impression that the other people he was talking to aren't happy about a certain thing. Insinuating the IRA were angry about something, when the IRA were oblivious to whatever the topic was, he hadn't been home in days to talk to anyone else, he just meant himself and he didn't know the right answer or he felt backed into a corner.'

One Irish minister said that on a number of occasions they took what he described as 'big chances' on the word of McGuinness without telling the British.

'I had to go on his word that he wouldn't let me down,' the official recalls. 'And he didn't. Would I have done that for Gerry? No.'

Officials would inform Ahern of every move, and whenever he was in doubt, he told them to err on the side of McGuinness's word.

Although they had different styles, Adams and McGuinness were completely in step with one another on the substance of the negotiations.

'When one would lose the head, the other would go silent and pick up the issue a different way,' the official recalls. But they always presented a united front, 'even when you could see that they'd have different views on the topic'.

The British government's chief negotiator, Jonathan Powell, referred to their 'good cop, bad cop routine', noting that the pair had been together 'longer than most married couples' by this stage.

One distinguishing feature of Sinn Féin's approach to negotiations was that they kept detailed notes of everything that happened.

A Fianna Fáil minister who negotiated with Sinn Féin during the peace process recalls: 'In Fianna Fáil, minutes of meetings are taken and they might as well be the fairytales of Ireland. In Sinn Féin, everything was logged, everything was detailed.'

Bertie Ahern once asked Martin McGuinness about the note-taking. The pair were attending the Forum for Peace and Reconciliation event in Dublin Castle in December 1997 and were speaking privately when the Taoiseach said he felt they were wasting time in meetings writing notes about trivial matters during negotiations.

McGuinness replied: 'Well, you'd keep the minutes as well, if the outcome was that you could get killed.'

If not Adams or McGuinness, another Sinn Féin staffer,

usually Siobhán O'Hanlon, a close aide of Adams, would always be taking notes.

O'Hanlon, a completely trusted member of the team, was part of the first Sinn Féin delegation to meet Prime Minister Blair. A niece of Joe Cahill, a former member of the IRA Army Council, she was convicted in 1983 on explosive charges, serving four years in Armagh jail. After three IRA members were killed by the SAS in Gibraltar in 1988 while allegedly preparing an attack on British forces, the *Sunday Times* reported that O'Hanlon had been part of the same Active Service Unit.

O'Hanlon denied that she had been involved in any illegal activity in Gibraltar, or that she was even an IRA member.

For its next meeting with Blair, in Downing Street on 11 December, Sinn Féin arrived with a big delegation including Martin Ferris, a convicted gun-runner, Michelle Gildernew, Lucilita Bhreatnach, Siobhán O'Hanlon and Richard McAuley. Dozens of photographers snapped pictures of the once unimaginable becoming imaginable, the political wing of the IRA invited to Downing Street by the Prime Minister of Great Britain and Northern Ireland.

A Fianna Fáil minister who participated in the talks describes O'Hanlon as 'meticulous'.

Whenever a negotiator suffered a genuine or deliberate failure of recollection, 'Siobhán would always pull out her notes and give them chapter and verse of what they said two months ago,' the minister said.

An air of physical danger played a part in how negotiations were conducted by the Sinn Féin leadership.

'There was always the impression that they were vulnerable,' an Irish official recalls.

'I suppose that was true. I mean, both from dissident types and some lawyers at times for sure . . . they had a different vulnerability and they also came with their own security, some level of protection with them.'

Adams and McGuinness both travelled with drivers for the entirety of their public life, usually ex-IRA prisoners whom they trusted, literally, with their lives.

'They could never believe that we took the bus,' the official says.

If O'Hanlon wasn't present, Adams and McGuinness would be scribbling notes constantly, sometimes passing them to each other. If they hadn't brought paper, they would write on napkins and paper coasters and stuff them into their pockets at the end of the meeting.

O'Hanlon wasn't the only trusted woman who took part in high-level talks.

Lucilita Bhreatnach didn't fit the Sinn Féin mould. She was from Dublin, and middle class. Her father, Deasún Breatnach, was a journalist who had served as editor of *An Phoblacht* twice. Her mother, Lucila Hellman de Menchaca, was born in Algorta in the Basque country. A language activist and co-founder of the first gaelscoil in Ireland, she was also a member of Amnesty International and the Irish Council of Civil Liberties.

Lucilita joined Sinn Féin at sixteen, and later worked for *An Phoblacht*. She was party general secretary from 1988 to 2003 – the only female general secretary of any party in Ireland at the time.

One negotiator recalls Bhreatnach as having been present at 'all the meetings in the nineties.' Whereas members of the Sinn Féin delegation usually left the talking to Adams and McGuinness, Bhreatnach was willing to speak up.

One person present at the talks describes Bhreatnach as having been 'very close' to the leadership. 'There was a lot of people who thought that she was a token woman, but she wasn't a token woman.

'They did bring in token women to meetings. They'd get their pictures taken going in with the likes of Michelle Gildernew, and then they'd either not be in the meeting room at all, or would come in and sit in silence.' Bhreatnach, by contrast, 'would speak and you could see her reacting to things and I always thought that she was probably more on the army side or speaking from their side'.

Each member of Sinn Féin's delegation was given a portfolio to be responsible for, such as prisoners or parades, the Irish language, policing and legacy.

One official recalls an occasion during negotiations in Belfast when the delegations spent until five in the morning going through an agenda of ninety items. As different agenda items arose, Adams would bring different people into the room. It was, according to the official, as though Sinn Féin had a bench full of substitutes ready to go on for each issue, while the others in the negotiating teams had played the entire game and were getting increasingly weary.

One Sinn Féin negotiator says that the party's use of a large team was partly for appearances.

'You'd have three or four people they would want elected in the next election so they'd bring them to Downing Street and they'd get their picture taken going in and it would boost their profile. It was so they could go back to the constituency and say they negotiated with the Brits.'

Even when the document that would become the Good Friday Agreement had been drafted, after months of painstaking back and forth, Sinn Féin were still unable to fully commit to supporting the agreement that they had helped craft. The party felt it had to commit to an elaborate process of internal consultation and voting.

Support for the Agreement was passed by Sinn Féin Ard Comhairle the following Tuesday. This was no surprise, as almost every policy submitted to the Ard Comhairle by the party leadership sailed through with little dissent. The real crunch would come for the party leadership on 10 May, when the agreement was taken to the Ard Fheis.

The leadership broke up into small units and travelled the country, North and South, to plead the case for politics. Martin McGuinness was in charge of convincing the IRA membership.

According to Powell's memoir, in order to sweeten the deal with current IRA members, McGuinness asked Tony Blair if he would consider taking down some military installations across Northern Ireland, but Blair refused.

The message that volunteers were given shifted from place to place, depending on the membership of the local unit and the level of their dedication to armed struggle. High-level Sinn Féin representatives would assure volunteers that what they were seeing nightly on the news wasn't the full story. Sinn Féin and the IRA would give them the full story, they said: they just had to be patient.

'When you look back, they'd have told us anything to get us to go along with it,' one IRA member says.

This person recalls Adams making 'his impassioned plea for [IRA] volunteers to join Sinn Féin'. He recalls IRA members feeling annoyed at the idea that they were viewed as 'dumb fucking soldiers', whereas they believed themselves to be 'political activists'.

A Sinn Féin official was called upon to collate prisoner

views on the peace process in advance of a special meeting with the Sinn Féin and IRA leadership in Dublin.

The staffer missed his deadline by a few days, and was coming under increasing pressure from head office in Dublin. Finally, the missing document arrived at the Falls Road office in a car. The staffer bounded up the stairs and began furiously faxing the pages away.

It was only when he had the final page in his hand that he realized he had just sent information about the party's policy direction and analysis of the Good Friday Agreement to a fax machine located in the hallway of an office with any number of people filing in and out.

'I thought, "Fuck it" and just filed the last page, too. The damage was done.'

The report from the republican prisoners appeared in a newspaper the following week.

One day before the Sinn Féin Ard Fheis, the Real IRA publicly announced its existence. The Real IRA statement said they had set up 'a caretaker IRA executive' as the 'true IRA' and that the ceasefire was over, with war set to continue against the British.

Many believed that the move was intended to show Sinn Féin members that an alternative was available.

Undeterred, voters at the Sinn Féin Ard Fheis supported the Good Friday Agreement 331 to 19. The result was an overwhelming vote of confidence in the republican leadership. Later that same month, voters in referenda on both sides of the border strongly supported the Agreement.

On 15 August 1998, the Real IRA would carry out one of the most horrific acts of violence ever seen in Northern Ireland and the single worst atrocity of the Troubles.

The group detonated a 500lb car bomb on a Saturday afternoon in the market town of Omagh, Co. Tyrone. Twenty-nine people were killed along with two unborn children.

The Omagh atrocity put Sinn Féin under pressure to respond. According to an RTÉ report at the time, Adams's statement was written in consultation with the British and Irish governments as well as senior White House officials. President Bill Clinton was due to visit Ireland two days later. Adams said:

[. . .] This appalling act was carried out by those opposed to the peace process.

It is designed to wreck the process and everyone should work to ensure the peace process continues as is the clear wish of the people of the island. Sinn Féin has called for a complete halt to such actions and has urged all armed groups to stop immediately.

Those responsible are aligning themselves with the forces opposed to a democratic settlement in the conflict here.

[. . .] Sinn Féin believe the violence we have seen must be for all of us now a thing of the past, over, done with and gone.

3. Sink or Swim

The Good Friday Agreement was ratified by large majorities in the North and South of Ireland on 22 May 1998. In the elections held just over a month later for the new devolved Northern Ireland Assembly, Sinn Féin might reasonably have hoped for a post-Agreement bounce. Instead, having received 16 per cent of the vote in the 1997 general election and 17 per cent in the local elections later that year, the party's support held steady at 17.63 per cent of the first-preference vote, which brought them eighteen out of 108 seats. Five of the new Sinn Féin MLAs were women, the highest number for any party.

Many of the elected candidates, including Adams, McGuinness, Gerry Kelly, John Kelly, Alex Maskey and Conor Murphy, had been either jailed for IRA activity or interned by the British government; and Adams, McGuinness and Pat Doherty have all been named as members of the IRA Army Council.

In this company, Bairbre de Brún was something of an anomaly. Born in Dublin, she attended University College Dublin for a Bachelor of Arts Degree in Modern Languages and a Higher Diploma in Education. She earned a Post-Graduate Certificate in Education at Queen's University Belfast and became a language teacher. She became involved in politics through the National H-Blocks/Armagh Committee while studying in Belfast, and joined Sinn Féin in 1982. During the peace process, she took a year off work as a teacher to join the party's negotiating team. She was one of four Sinn Féin candidates elected to represent Belfast West in the Assembly.

Owing to delays in IRA decommissioning, it was 3 December 1999 before the new ministers took charge of their briefs in Northern Ireland. The UUP's Michael McGimpsey, who was appointed culture minister, would later recall de Brún being under 'huge pressure' on the Assembly's Executive Committee:

> People were merciless with her as minister for health. I always got the sense with Bairbre that she actually cared about the job, but she was slaughtered in the chamber. The crowd that we had round the table wasn't the happiest of groups; we weren't the most sympathetic with each other.

A former MLA told me that the Sinn Féin members and staff were ill prepared for their roles in the Assembly: 'It was sink or swim when you got there and to be honest, we hadn't a clue.'

Some MLAs were out of their depth. Others took to their new roles easily, despite the deep mistrust with which the unionist parties and public viewed Sinn Féin.

The contrast between the wartime republican movement and the peacetime republican movement could be stark. One bright-eyed MLA who had set their sights on changing the world away from conflict recalls walking into their grim-looking office on their first day and being greeted by a former blanket-protestor who opened the door and exclaimed: 'Welcome to the rest of your life.'

McGuinness's new role as education minister caused huge upset in the unionist community. A protest was organized in one school and students boycotted classes. DUP leader Ian Paisley said: 'We never thought we would live to see a Sinn

Féiner in charge of education. The people of Northern Ireland need to realise that this is not a game. The IRA have designs on their children and their education.'

McGuinness – who had left school at fourteen, and now found himself presiding over a £1.4 billion education budget – was unperturbed.

'People, particularly those of a different political opinion, will be concerned that I may not serve the interests of all the children in Northern Ireland,' he said at the time.

'They could not be more wrong. I'm prepared to learn. I'm prepared to work hard. No-one could ever accuse me of shirking my responsibilities.'

McGimpsey later recalled:

Martin was enjoying it. He felt that it was another step forward, an achievement, so he was generally very cheerful and practical round the table. [. . .]

I got the sense that he didn't think he'd get as far as he did, so he felt he'd achieved something. He was fully energetic and energised when it was an armed struggle, and once that changed and it was politics, he gave it 100 per cent.

If McGimpsey and others in the UUP were willing to work constructively with Sinn Féin, the DUP was a different story. Sinn Féin women were particular targets. 'There was a core of the DUP MLAs who just couldn't get their fucking head around the fact that you had a brain,' one female former MLA recalls. 'One in particular used to say to me; "Who's advising you?" He was basically saying; "You're a woman and Republican and yet you know that?"

'The base sectarianism was constant. The same man came bounding over to me in the canteen in Stormont while I was having carrot soup, and said: "Told you it would all go orange eventually."'

Some within the Sinn Féin viewed the Assembly as a stop-gap, a temporary step on a rapid path towards Irish unity. Others, with a more realistic understanding of political reality in Northern Ireland, made it clear they were there for the long haul. The leadership, as usual, strove to keep both tendencies on board, and urged MLAs and staff never to lose focus on the end goal of a united Ireland, no matter how far off it might be.

The former MLA was among those who viewed Stormont as a 'stepping stone', but embraced the workload nonetheless: 'I wouldn't have been up and down that road four times a week or sitting on a seven-hour committee meeting or looking to pass legislation far beyond your comprehension and taking shit wages if you didn't think this was all worth it.'

The 'shit wages' received by Sinn Féin MLAs and staffers is a story unto itself.

The party's unwritten policy was that elected representatives should be living on the 'average industrial wage' and contributing the rest of their salary to the party and constituency services.

When the party entered Stormont, it had an odd way of making sure that was the case.

A number of previously elected MLAs and staff, including ministerial special advisors, have told me that upon their first days of entering the Assembly, they were asked to either open new bank accounts or to sign papers to open bank accounts in their name. Their Assembly salaries were to be paid into these new accounts which were controlled by the Sinn Féin leadership.

One MLA recalls having 'no fucking control' over the account, and 'never saw a bank statement: they were all managed by head office'. Wages for MLAs and staffers – the average industrial wage – were paid directly by the party. In 1998, an MLA's wage was £22,457. The average wage for a worker in Northern Ireland at the time was around £13,000.

One MLA told me about being instructed to open a new bank account, controlled by the party, into which the MLA salary was to be paid. 'I didn't do anything other than sign a form that was put in front of me,' this MLA says.

A ministerial special advisor told me he had trouble getting a mortgage because he could not explain to his mortgage advisor why he did not receive the salary publicly specified for his job. Adding insult to injury, MLAs and staff would receive payslips from Stormont detailing salaries that they would never actually see.

A staffer who worked in Stormont in 2015 recalls: 'I opened that separate account myself . . . your Stormont wage went in there, and then you get paid your normal wage into a different account you used personally.

'So I got a payslip for the Stormont salary, showing you're paying taxes and dues, for the full amount, as you normally would.

'We were buying the house and I think my pay band was £62,000 or something. So we were applying for a mortgage at the time and in reality I was only being paid £26,000 or £27,000 and I had to explain this to my mortgage advisor, who thought it was completely mental.'

This staff member says that not everyone in Sinn Féin was restricted to the average industrial wage. 'I also know that there's some chancers, they're getting paid [a] complete fortune because of the nature of the party: if you can get away with it, you will.

'I think if you want to professionalize the party you need to professionalize the party properly, you needed to treat people like they're employees, and that's hard for a revolutionary organization to do.'

Sinn Féin's unusual approach to money at Stormont was not restricted to the arrangements the party made for Assembly salaries. A BBC investigation in 2014 revealed that thirty-six Sinn Féin MLAs had claimed nearly £700,000 in expenses over the previous ten years to cover payments to a research company, Research Services Ireland (RSI), which was run by the party's own finance managers, Seamus Drumm (the son of Maire Drumm) and Sinead Walsh (the wife of Seanna Walsh, who read out the statement announcing the end of the IRA armed campaign).

The BBC *Spotlight NI* programme was 'not able to find any evidence of research that had been carried out by RSI'. One Sinn Féin MLA said they had 'never heard of the company until they saw it on their annual expenses'.

Sinn Féin had evidently worked out a new way of raising money for the party: claiming expenses from the British Exchequer to cover payments to an in-house company.

After the Police Service of Northern Ireland was alerted to the issue in 2009, they decided that an investigation was not necessary, and a 2016 report by the Assembly Commission, which oversees the day-to-day running of Stormont, found that the Sinn Féin claims 'were made for admissible expenditure'. The company folded in 2017.

The *Spotlight* programme also looked at other alleged financial irregularities in the party. A former Sinn Féin MLA, Davy Hyland, told the BBC that an expenses claim form for mileage, amounting to almost £5,000, was signed without his knowledge.

Hyland, who does not drive, said he knew nothing about most of the mileage claimed on his behalf, only finding out when he had approached a bursar for information after he decided to leave the party and the Assembly.

Other MLAs spoke to me of having no control over their expense claims or later finding claims they had not submitted themselves.

'These are all just examples of Sinn Féin really milking the system, milking it dry,' one ex-MLA told me.

'I was amazed when I saw my own expenses file, the fact that my signature was included, which it obviously wasn't, it was forged in.'

Sinn Féin had a steep learning curve at the Northern Assembly, in part because the party had never taken the seats it won at Westminster. But just under a year before the first Assembly elections, Caoimhghín Ó Caoláin became the first Sinn Féin TD to be elected in the Republic since 1957, and the first to take his seat in Dáil Éireann since 1922.

Born in the border county of Monaghan in 1953, Ó Caoláin was an official with the Bank of Ireland in the 1970s. As Director of Elections in the Anti H-Block campaign of 1981, Ó Caoláin helped elect hunger-striker Kieran Doherty to Dáil Éireann in his home constituency of Cavan–Monaghan, just eight weeks before Doherty died.

He was general manager of *An Phoblacht* between 1982 and 1985, before being elected to Monaghan County Council. He had unsuccessfully contested general elections in 1987, 1989 and 1992 before joining the Sinn Féin negotiating team during the peace process and finally being elected in 1997.

The peace process had persuaded some in the Republic that Sinn Féin were dedicated to peace, the Cavan–Monaghan first preference vote for Sinn Féin rose by 7,000 to 11,500, and Ó Caoláin was in. Himself, alone.

The election of a Sinn Féin representative shocked some of the Leinster House establishment, and the lone Sinn Féin TD said he suffered 'lots of abuse' upon entering Leinster House.

I was there to represent the electorate of Cavan-Monaghan but also, as the sole Sinn Féin TD over that five-year Dáil term, to represent the republican analysis on behalf of republicans the length and breadth of Ireland.

It was a cold house for Sinn Féin.

Despite the hostility, we just got on with it. We had a job to do.

In the 2002 general election, the party fielded thirty-seven candidates and Ó Caoláin was joined by four other Sinn Féin TDs: Sean Crowe, Aengus Ó Snodaigh, Martin Ferris and Arthur Morgan.

Ferris joined the Provisional IRA at age eighteen. He was a gifted Gaelic footballer and had lined out for his county team in under-21 and senior championships. One of the men who swore him into the IRA was Liam Cotter, a former vice-chairman and cultural officer of the Kerry County Board of the GAA.

Ferris had served a number of stints in prison for being a member of the IRA before he was arrested in 1984 after attempting to import seven tonnes of arms, including a .5 Browning machine gun, 300 rifles and 50,000 rounds of ammunition on a boat named the *Marita Ann*, which left

Boston for the coast of County Kerry. The guns were supplied by an organized-crime gang.

The *Marita Ann* was intercepted by the Irish Navy vessels the LÉ *Emer* and the LÉ *Aisling* off the south coast, with Ferris on board. He served ten years in prison.

Arthur Morgan, from the Cooley Peninsula of Co. Louth, joined the IRA while still in secondary school in 1971, aged seventeen. In 1977, he was arrested by the British Army aboard a boat on an IRA operation in Carlingford Lough alongside Paddy Agnew. He served seven years in the H-Blocks, where he joined the blanket and no-wash protest and served his sentence during the 1981 Hunger Strike. He was elected to the same seat that Paddy Agnew had won in 1981.

'It was all a bit shambolic,' one early staffer says of Sinn Féin's experience of being a small opposition party in Dáil Éireann. 'We were still getting our heads around the implications around having five TDs in a Dublin parliament for a party with a very centralized policymaking structure, 99 per cent of which was based in Belfast.

'We had five TDs and every single day something will come up in Leinster House that you had to have a policy or stance on, and really none of us had a fucking clue. So it was all a bunch of people who were thrown together and kind of making it up as we went along.'

One of the party's press officers was a young party member who knew little to nothing about communication strategy.

This person told me: 'My thought process was, "Hopefully the coverage will work if we send as many press releases as possible, send nine press releases this morning about anything and everything. If we send a press release on everything, one will be picked up on and thrown in."

'Not long after I left the job, I ran into a Newstalk journalist and they said we were a laughing stock.

'Journalists were busting their arses laughing at the press releases we were sending out, an opinion on literally anything that was happening.

'Media really was a struggle for us, back then there was a willingness to ascribe bad media performances to bias or to overly aggressive interviews. So you'd watch Martin Ferris, for example, or somebody who maybe wasn't a fantastic media performer on *Questions and Answers*, and it will be a shambles.

'Then our people will say, "Yeah, but the presenter was a bollocks to him. The audience is biased against him."

'Well, yeah, but, one: we would have known that going in, why didn't we prep for it?

'Two, actually some of those are really fair questions. So we should just have better answers for that. There was almost a reluctance to do media training or to sit down with somebody and say; "Look. I love you but that was not great", because it would undermine their confidence.'

What the press office did instead, even after the most shambolic media outing, was to tell the TDs that they were great, hoping that a confidence boost might improve their next appearance. They also continued to blame the media, which was openly hostile anyway.

The small Sinn Féin office staff loved Ó Caoláin, who was the leader of the group in the Dáil. He was conscientious and hardworking, and his banking background made him suited for office life. The other TDs struggled.

'I genuinely think Martin Ferris and Arthur Morgan thought they were still in prison,' one staffer says.

'They could not wait to get out of there on a Thursday,

they did not want to be TDs, they never liked it. They took up their obligation to the party to take on the roles so that's what they were doing. Caoimhghín took it quite seriously to be part of Sinn Féin politics.'

Morgan admitted as much upon his retirement in 2010. 'I think it's no secret that I was quite reluctant to go into the Dáil in the first place,' he said at the time.

He added that 'there are conventions about the Dáil that are extremely frustrating', and described it as a 'very stuffy and a very restrictive place'. When you have decided a cause is worth killing and dying for, the adrenaline rush of proposing an amendment on road traffic or marine legislation surely pales in comparison.

As it was in the North, money became a recurring problem in the South, because some staff weren't as keen to take the average industrial wage as others.

In contrast to the situation in the North, where MLA and staff salaries were paid into accounts controlled by the party, in the South TDs and staff were allowed to receive their Dáil salaries – but were then expected to donate to the party the difference between the salary and the average industrial wage. On two or three occasions at the Coiste Seasta, it was noted that a certain staff member who worked for Martin Ferris in his Kerry constituency office was not making the expected donations.

'He wasn't doing it,' recalls one party member from the North who attended the meeting. 'And I don't mean like, he didn't do it for a month: he never fucking did it. I used to get annoyed about it and then I started finding it quite funny.

'I used to love coming to the Coiste Seasta because some of them would be spitting fire about some ridiculous

Southern issue while we had real fuckin' problems we were dealing with, with our squad in the North.'

Another few months would pass and the issue of the non-contributing staff member would be raised again.

'He says he's gonna do it,' came the reply.

'We'd pull up minutes of the last meeting, he said he'd do it then too.'

Upon some digging, it was found that the staff member had said he had forgotten, then he lost his bank card, his car had broken down and a range of other unfortunate events had befallen him before he was able to donate a chunk of his salary to Sinn Féin.

'If it was me, I'd be embarrassed every time I saw you, I'd be hiding this behaviour from Martin [Ferris] first. [But] Martin wasn't one bit arsed, and then it dawned on me: Martin Ferris is the problem. Martin told him to ignore them.'

The money was never paid. The staffer continued to work for the party.

The Northern party member who attended the meeting about the non-contributing staffer recalls realizing the depth of the difference between the way the party operated in the North and the South.

'If somebody in Strabane or Derry or Antrim fucked about, some of us could get into a car and call to their house. If we have someone acting the maggot in Cork or Kerry, who from Dublin leadership is gonna drive four hours in the car and you meet this guy and he goes; "Ah yeah, I forgot, I'll do it next week"?

'There's a degree of that in Sinn Féin in the South, they don't give a fuck about head office. In the North, everyone's within the range. Everyone's at the meeting, everyone holds the line.

'Early on in the South, you could do that, there's hardly any TDs, he's rarely in Leinster House, you're rarely in contact. You can see their number coming up on the phone, just don't answer the call. So he didn't.'

In 2016, following complaints that Sinn Féin representatives could not afford to pay their bills, an internal review determined that the party would end the rule regarding TDs' pay. Earlier that year, the *Irish Independent* had reported that Dublin TD Dessie Ellis had been taking his full TD's salary since 2011, having agreed the arrangement with the party. Some of his colleagues who were still giving up much of their salaries were unaware of Ellis's arrangement.

Party organizers in the South kept an eye on young members who had good speaking and debating skills, and who could be honed by leadership. Sometimes the desired skills were fairly rudimentary.

'I got the job of writing up minutes for the Ard Comhairle meetings in around 2001 on the basis that I had a laptop and could type,' one member recalls. 'I once left the laptop at the gym in college and it's the fastest I've ever run for a consistent period of time, once I realized and had to run back and get it.'

At one Ard Comhairle meeting, the member recalls, there were hours of debate about fluoride in the water system.

'Basically Sinn Féin in the South wants to [get] fluoride out of the water system and Sinn Féin in the North wants to [keep] fluoride in the water system, and we were two hours in [to the meeting] and I couldn't take it any more,' he recalls. 'I told them I had something to do, and I actually went down the bar down the street and I actually started crying in Conway's pub. I went in and asked for double whiskey and I just sat there I had a bit of a cry because it's just typing constantly and the entire debate was so stupid.'

Sinn Féin's backroom staff in the Northern Assembly took instructions directly from the Sinn Féin leadership and relayed them to MLAs. MLAs were told in no uncertain terms that these staff 'ruled the roost'.

Despite the triumph of the party's political strategy and the end of the armed campaign, the IRA's dominance of the republican movement in those early days remained very apparent. MLAs recall that when they held constituency meetings in community centres, about fifteen minutes after the meeting started a group of 12–15 men would troop into the hall, sit at the back and not say a single word. This was seen as a show of strength by the local IRA, letting Sinn Féin MLAs know who was really in charge.

'You couldn't do a solo run in Stormont, you don't do any-thing without checking,' one MLA told me. 'You didn't speak to press, or put out statements or vote on anything without consulting the leadership.

'There's a hierarchy, [and] we were the lower-archy amongst the Sinn Féin people because we were just sort of dependent on them for orders, we were foot soldiers, you were supposed to just do what they want.'

Policy discussion for how Sinn Féin would vote or behave at Stormont did not, in the early days, involve the MLAs at all. No opinion could be formed without prior say-so.

In October 2002, Sinn Féin's chief administrator at Stor-mont, Denis Donaldson, was arrested in connection with allegations about a republican spy ring at Stormont.

Donaldson, born in 1950 in Belfast, befriended Bobby Sands when the two of them were imprisoned in Long Kesh.

The iconic image used of Sands in a red jumper is a cropped image of a larger picture in which Donaldson's hand is slung around Sands' neck. Donaldson was also close to Adams. After his release from prison, according to the journalist Henry McDonald, Donaldson 'acted as Adams' political enforcer, ensuring that branches, constituencies and even its fund-raising arm in North America, NORAID, toed the party line'.

Donaldson was charged in connection with computer disks and thousands of documents in his possession which were described as 'likely to be of use to terrorists'.

The 'Stormontgate' arrests led to the suspension of the Assembly and the reimposition of direct rule. And so things still stood in December 2005, when the Public Prosecution Service dropped all charges against Donaldson and two other defendants, on the grounds that it was 'no longer in the public interest' to pursue them.

The decision to drop the charges baffled republicans and others. Donaldson seems to have been seen as above suspicion, even in an organization obsessed with 'touts'. But later that same month, it emerged that Donaldson had been operating as a British agent for twenty years.

Donaldson told RTÉ he had worked for the RUC, the PSNI Special Branch and British intelligence at different times since being recruited in the 1980s, but denied any involvement in the so-called Stormontgate republican spy ring:

> I was not involved in any republican spy ring in Stormont. The so-called Stormontgate affair was a scam and a fiction, it never existed, it was created by Special Branch [. . .]
>
> I deeply regret my activities with British Intelligence and RUC/PSNI Special Branch. I apologise to anyone who has

suffered as a result of my activities as well as to my former comrades and especially to my family who have become victims in all of this [. . .]

Sinn Féin had long denied that there was anything to Stormontgate, but now Taoiseach Bertie Ahern too claimed to have been 'totally sceptical' about the idea of a republican spy ring in Stormont:

This was a huge case – it doesn't get much bigger than bringing down democratically elected institutions that people have voted for.

What this [Stormontgate] was about, I just don't know.

I'd just like to hear all the sides in this.

We're asked to believe that the person Sinn Féin had in there looking after the administration [Donaldson] was also in there by the British security [services].

So he had the confidence of Sinn Féin and he had the confidence of British security to be in a key position that, ultimately, brought down the whole institutions.

I tell you, it even stretches my imagination at 4 in the morning. [. . .]

It never added up [. . .] The storm troopers charging up the stairs with heavy armoury to collect a few files.

Last week when I asked Tony Blair why did the trial of the three men charged collapse, he couldn't understand it either. I've never been happy with it. And it created enormous grief for us because all the institutions were brought down, it created huge difficulties.

In the aftermath, according to a secret dispatch sent to Washington by US embassy officials in Dublin, the then Irish justice minister, Michael McDowell, told officials that he believed revealing Donaldson as an informant was 'a clear message from the British government that it had another, more valuable, source of information within the republican leadership'.

Denis Donaldson was murdered in a Donegal farmhouse by the Real IRA on 4 March 2006.

After a gap of almost five years, and following a pledge by Sinn Féin to support the PSNI, the Assembly and other devolved institutions were restored in May 2007. Among the new MLAs elected that month was Martina Anderson, the former IRA member from Derry, who was a close confidant of McGuinness and quickly became the voice of the party leadership at Stormont.

Almost every morning, the person who came in to give MLAs a pep talk was Anderson.

'She'd always be gushing about how well the party was doing or [the] leadership or the negotiators were doing. She'd say, "We have the Brits on the run now" – this commentary every day.

'"There's more and more evidence of it, we're winning" – whatever debate was going on with the Brits at the time.

'I remember thinking, I don't see where the evidence is, but she was obviously there meaning to inspire people, keep the morale up, when we were all bored out of our heads.

'Every so often they'd send some people there who were obviously IRA people and every so often they'd come in so the MLAs could be given the sort of stern warning: "You're not doing enough here. You need to be doing more. We needed to keep going. We need to get more MLAs – blah blah, blah,"' one MLA told me.

The war was over, but the men of war were still around, still part of the movement.

'Them people don't just fucking evaporate,' says a former close aide of Martin McGuinness. 'They ended up in party positions ... I remember decisions being made and being told about decisions – even from a local perspective – that there was no conversation on. It was clearly an army thing. You were told and never questioned it.'

Even when Stormont got up and running again in 2007, Sinn Féin were on the back foot.

'I remember when I went into Stormont, I was thinking, "Right, I'm going to have this whole team of people around me and they're going to take the committee papers every week and do that bit and that bit and we'll all just pull it together,"' one former MLA told me.

'No, not at all. That first Christmas, I was sitting reading up on a Health Department committee document and I phoned another one of our MLAs to ask about it.

'She was like, "Are you fucking mad?! Why are you doing this at Christmas?" But you just had to do it yourself. It was that notion of "If I don't do it, it wasn't getting done", and that's not easy to carry.'

For most of the 2000s, Sinn Féin's Stormont operation was managed by Leo Green and, to a lesser extent, Jackie McMullan.

Originally from Lurgan, Green spent time in prison for IRA involvement, as did two of his brothers. One of them, John Francis Green, escaped prison in 1973 and was assassinated by loyalists in a farmhouse in County Monaghan in 1975.

Leo Green was arrested in 1977 and sentenced to life imprisonment. He took part in the 1980 Hunger Strike, going fifty-three days without food before it was called off. He spent over seventeen years in prison.

He told *An Phoblacht*:

> It was certainly a bit strange coming to work here in Stormont initially. And presumably it was the same for other Sinn Féin people who had experienced imprisonment.
>
> Some of the people we've had to work with here were knocking about the NIO during the height of the prison protests. And some of the staff who now work at Stormont are former prison officers who we knew in jail. I'm guessing at this but whereas we would have found it a bit surreal, I'd say some of them found it more uncomfortable than we did.

Jackie McMullan was born in Belfast, the third of seven children. He joined Na Fianna Éireann, the IRA's youth wing, after his older brother Michael was interned. He joined the IRA aged seventeen, and in 1976 he was arrested and charged with attempting to kill RUC officers. Sentenced to life imprisonment, he joined the blanket protest and was twenty-five when he replaced Thomas McElwee on the 1981 Hunger Strike. He was released in 1992 and went on to work his way up through the ranks of Sinn Féin.

The decision to employ so many former IRA prisoners in Stormont was a deliberate one, McGuinness explained in a speech in 2009:

> Every Monday morning, without fail, I look around that room and I see former hunger-strikers and freedom fighters staring back at me [. . .]
>
> People like Leo Green or Raymond McCartney or Jackie McMullan who were – like [the hunger-striker] Kevin

Lynch – literally prepared to give up their lives on hunger strike for justice in the jails.

People like Sean Lynch or Alex Maskey or Gerry Adams who carried the burden of the freedom struggle and who still bear the scars of the battle.

People like Martina Anderson or Sinead Walsh, people like Cáral Ní Chuilín or Jennifer McCann or Mary McArdle, all of whom endured the brutality of state-approved strip-searching in prison and yet who maintained their republican dignity – and their good humour.

People like Gerry Kelly or Bobby Storey, people like Conor Murphy or Padraic Wilson or Sean Murray, who helped lead the Long Kesh prisoners and who took the entire System apart – block by block – from the inside out.

People like Francie Brolly, a civil rights veteran and former internee, or Francie Molloy, a veteran of Caledon and the civil rights struggle.

[. . .] So when you see the Assembly on TV, or look at Gerry Adams or Bairbre de Brun or myself in the media, always remember this: standing at our shoulders are the women and the men who stood at the front of the struggle when there was no alternative option but war, and who – when the time was right – had the courage and commitment and skills to create the new phase of peaceful and democratic change into which we have successfully led this society.

The management style had been unpopular with the MLAs over the years and people were becoming disillusioned.

'It was just really dysfunctional,' one MLA told me. 'I kind of started just with an open mind and then after a couple of months, I said to someone, "This is not working. Whatever system up here is completely broken. There's no team morale."'

In the aftermath of the global financial crisis that erupted in the late 2000s, a row over welfare reform caused huge tension within the party and tested Adams's leadership. Sinn Féin was in government in the North but in opposition in the South, and the issue exposed the political difficulties of operating in multiple jurisdictions.

In 2012, the Conservative–Lib Dem coalition in Westminster announced a plan to introduce the biggest change to the welfare system in decades. It included a freeze in child benefit, ending child benefit for higher earners, and a change to housing benefit.

Social welfare in Northern Ireland is, in theory, a devolved matter. In practice, under what is known as the 'parity principle', social welfare provision in the North tends to match Britain's. The social welfare legislation that came before the Assembly included the same austerity measures that had been approved by Westminster.

If the Assembly did not approve welfare changes along the lines set out in the Westminster legislation, the management and vast costs of the computer system needed to run the unreformed welfare system would become the responsibility of Northern Ireland, and financial penalties would be imposed by the Treasury.

Sinn Féin's problem was that it would be jointly responsible for any changes to social welfare provision, with McGuinness serving as Deputy First Minister alongside the DUP's Peter Robinson as First Minister. The party that had called itself socialist and on the side of working people was about to oversee a move that could take millions of pounds out of the hands of the people who needed it most. The party had lambasted the Labour–Fine Gael coalition government in Dublin for embarking on a series of cuts to welfare services. Now they were faced with the prospect of having to oversee a similar austerity regime in Belfast.

From the outset Adams was clear that Sinn Féin could not be seen supporting any cuts to welfare. A senior party staff member at the time told me that Adams called on the senior staff to 'contact the Brits, the Labour Party, the Irish government, at one point he suggested getting the Americans to lobby the Brits'.

It was clear Adams was determined not to support this without expending every option, no matter how ridiculous it seemed.

'I said to him, "Gerry, the Irish government are doing the same fucking thing. The Americans don't do welfare reform. If you think they're going to roll in behind some campaign against the Brits – get real."'

Others who took the view that welfare cuts were unavoidable included MLA Caitríona Ruane, Leo Green, Jackie McMullan, and staffers like policy head Michelle Rouse and Clíona O'Kane.

A consultation with party members suggested that social welfare was not the hill they wanted to die on. At meetings, members would be asked to list the most important issues for the party in order of priority. Welfare never featured in the top five.

A series of meetings were set up between the DUP and Sinn Féin staff in charge of welfare reform. Those in the welfare policy group listed the party's major concerns, and the parties went back and forth attempting to put together solutions. Any outstanding problem was marked in red; as issues were resolved, they were marked in black.

Sinn Féin were keenly aware of the negative press they would receive if they appeared to be on different sides of the welfare argument North and South. Leo Green in Belfast and Dawn Doyle in Dublin organized a North–South meeting on the party's position on welfare on a Sunday in late 2012. Thirty people were present, including Adams and McGuinness.

Following a summary by the chair of the general situation, Adams stood up.

'Look, folks, I have a constituency meeting to go to, but just generally, we need to be very careful and make sure everybody's on the same page.' He turned and left.

McGuinness turned to the man beside him, looked at him and said: 'What is he doing?!'

The man to whom McGuinness spoke told me: 'Gerry was doing what he always did. He doesn't want to be pinned down on an opinion, he doesn't want to give an opinion, we had agreed things with the DUP and he doesn't want to say if it's good or bad.'

Following Adams's departure, the meeting was cut short, lasting only an hour, and cast as a briefing.

Adams believed that Leo Green and the MLAs and staffers who were loyal to him had been agreeing to things with the DUP that would be unacceptable to party representatives and members. There was also a belief within Sinn Féin that, in building up their influence on events at Stormont, Green and McMullan strategically kept McGuinness at arm's length.

One MLA told me: 'I'm not sure to what extent he knew what was happening with welfare reform. We would rarely see Martin at Monday morning meetings. He was seen as leader in public but privately very hard to reach.'

A week later McGuinness told senior staff that Adams had said implementing welfare reform with the DUP is a non-runner. Adams continued to claim it was the biggest issue for the members, despite the evidence arising from consultations. The party leader told his allies he had found out how far Green had gone on welfare and had put a stop to it.

McGuinness rang the First Minister, Peter Robinson. The pair agreed to meet with their staff at Stormont Castle. It was a Saturday night.

McGuinness told Robinson that, despite what they had agreed over months of work on welfare reform, the party had now decided they couldn't run with it.

Robinson said: 'Well, Martin, we'll just pick up the pieces.'

As it turned out, the pieces would remain scattered for a long time.

Shortly before Christmas 2014, Sinn Féin signed up to the Stormont House Agreement, an attempt to resolve a number of issues that had bedevilled Northern Irish politics, including welfare reform. Weeks later, though, Sinn Féin accused the Minister for Social Development, the DUP's Mervyn Storey, of reneging on what had been agreed.

The party released a twenty-five-page dossier on the issue. The DUP's deputy leader, Nigel Dodds, described the dossier as an attempt 'to confuse people about their U-turn on welfare'.

In May 2015, the welfare legislation was supported by a clear majority in the Assembly, but it was blocked by a Petition of Concern tabled by Sinn Féin, the SDLP and the Green Party. The Petition of Concern is mechanism that allows a group made up of at least thirty MLAs to block a bill or motion that lacks the support of both a majority of designated unionist MLAs and a majority of designated nationalist MLAs.

Martin McGuinness told the Assembly before the vote:

> The immediate difficulties we are facing into have been triggered by the DUP's decision to bring forward a Welfare Bill to the Assembly which does not implement the protections agreed at Stormont House for children with disabilities, adults with severe disabilities, the long-term sick and large families.
>
> It appears that the DUP is responding to pressure and demands from the Tories in London. In my view, that is a major tactical error.
>
> The crisis has been created by the austerity cuts agenda of a Tory administration in London which is attempting to decimate our public services and punish the most vulnerable people in society.
>
> Sinn Féin stood in the recent elections against Tory austerity and for social justice and equality. Our approach was mandated by over 176,000 voters, almost 25% of the popular vote.
>
> In contrast, the Tories received only 9,000 votes in the North, just over 1% of the vote.
>
> This is a party which doesn't have a single Assembly or local council seat. They have no democratic mandate for their austerity policies in the North of Ireland.

The logic of McGuinness's ringing words was soon abandoned. In 2015, Sinn Féin joined the DUP in pushing through a legislative consent motion which allowed Westminster to implement welfare reform in Northern Ireland. Under the plan, the Executive was called on to find £585 million from its own resources over four years to mitigate the effects of the reforms.

Sinn Féin were hounded North and South for the decision. The republicans had paired up with the unionists to hand control back to the British.

Some in Sinn Féin felt the party's actions had been misrepresented, and pointed the finger of blame for the communication and messaging failure at Mark McLernon, who ran Sinn Féin's Stormont press office at the time (and now is a senior member of the party's staff in Leinster House).

'The press office was an absolute mess until [Seán] Mag Uidhir took over – you'd walk in there to get a statement done and nobody would even look up or speak to you,' says one party figure.

Whatever about the party's messaging, welfare reform exposed the fault lines in Sinn Féin's political situation. Total and unrepenting dedication to your principles is rarely manageable in any government, let alone in a power-sharing administration with your polar political opposite. In the end, the party had an unpalatable choice between a painful U-turn – signing up with the DUP to a welfare reform package it had disparaged – and the even more painful prospect of implementing cuts on those already in poverty. The party stalled for as long as it could, but in the end no escape route presented itself, and they bit the bullet.

Sinn Féin's support slipped by 2.9 per cent in the Stormont election in 2016, and the party lost a seat, but no lasting damage was done. Six years later, it would become the most popular party in Northern Ireland.

4. Wrapping It Up

The evening was still warm as the sun began to disappear behind the hills of Donegal. The pub owner shifted his weight from one foot to another behind the bar as punters came and went. Through the windows he watched the main road outside, delicately checking if the same car passed more than once. He had been told to observe traffic outside and whether the premises were being watched. If he felt something was off, he was to phone those who had given him the instructions.

All seemed clear.

When darkness fell, he set out in his van: a large and noisy vehicle that had been battered by beer kegs rolling around inside.

Alone in the cab, he drove in silence up a narrow laneway close to the border with Co. Derry. At 9pm there would be another van waiting. He knew these roads like the back of his hand from boyhood summertime adventures, when he hitchhiked to the beach.

The two vans pulled up side by side, perfectly parallel. Without saying a word or making eye contact with the other driver, the publican got out and slid open his van's side door. He walked silently back to the driver's seat and waited in the darkness.

The other van's door slid open, and he could feel the weight of a man climbing into the back of his vehicle. The door snapped shut. The pub owner had no idea who his passenger was. He heard his new passenger lie down and roll himself close to the back of the van's partition, as to avoid being visible from the window if anyone stopped them.

He had been given strict instructions from his IRA handlers: You stop for nothing. Not for gardaí. Not for an accident. Not if you hit something. You keep driving. These weren't orders, exactly. The man wasn't a member of the IRA, so couldn't be ordered to do anything. But this was a request from the IRA, for which he was doing a favour. His bit for the cause.

The driver and his hidden passenger travelled the long Donegal road in silent darkness. No radio played.

Then the pub owner saw him – the Garda for the local village. His squad car was parked up at the side of the main road: a mini checkpoint manned by the lone garda. The garda who drank in the pub and brought his family there for a roast on Sundays.

His heart was pounding, ringing in his ears. He slowed the van down and said loudly to his hidden passenger: 'There's a guard here who knows me, I have to stop.'

From the back of the van, in a thick Belfast accent, the passenger said: 'No you fucking don't. Keep driving.'

He continued to slow down, then stopped at the checkpoint and lowered his window. He was struggling to breathe as he greeted the friendly face.

'Alright Pat [not his real name], how's it going?'

'Joe [not his real name], are ye well?'

'Well enough, any craic?'

'Not a bit, stuck out here for the foreseeable.'

'Well, at least it's not raining, says you. I better get on.'

'Good luck, Joe.'

He pulled away from the checkpoint and wound the

window back up. His hands sweated on the steering wheel. He told his passenger: 'If I had driven through that checkpoint and past that man, he would've followed me to the pub to ask me what was wrong.'

His passenger replied coldly: 'You're a lucky boy.'

He pulled the van up near the back door of his large country pub. He got out and opened the rear door of the building. Then he slid the van's door open, and the passenger climbed out quickly. The pub owner was so occupied with closing the back door that he barely looked at his passenger's face until they were both safely inside. The passenger was a man he knew only from seeing him on TV.

Gerry Kelly reached out his hand and says: 'Good man. We appreciate this.'

The back stairs were old wooden and rickety, and rarely used. The upstairs of the pub was used for storage: old Christmas decorations, extra crockery for funerals and christenings. There were no radiators or heating, and the barman had been told by his IRA contacts not to turn on the old strip lighting, lest it attract attention. He had moved a few lamps upstairs, and unstacked some spare chairs. Everything was covered in a film of dust, and there wasn't time to wipe each chair before heading out to collect his passenger at the border.

The bar was still open, but it was quiet and customers in the front of the building couldn't see into the back or the stairs, or hear anything in the attic.

The publican had told one person about the plan for the meeting: his most trusted staff member. A local woman in her fifties. He tried to tell her as little as possible, only that he had allowed 'some boys' to use the upstairs and he would be absent for a while.

'Don't let anyone out the back, no matter what, no smoking, nothing. Serve the drink, chat to the customers, I'll come back when it's over.'

She looked nervous and nodded. Such a woman in such a border town knew who such 'boys' were.

At the top of the stairs, a man stood holding a cardboard box. The publican was told to hold the box and to collect people's mobile phones and watches – anything that could be bugged – as they arrived. He stood there as the men and women trickled through the back door. Faces he recognized and faces he didn't. Local IRA men. A few solicitors. Teachers, GAA players, men he knew from school. The priest who married him and his wife.

When all the invitees had entered, he closed the door behind them and stood outside in the cold, dimly lit silence, brushing dust off his black work trousers.

The meeting in that Donegal pub, with all its cloak-and-dagger security measures, took place not in the 1970s or 1980s, or even during the most sensitive stages of the peace process in the 1990s. It happened in September 2004 – six-plus years on from the Good Friday Agreement, and seven-plus years on from the final IRA ceasefire.

It was one of many such meetings held across the island as the leadership of the republican movement attempted to sell the rank and file on the necessity of decommissioning the IRA's remaining weapons. The Sinn Féin leadership had accepted the need for decommissioning back in 1997, when it signed up to the Mitchell Principles as a precondition for entering the all-party talks. The Good Friday Agreement linked the decommissioning of paramilitary weapons to the 'normalization' of the British military and security apparatus in Northern Ireland. Three rounds of decommissioning had already happened, but progress would remain stalled until the IRA eliminated the remainder of its arsenal.

Fully six years earlier, Gerry Kelly had sat at a table with the Prime Minister. The message he brought to that Donegal pub – that the IRA needed to get rid of the rest of its weapons – was hardly subversive. So why was he now lying down in the back of vans?

Republican distrust of the British state, and the fragility of the peace process, dictated that these meetings were conducted in conditions of secrecy and high security. Many of those who attended them were not known members of the IRA, or members at all. Many had never been convicted of any crime, and held respected roles in their community or professional life. If priests and solicitors were found in the company of convicted IRA prisoners, it could have a negative effect on their life and livelihood. In addition, the republican movement, which had been infiltrated by multiple British spies over the decades, had good reason to fear that the British were still watching and listening.

The briefings were led not by the movement's best orators or sharpest policy people, but by those whose military credentials could not be questioned. Gerry Kelly was ideally equipped for the role.

Kelly was born in the Falls area of Belfast on Easter Sunday 1953. In 1971, he escaped from St Patrick's Juvenile Prison, where he had been sent after a botched robbery for Na Fianna. Later, as we have seen, he was part of the IRA unit that perpetrated the Old Bailey bombing, and he spent a total of 205 days on hunger strike in 1973 and 1974; for 167 of those days he was force-fed.

He reached mythical status in republican circles for being one of the minds behind the escape from Long Kesh in 1983.

On 25 September, in what was generally thought of as Europe's most secure prison due to the fact it was not merely a prison, but a prison located inside an army camp, thirty-eight IRA prisoners escaped.

The escape was masterminded by Larry Marley, who had painstakingly learned the layout of the prison in order to facilitate the plan. The prisoners – including Kelly, Bobby Storey and Brendan McFarlane – hijacked a lorry delivering food to the prison and forced the driver to drive to the main gate.

Speaking about Kelly's character, comrades often mention his fondness for the opposite sex and his dancing abilities. One former comrade remembers being taken with Kelly through an airport while being extradited to Britain, hand-cuffed to a prison officer on each side.

While they were waiting for the plane, Kelly started making flirty eye contact with a tall, blonde and attractive airline worker. When one of the prison officers lifted his arm to scratch his nose, Kelly's lifted too, and the handcuffs became visible. The woman, horrified, did not look at Kelly again.

'That was Gerry,' his comrade says. 'Even when he was handcuffed to two other men, he would still fancy his chances with a woman.'

Following his release from prison, Kelly joined Sinn Féin and remains a key member of the party. He was involved in secret talks with the British government between 1990 and 1993 and part of Sinn Féin's negotiating team for the Good Friday Agreement. Thus he came into these meetings with impeccable credentials as a combatant, as well as genuine stature as a leading republican politician.

The meetings were attended by IRA volunteers and others who held sway within the republican community. What generally happened was that senior republicans talked about the movement's strategy and the necessity of decommissioning. When IRA members spoke, things sometimes became heated. One former bomber wept when telling me about challenging Gerry Kelly, with whom he had joined the Belfast Brigade of the IRA when they were both teenagers.

Kelly's co-chair for the meeting in the Donegal pub was Martina Anderson.

Anderson was born in the Bogside in Derry on 16 April 1962, the ninth of ten children, into a well-known republican family. Her father was a member of the Church of Ireland who converted to Catholicism when he married her mother, Betty, who Anderson has described as the more 'militant' of the two.

The house was raided constantly due to the IRA connection of her older brother Peter, and Anderson was first arrested and fingerprinted at sixteen. At eighteen she was charged with possession of a firearm and causing an explosion. She was released on bail after spending two months in Armagh Women's Prison and fled across the border to Buncrana in Co. Donegal.

She says that before she decided to go on the run she was warned she would never see her family again, but felt she had more to give to the movement.

Anderson was arrested on 24 June 1985 at a flat in Glasgow with four other IRA members.

Anderson and the others in the Glasgow flat were jailed as part of an IRA active service unit planning a bombing campaign on sixteen targets in England, many of which were holiday resorts. If carried out as planned, the campaign would have caused an unimaginable level of carnage and death among innocent civilians.

Anderson was jailed for life, with no recommended minimum sentence. A republican to the end, she and her co-accused Ella O'Dwyer dressed in green, white and gold for the last day of the trial at the Old Bailey.

In Brixton Prison, there were over 600 men, and just two women: Anderson and O'Dwyer. They spent thirteen months there.

Anderson has spoken about the sexual and physical abuse she suffered in prison in England and the trauma it has caused her in later life. She wrote in 1985 that was subjected to daily strip searches in Brixton, 'sometimes six times a day'.

At Durham, she wrote in *An Phoblacht*, the governor of the prison gleefully told her that he had been governor of Wakefield prison when IRA prisoner Frank Stagg died there on hunger strike and 'he would happily send us home in boxes'. She spent eight years in Durham, successfully cam-paigning for better conditions and earning a first-class honours degree in social sciences.

While in prison, Anderson married Paul Kavanagh, with whom she had been arrested in Glasgow. The couple would not be able to consummate the relationship until seven years later.

Anderson and O'Dwyer were the 200th and 201st prison-ers released under the Good Friday Agreement. They were greeted by their comrade Gerry Kelly as they climbed out of the van as free women.

For years, decommissioning was the spanner in the works of Stormont. The fledgling devolved assembly collapsed over

IRA weapons for the first time while still in its infancy in February 2000.

Around that time, BBC journalist Brian Rowan was given a police Special Branch 'guesstimate' of the arsenal of the IRA: '1,700 weapons, over 1,000 of which are long arms, nearly all rifles, 500–550 handguns, 50 heavy and general purpose machine guns, two and a third metric tonnes of the explosive Semtex and a huge quantity of ammunition.'

Those involved in the briefings say the leadership instructed them to emphasize that the act of destroying weapons was symbolic.

The IRA was not handing weapons over. It was throwing them away.

'Part of the difficulty is that people in the briefings were given a very, very tight bullet-pointed brief,' one said.

'Some people weren't there for the actual discussions on how it would work, their knowledge was lacking and it's like the would-be Sinn Féin politician coming out of Downing Street standing at the door with Adams, as if they were in there giving Blair what for, and they probably weren't even in the meeting.

'I remember being at one where I wasn't giving the briefing and there are people talking about stuff that they've not been involved in any discussions about, and when someone asks a question, they're not saying; "I don't know. That's not on my list", so they spoof beyond belief.

'I was able to interject in that instance, God knows how many other meetings there were without someone to set the record straight.'

One attendee recalls being told that if decommissioning was completed, Gerry Kelly would be appointed justice minister.

'That's when I realized this was all bollocks,' they said.

'They would've said anything to get us on side and insulting our intelligence. As if the man who bombed the Old Bailey and masterminded the escape would be in charge of police and prisons. It was ridiculous.'

The meetings sometimes got argumentative. Many of these former combatants had made major life sacrifices and suffered severe trauma for the cause of Irish Republicanism. Now they were being told they were going out with a whimper and not a bang. For some, after a life of being the IRA hardman around town, the idea of disarming was felt as a loss of identity.

Some people left the IRA over decommissioning. But it was a trickle, not a flood, and the leadership felt that they could weather it.

There were a younger cohort, more politically sophisticated, who stayed on, who were willing to allow the process to run its course to see what could emerge.

'I could see that there was no future for armed struggle,' says one such member.

'It became clearer to me then from way back, even when I had joined in 1994, I was twenty years of age and up for anything.

'Young men want to fight: "Let's fucking go", you know?

'A lot of people in 1994 felt that the army had more capacity than we were told. Many of us thought practically, we could continue the war for a good while in terms of weapons and men. In reality, I've come to understand the movement and the nature of politics and it was over even then.

'There was no future for armed struggle.'

Many say the idea of decommissioning was sold on personal trust. A lot of members didn't really buy into the strategy, but the trust in the leadership of Gerry Adams and Martin McGuinness kept them in line.

'The plan was always just keep them on board. Keep them aboard all the time,' the source added.

In some ways, decommissioning was harder for the republican rank and file to swallow than the end of the armed campaign or the other compromises of the Good Friday Agreement. It was seen by many as symbolizing defeat. 'Only surrendering armies give up their arms,' one IRA bomber told me.

In 1999, the IRA appointed Brian Keenan as its representative in secret talks with the disarmament chief, Gen. John de Chastelain of Canada. Like the combatants who conducted the briefings for volunteers, it would have to be the most respected and hardened of IRA men who would negotiate decommissioning.

In his book *Great Hatred, Little Room*, Jonathan Powell said if Keenan had opposed decommissioning, it would not have gone ahead.

Considering Keenan once said the only thing that would be decommissioned in the province would be the British state, it was a testament to how far the republican movement had come.

During the decommissioning saga, Brian Keenan developed cancer.

Keenan, born in Belfast and brought up in rural Co. Derry, was a member of the Army Council. Once the IRA's quartermaster-general, he helped to organize the 1970s bombing campaign in London. He was jailed for eighteen years in 1980 for his involvement in the deaths of eight people.

At one point during the early stages of his illness, he was being treated in Dublin's Mater Private Hospital, his bills covered by the republican movement.

The Sinn Féin leadership knew that there were plenty of

guns and explosives hidden across the North. Should some disgruntled volunteers feel the need to fight on, they could do so, with fatal consequences. The Omagh bomb had shown that those with expertise in explosives were still able to get their hands on them, and McKevitt, among others, knew where most of the weaponry was held.

After two deadlines passed without any IRA weapons being decommissioned, the post-Agreement peace process hit a crisis in summer 2001, leading to the suspension of the Assembly.

The Al Qaeda attacks on the United States in September of that year shifted the political dynamic. America's influence and support were essential to the republican movement, and the climate in America had now dramatically shifted.

Four days after 9/11, Gerry Adams phoned Tim Dalton, the Secretary General of the Irish Department of Justice, and told him the IRA would decommission for good, but he needed more time to make it possible.

After the Army Council had decided to put arms beyond use, a planned October 2001 Army Convention was abandoned, lest dissidents use it as a chance to rally others to their point of view.

On 22 October, in Belfast's Conway Mill, Adams stood at the top of the room and told those present that he and Martin McGuinness had spoken to the IRA leadership and told them that a 'groundbreaking move' on decommissioning would save the peace process.

Adams later released a public statement calling on the IRA to lay down its weapons:

I do not underestimate the difficulties this creates for the army. Genuine republicans will have concerns about such a move. The naysayers, the armchair generals and the begrudgers and the enemies of Irish republicanism and the peace process will present a positive IRA move in disparaging terms. This is only to be expected.

The next day the IRA released its own statement, confirming that some weapons had been decommissioned. The Independent International Commission on Decommissioning confirmed it had witnessed an event in which the IRA had put a quantity of weaponry 'beyond use'.

McGuinness spoke to Brian Rowan about the almost visceral objection IRA members felt towards decommissioning:

I went through that journey maybe long before they did, and as they were going through the journey after the announcement, I was still going through it. So, there was a lot of pain and emotion in it for me and for everybody who was connected to me within republicanism, but it was a journey that had to be travelled and it was a journey that hopefully is going to lead us to a whole new situation on this island.

The leadership needed time and space to assess the fallout of the first act of decommissioning. It had not been universally popular within the rank and file and there had been defections to the Real IRA.

One IRA leader at the time told the BBC in Belfast: 'What we have to do is weigh up the impact – the internal reaction.'

The second act of decommissioning came in April 2002, and the third in October 2003. The republican movement was trying to strike a balance between what was tolerable to the IRA rank and file, and what was necessary for Sinn Féin to succeed politically. Even after three rounds of decommissioning, the troops were uncomfortable – and that is why, in order to prepare the ground for the final act, leading republicans were addressing secret meetings around the country.

The announcement that decommissioning was completed finally came on 26 September 2005.

By this stage, all local army departmental structures had been reduced down to almost nothing ahead of the announcement of the final round of decommissioning. There had been no operations, no planning or meetings other than those about the political situation. Armed support units lay dormant.

But there could be no announcement that the war was over without a number of high-level meetings of the IRA leadership.

The main defender of the decision was Brian Keenan. Keenan had resigned from the seven-member Army Council by this time, but was still a leading figure in the movement.

'I have studied this constitution,' he said at one meeting. 'I have studied the rules, this is all 100%.' He raged against 'those who dare to challenge the constitution of the IRA'.

One person present remembers 'sweat pumping out of him, he was a fucking madman'.

Thomas 'Slab' Murphy was asked to read a statement about 'wrapping it up'. A native of South Armagh, Murphy is alleged to be a former IRA chief of staff. He had sued the *Sunday Times* newspaper in 1990 over an article claiming he was an IRA commander who had helped organize IRA bombings in Britain and import weapons from Libya. He lost the case, appealed the ruling, and lost again.

More recently, in 2004, the BBC's Underworld Rich List had named Murphy as the wealthiest smuggler in the UK, claiming he had generated £40 million through smuggling cigarettes, oil, grain and pigs. He would eventually be convicted in 2015 in the Republic's non-jury Special Criminal Court for tax evasion.

Murphy – once described by Gerry Adams as 'a key supporter of the Sinn Féin peace strategy' – was presumably asked to read the statement to his comrades due to his standing within the movement. But no matter how highly regarded he was by his colleagues, the task was an uncomfortable one.

'Never saw a man looking so awful,' one witness told me. 'He was standing there, with his trouser legs too short, his white socks on show, he just looks like a simple farmer who just stuttered his way through it and there was fuckin' silence in the room.'

Some felt that the IRA had given up or given in. Many felt that Adams and McGuinness had been romanced by the British. But these elements were a clear minority. Time was up for the IRA.

On 28 July 2005, former IRA prisoner Seanna Walsh read out the IRA statement on a DVD distributed to broadcast media.

The Belfast native had spent a total of twenty-one years in prison and was first arrested at sixteen in 1973 for robbing a bank. Upon his May 1976 release, he managed only three months as a free man before he was charged with possession of a rifle and sentenced to ten years. He joined the blanket protest when he arrived in the H-Blocks, where he served seven years and seven months. Upon his release, he was caught making explosives and sentenced to another twenty-two years in prison. He was released under the Good Friday

Agreement, aged forty-two, having spent over half his life in jail.

In the video, Walsh was dressed in a plain white shirt: the days of balaclavas and flak jackets were over. The statement began:

> The leadership of Oglaigh na hEireann has formally ordered an end to the armed campaign.
>
> This will take effect from 4pm [1600 BST] this afternoon [Thursday 28 July 2005].
>
> All IRA units have been ordered to dump arms.
>
> All Volunteers have been instructed to assist the development of purely political and democratic programmes through exclusively peaceful means.
>
> Volunteers must not engage in any other activities whatsoever.
>
> The IRA leadership has also authorised our representative to engage with the IICD [Independent International Commission on Decommissioning] to complete the process to verifiably put its arms beyond use in a way which will further enhance public confidence and to conclude this as quickly as possible.

The DVDs were distributed to media outlets from 10am, under a strict 2pm reporting embargo. However, shortly after 12.30pm, the statement was posted, apparently in error, on the website of the republican newspaper *Daily Ireland*.

At 12.49pm, according to Senan Molony's account of the day's events in the *Irish Independent*, RTÉ Radio 1 interrupted the John Creedon programme to report the news: the IRA's war was over.

The IICD reported that the IRA had decommissioned 'very large quantities of arms', which their representative stated 'includes all the arms in the IRA's possession' on 26 September 2005. It was impossible, of course, to know if the latter was true.

The final inventory of the Independent International Commission on Decommissioning remains classified.

Those involved say it might never be truly known if all the weaponry was given up, due to the sheer volume of arms that had been accumulated and the clandestine way in which weaponry was moved around the island. Even IRA leadership may not have known the full extent of the arsenal. In 2006, MI5 and senior officers from the PSNI's Crime Operations Department told the Independent Monitoring Commission that it had received reports that not all IRA weapons had been decommissioned. However, they also said that 'These same reports do not cast doubt on the declared intention of the PIRA leadership to eschew terrorism.'

One republican, deeply connected to the decommissioning process, spoke to me in his home in rural Ireland. I sat under a wooden shelf that held a number of bullets of different calibres. The source told me that he kept them as souvenirs. They sat next to miniature action figures belonging to his grandchildren.

'I mean, technically speaking, that shouldn't be there,' he told me. 'But that's not going to cause any harm.'

5. Crime and Punishment

The republican movement has long been steeped in hypocrisy when it comes to dealing with its own. In neighbourhoods where calling the police was often not an option, many people relied – or were forced to rely – on their local Provisional IRA unit to iron out disagreements and, in many cases, dole out vigilante justice to those who had been causing trouble. Not everyone who was targeted by the vigilantes had committed an actual crime. Sometimes the person's offence had simply been to annoy a senior member of the IRA.

Punishments were usually 'PBs' – punishment beatings – or kneecapping, a catch-all term for a non-fatal shooting in the knees, arms, legs or thighs. The victim, usually a young, working-class man, would be taken to, or, having been summoned, would arrive voluntarily to a location where the allotted punishment, decided on by the local IRA leadership, was carried out. Weapons used for beatings included bats, wooden planks with nails driven through them and hammers.

The branch of the IRA that policed republican heartlands was known as the Civil Administration, and sometimes as the Administrative IRA. By 2003, five years on from the Good Friday Agreement, punishment beatings reached an all-time high. At the time, Sinn Féin said blandly that 'these sorts of things can happen in the vacuum that exists because of the lack of effective policing'.

In 1981, the *New York Times* published an article on the practice:

According to Richard McCauley [recte McAuley], press officer of the Provisional Sinn Féin, the IRA's political wing, there are firm rules governing kneecapping. 'No one is kneecapped who is below the age of 16,' he says. 'If he is under 16, he might get a beating. I'm not talking about breaking his arms or legs, but a beating is a beating.' Before anyone is kneecapped, the press officer says, he is given a series of warnings.

McCauley [recte McAuley] says that most people are actually shot not in the knee but in the thigh. 'They're in the hospital for a day or two,' he says, 'and they hobble around for a week after. It's more the scare that's effective than the injury itself. It's awfully frightening to sit and watch a man pointing a gun at your leg. You have to be very bad to be shot in the knee, and if you are very, very bad, you are shot in the kneecaps and elbows.'

Kneecap victims have little choice but to go back to their neighborhoods, where they are intended to be limping examples for those who would stray from the straight and narrow. In a study conducted six years ago of 86 punishment shootings, Dr. James Nixon, an orthopedic surgeon at Belfast City Hospital, found that amputation occurred in about 10 percent of the cases. He estimates that one in five kneecap victims will walk with a limp for the rest of his life.

A 1982 article in *An Phoblacht* laboured to create the impression that communities were pressing the IRA to be even harsher:

The Derry Brigade of the IRA are under considerable pressure from the nationalist community to kneecap more people than they actually do. Often this comes from those who fail to realise that kneecapping is brought in only as the absolute last resort for someone who persists in serious offences against the community despite numerous warnings. A strict procedure governs handling all complaints made against anyone. Statements are taken from all parties concerned including, of course, the accused, and unless the IRA are completely satisfied with the proof of guilt, no action of any kind is taken.

The article went on to detail a case of a child molester who was only fifteen when he was first brought to the attention of the IRA: 'too young to be kneecapped, in any event'. The article claimed that the IRA informed the boy's parents of his actions and 'ensured' he received psychiatric treatment. Upon his release from hospital, he molested another child. The IRA decided that, due to the young man's mental state, they would 'put him out of Derry' rather than kneecap him. He joined the Irish Defence Forces and was dismissed for the same kinds of offences against children. At this point the IRA 'finally' kneecapped him, the story states. 'Many in the community regarded republicans' treatment of this offender as too lenient.'

A 1993 survey of victims of domestic violence in Northern Ireland, by Monica McWilliams and Joan McKiernan, quoted the response of one woman who was asked if she would call the police if she was being abused by her partner: 'They are not there to help. In this area police are not people that you normally go to. I mean, to walk out and stop them in the street, they would laugh at you – I mean they don't have any contact with this community whatsoever.'

Derry Sinn Féin had its own guidebook for dealing with violence against women. 'Any woman seeking assistance from SF because of an abusive relationship is to be believed

and supported. Violence against women is in no way tolerated, and Republican men accused of beating their wives or
partners are to be suspended automatically from the organization, pending a full inquiry,' the guidelines state.

According to the Derry guidelines, a man accused of
abusing a partner would be asked to come down to the local
Sinn Féin centre. There he would be informed that the
request had been made because his violent behaviour was
unacceptable. If the woman wanted the violent partner per-
manently out of her life, Sinn Féin would order him to leave
her alone. The man would be left in no doubt about the
consequences if the abuse continues: the problem would
be passed on to the IRA.

If the abuse continued, the IRA either 'put out' the abuser,
meaning that he would be expelled from the city or county
where he lived, or from Ireland. In some instances he would
be beaten or kneecapped. This punishment structure applied
for all kinds of criminality, including petty theft, joyriding
and drug use.

In a 1993 interview, Freddie Scappaticci talked about how
the IRA and Sinn Féin worked hand in hand on policing their
communities. Scappaticci was, for years, at the very heart of
internal security in the IRA – while also acting as a British
spy. The 'nutting squad' of which he was a member became
infamous for shooting suspected informers in the head after
hours of torture.

'The IRA appointed a person in Belfast, and his sole job
was to look after Sinn Féin/IRA-type things – co-ordinate
publicity campaigns, etc,' Scappaticci said.

'If Sinn Féin wasn't doing too well in an area the IRA
could be deployed in that area to do various things, to work
alongside Sinn Féin.

'Part of this co-ordination would have been "civil administration" – that is, the people who kneecap people, baseball-bat people, who break legs, arms, is what their "civil administration" is.

'The IRA made a conscious decision along with Sinn Féin to clean up the Divis Flats [a complex of high-rise flats in west Belfast] because of the crime and drug dealing. An IRA man was put in to call on people to band together and make the flats a hoods-free area.

'The IRA moved in and kneecapped four or five people. Then they gave a particular drug-dealing family forty-eight hours to get out of Belfast or be "stiffed". They left. The Lower Falls became quiet. Sinn Féin got their act together and got two seats in the Lower Falls.'

Into this environment, where Sinn Féin saw a direct link between the harshness of its vigilantism and its electoral fortunes, were born two women, unrelated by blood but connected by trauma, who came close to bringing the republican movement to its knees. The story of one of them, Mairia Cahill, will be told in a later chapter. The other was Áine Adams.

Áine Adams's father, Liam Adams, began sexually abusing her in 1977, when she was just four years old. The first rape she remembers took place that year, while her mother was in hospital giving birth to her younger brother, Conor.

Aged thirteen, at a time when she was struggling with behavioural issues, Áine told her mother, Sally Adams, she was being abused. She did it in writing: 'Mummy this is why I am like this, because my daddy made me sleep with him.'

Sally, who had split up with Liam due to the violence he inflicted upon her, reported it to the Grosvenor Road RUC station in January 1987. Áine and Sally withdrew the complaint shortly afterwards. 'Police were more interested in who [Liam] was,' Áine would tell a police officer in 2006.

In 1987, Gerry Adams met his brother Liam in Buncrana, Co. Donegal, where Liam was then living, to challenge him about the allegations. He brought Sally and Áine with him.

Gerry Adams felt this was an internal family matter and could be settled in-house, literally. Áine recalled in later interviews they had tea and Mikado biscuits.

When Liam denied the allegations outright, Áine recalls that Adams stated: 'It's like trying to prove who stole the apples from a cart.' After that, Áine said, 'we received no support from Gerry.'

Gerry and Liam remained in contact, photographed together on occasions such as Liam's wedding in 1996 and the christening of his baby daughter in 1997. Liam Adams was also active in Sinn Féin well after Gerry Adams was aware of Áine's allegations. He was chair of Sinn Féin's Louth Comhairle Ceantair for two and a half months in 1996. He sought the nomination to be Sinn Féin's candidate in Co. Louth for the 1997 Irish general election, but was defeated by local Owenie Hanratty.

A source told the *Sunday Tribune*: 'It is impossible that Liam sought the Dáil election nomination without Gerry knowing about it – absolutely impossible. Liam was very much the Belfast leadership's man in Dundalk, pushing their line all the time.'

In January 2006, Áine made a formal complaint against her father. She was thirty-four, and her married name was Áine Tyrell. When interviewed by police, Liam denied the allegations.

The allegations about Liam Adams were first made public

when Áine took part in a TV documentary that was broadcast in December 2009. UTV's *Insight* programme featured Áine on camera, documenting the abuse her father had subjected her to and the failure of the police to protect her.

Gerry Adams appeared on the programme too. He said he was shocked when he first heard the allegations. He confirmed he had made a statement to the PSNI and was prepared to go to court to testify against his brother.

On Sunday, 20 December 2009, shortly after the airing of the documentary, a statement was released to the media by Gerry Adams. The statement purported to be from 'the Adams family', though no detail was given about who in the family had agreed that it be issued in their name.

In the late 1990s we discovered that our father had been sexually, emotionally and physically abusing members of our family.

This abuse happened over many years.

This discovery and the abuse which preceded it have had a devastating impact on our entire family.

We are still struggling to come to terms with what happened.

We live with the consequences every single day.

We have been dealing with this with the support of a number of professionals who have the expertise to deal with these matters.

We thank them for their help.

Abuse of any kind is horrendous but sexual abuse, particularly of a child, is indescribably wounding and heartbreaking.

Our family have debated for some time whether we should publicise our father's abusive behaviour.

We do so now in the hope that, in time, this will assist the victims and survivors to come to terms with what happened and help them to move on from these dreadful events.

All citizens need to be educated and children need to be listened to, empowered and protected.

Many people in other families have suffered from abuse.

Our family knows how deeply hurtful and traumatic that can be. No-one should have to deal with abuse or its consequences in isolation.

Victims of abuse in our family are still, years later, recovering from the trauma inflicted on us.

Our prayer is that everyone will be healed.

Most of us have grown in strength with the help of other family members, partners and friends.

We know this will continue. Our family are united.

We believe that there is a way out of this awfulness.

We hope this knowledge can be of some help to other families who are in the same situation.

Anyone affected by these issues should contact the Samaritans or any appropriate agency.

We would ask the media to give us some privacy, particularly over this Christmas period.

Just as Áine's allegations entered the public domain for the first time, her uncle Gerry – sensing the danger to him personally and to Sinn Féin – changed the narrative. Gerry Adams Snr was dead, and there had been no public allegations against him. But now, in the public mind, Áine's allegations did not stand alone; and Gerry Adams's statement opened the possibility that Liam was a victim too. The story became one of a traumatized family who had all suffered, rather than one of a child repeatedly raped by her father and let down by her family.

Gerry Adams's claim that 'Our family are united' was extraordinary under the circumstances – and demonstrably wrong, considering Áine's feelings towards him.

Sinn Féin's statement sought to distance the party and its leader from Liam Adams, and to pin the blame for his continuing access to children on the police:

Sinn Féin have confirmed that Liam Adams was a party member for a period in the 1990s in the Dundalk area. A party spokesperson told An Phoblacht that 'contrary to media reports, Liam Adams was not proposed as a party candidate in Louth and he left the party after an intervention by the party president. Nobody in the party in Louth was aware of the allegations against Liam Adams.'

It has also come to light that Liam Adams received both RUC and PSNI clearance to work in a number of youth projects in Belfast. He also worked in a similar project in the Dundalk area. This happened despite the authorities being in possession of a statement from his daughter alleging serious sexual abuse. Gerry Adams has made it clear that when he discovered his brother was working in the Clonard Youth Club he ensured that authorities in Clonard were informed about the allegation against Liam Adams. He also personally intervened to get him to leave the other project in the Beechmount area. He was not aware of the nature of his brother's work in Dundalk, having had limited contact with him from the late 1980s.

In the weeks since the UTV Insight programme much of the media focus has shifted from the need for Áine Tyrell to get justice, and the need for Liam Adams to appear in court to answer these charges, to a political witchhunt against Gerry Adams by predictable elements in the media. This is quite disgraceful. The victim in this case is Áine Tyrell and the alleged abuser is Liam Adams. At all times Gerry Adams has sought to carry out the wishes of his niece. It is quite shameful for a small number of media outlets to allow those opposed to Sinn Féin to attempt to hijack a young woman's demand for justice and the very serious issue of sexual abuse to further their own political aims.

This issue can only be dealt with through the courts. And the sooner the PSNI complete the necessary EU warrant and Liam Adams is given the opportunity to answer these allegations in court, the better.

Sinn Féin's message was clear: everyone needs to stop talking about Gerry Adams or else you're letting down an innocent victim.

Gerry Adams gave an interview to RTÉ in the aftermath of the UTV documentary and his own statement about his father. 'I don't want to distract for one second from Áine's plight,' the Sinn Féin leader said. 'I have felt for some long time we should go public about my father as part of the healing process within my own family and to try and help other families who are in the same predicament.'

Adams said he had no recollection of being abused himself.

Gerry Adams Snr had died in 2003. He was given a full republican funeral, with a tricolour on his coffin. This could not have happened without the knowledge and blessing of his son. When asked about it, Adams shifted responsibility to other, unnamed members of the family: 'Personally that was one of the great dilemmas for me because I'm a republican. I'm speaking here as a human being, as a family member.

'I didn't want him buried with the tricolour. I think he besmirched it but it was a dilemma for other members of my family who felt that they didn't want this at that time out in the open.'

The public were supposed to believe that despite the death of Gerry Adams Snr in 2003 and despite Gerry Adams's suppression of his own wish to go public earlier about his father's abuse, the 'family' decided that the perfect time to come forward with the truth about Gerry Adams Snr was in the immediate aftermath of the extremely damaging allegations by Áine Tyrell.

In the aftermath of the UTV documentary, questions were asked about what Gerry Adams knew, when he knew it, and what he had done or failed to do in relation to the allegations about his brother. Mary Lou McDonald, who had that year become vice-president of Sinn Féin, spoke up in defence of her party leader:

> I am absolutely satisfied that Gerry acted to the very best of his abilities throughout all of this. I know that Gerry cares about Aine and that he acted in her interests as her uncle. I'm satisfied that as a public figure, any of the questions that have arisen – and legitimately arisen – have been answered by him fully and frankly.

The following month, Áine told the *Sunday Tribune*: 'All I hear is "We can't address this or that question because of Áine. We have to protect Áine; she is the victim." They don't know me so I find it hard to believe they have all this sympathy for me. I want them to stop using my name.'

She also directly criticized her uncle:

Gerry has said that when he found out Liam was in Sinn Féin, he couldn't tell his colleagues Liam was a suspected paedophile in order to protect my anonymity.

That's nonsense. I didn't know Liam was in Sinn Féin but had Gerry bothered to tell me, I would have waived my anonymity without hesitation. I'd have accompanied Gerry to meet his colleagues in Sinn Féin, to talk to the Ard Chomhairle about what Liam had done to me so they could expel him from the party. But Gerry never gave me that option [. . .].

I'd heard Liam was working in youth projects in west Belfast but not which ones. I repeatedly raised this with Gerry. I said I was very concerned that Liam was seeking jobs working with children. Gerry told me that was Liam's way of trying to make up to the community for what he'd done to me. I asked Gerry how Liam had been successfully vetted for these jobs.

I told Gerry I believed children were at risk. I said that if something happened to another child, it would be on my conscience and I couldn't sleep at night from worrying about it. Gerry said it wasn't my responsibility. I kept telling Gerry to get Liam out of the youth groups. [. . .]

I didn't know which groups Liam was in but I even thought of standing on the streets of west Belfast handing out leaflets saying 'Liam Adams is a paedophile'. I thought of writing it up as graffiti on the walls. That's how desperate I was.

Áine said that, in 1996, after she broke off contact with her uncle, she received a signed copy of his memoir *Before the Dawn* in the post.

In the foreword Adams thanks his brothers and sisters, 'especially Liam'.

Áine said: 'I threw the book in the bin. It made me feel sick. Imagine sending the person you believed had been abused by your brother a book thanking that brother?'

The allegations against Gerry Adams sent shockwaves through Sinn Féin and the wider republican community. One former senior Sinn Féin figure in Stormont told me that the party went into overdrive in order to cushion Adams from damage.

'Gerry wouldn't take any responsibility for anything,' this figure said.

At a meeting in late 2009, it was decided by the party leadership and officer board that Adams should say nothing about the Liam Adams case unless it was approved by the party. Days later, Adams put out a statement.

'So, we have another meeting which Gerry doesn't bother attending and I'm saying: "Hold on a fucking minute, didn't we all agree last week he was saying nothing? Who was this run by?"

'The answer was nobody.

'I lost it, shouting: "So what are we gonna do here? What is the point of all of us being here?"'

Speaking out of turn in such a way was dangerous, because almost all of what was said was relayed back to Adams himself, such was the loyalty of his inner circle in Stormont.

At one point, Sinn Féin staff had created what one of them called 'a fucking spreadsheet' on Áine. There were columns listing every allegation Áine had made in public and what Gerry Adams had said publicly, in order to keep track of both.

When the senior Sinn Féin staffer questioned the

spreadsheet, they were told it was party chairman Declan Kearney's idea.

The senior staffer exploded: 'Please, do not have a meeting which is minuted or which, in practice, deals with Áine Adams as a fucking column in a spreadsheet,' he said. The other men stared blankly back at him.

At the time, Sinn Féin was involved in fraught negotiations with the DUP, the UUP and the SDLP over the transfer of powers over criminal justice to Northern Ireland. The province was on the cusp of having its own justice minister for the first time in four decades.

There was an open row between Sinn Féin and the UUP, and DUP leader Peter Robinson was struggling to persuade his thirty-six MLAs to sign up to a policing board which would include Sinn Féin members.

According to a senior Sinn Féin Stormont source, one late-night meeting saw a small group of men meet in Martin McGuinness's office. Gerry Adams was there, as were Gerry Kelly, who was a junior minister and the party spokesperson on policing, and senior Sinn Féin staff members Leo Green and Ted Howell. Howell, a west Belfast native and Adams's most trusted advisor, attended St Mary's Grammar School a few years ahead of Adams. He kept a low profile, but held huge sway in Sinn Féin, especially for those in Stormont. A number of other senior Sinn Féin members were also present.

Leo Green was chairing the meeting. People were coming and going from the room, so that conversation was disjointed. One witness, puzzled by all the coming and going, asked a colleague what was going on.

The reply: 'We're working on publicity lines on Liam Adams.'

Senior staff were becoming impatient. One staffer took Adams aside and told the party leader that something had to give. 'I said; "Gerry, I wanna talk to you, we can't have a negotiation going on here [about policing] and prioritize what we're doing when you're pulling people out of meetings for this, that should not be discussed here. That's a personal issue."'

Adams agreed, and let a small group of trusted staff – all male – read the notes that had been drafted to guide party members in answering questions about Liam Adams.

Upon first glance, McGuinness noticed a huge problem in the draft. Adams was already trying to leave the room: it was clear he knew what was coming. He told the others that there wasn't time for a discussion.

The draft 'publicity lines' stated that if Martin McGuinness was asked when he first heard about allegations that Liam Adams had raped his daughter, he should say two years ago.

McGuinness, according to the senior party source, was shocked that Adams wanted him to say that he had sat on such information.

Another staffer said angrily: 'If Martin McGuinness goes out of here today and he says he knew about this two years, he's in trouble.'

McGuinness agreed.

'This is wrong. We need to get this right,' he said. He told Adams that if asked about Liam and Áine he would not say he had any prior knowledge of the issue before 2009.

Whether McGuinness knew about the allegations against Liam Adams before 2009 is unknown. Whatever the truth of the matter, it seems clear that Adams wanted McGuinness to help take the heat off him.

'It was all about Gerry,' one witness said. 'I have served in the IRA and spent my life in Sinn Féin and it was during the Áine Adams revelations that I realized that Gerry Adams is a terrible person, and I don't say that lightly.

'In terms of manipulation and control, when you watch this guy work and how he interacts with people you just see something else . . . I started to see him in a totally different light. There's no empathy, no warmth.

'For me, republicanism had been taken down a line where the primary, main thing was for Gerry Adams to maintain his credibility till the end. That's how it felt.

'So when he is confronted with any uncomfortable truth his first instinct is to lie to everybody. That's part and parcel of politics, but this guy has no qualms at all. And this guy has no conscience about stuff, he's not troubled by anything.'

Liam Adams contested his extradition from the Republic on the grounds that the media coverage of the allegations against him had made it impossible for him to receive a fair trial in the North. The extradition was granted, and the trial began on 9 April 2013 – but it was quickly abandoned because the judge had failed to make a social work file regarding Áine Adams available to the defence.

Before the trial collapsed, Gerry Adams was called to give evidence against his brother. He did, however, reveal that in 2000 Liam confessed to him that he had sexually abused Áine. (When questioned by detectives about Áine's allegations in 2007, he had not seen fit to mention Liam's admission.) Gerry Adams testified that during the course of a walk the brothers took, Liam

acknowledged that he had sexually abused Áine. He said it only happened once. [. . .]

He was very upset. I remember it was raining. [. . .]

To the best of my recollection the terms that he used were that he had molested her or that he had interfered with her, that he had sexually assaulted her.

[. . .] Let me say that I didn't want to know the detail, and I consciously (because this is a dreadful thing that allegedly happened) didn't want to know the detail. [. . .] the specifics of Liam telling me that he had sexually interfered with her, that he had assaulted her, and molested her — I was conscious of that.

Under cross-examination, Adams repeatedly failed to remember crucial details. When pressed on the meeting in Buncrana, Adams told the court:

When that concluded, I spoke to Liam on my own and said to him that I was very aware of the situation, that he needed to reflect on and needed to acknowledge what Aine was saying. Why should she make it up? There was no reason why she should make any of this up.

He did not tell police about the confession until 2009, when UTV's *Insight* programme was being made.

When Liam Adams was tried again later in 2013, Gerry Adams was not asked to reappear as a witness. The jury in the second trial queried his absence when they retired to consider the verdict. The answer was not made public, but Ed Moloney has reported that the explanation lay in Adams's performance under cross-examination in the aborted first trial:

Gerry Adams had been caught out in so many contradictions and factual errors during a bruising cross-examination by Eilis McDermott, QC, that when the retrial was ordered, the defence legal team served notice on the Crown that they planned to make 'a bad character application' in relation to the Sinn Féin president.

If the application was granted, the defence would have been allowed to introduce in court evidence of Gerry Adams's 'bad character'. According to Moloney:

> This would have enabled Liam Adams' barrister, Eilis McDermott, to cross-examine Gerry Adams about his alleged IRA career and his denials thereof, as well as to delve into some of the more controversial episodes with which he has been associated, including the IRA disappearance of a number of people in the 1970's such as the widowed mother-of-ten Jean McConville.
>
> The purpose of this would be to demonstrate a history and pattern of deception and untruthfulness by Gerry Adams which would make the allegations he made against his brother Liam suspect and dubious.

According to Moloney, after the defence served notice of its intention to file the application, the prosecution withdrew Adams as a witness, on the grounds that it would take too long to file a response to the application.

On 1 October 2013, Liam Adams was convicted of raping and abusing his daughter Áine over a six-year period, beginning when she was four years old. A jury of nine men and three women, by an eleven to one majority, found Liam Adams guilty of all ten charges against him: three of rape, three of gross indecency and four indecent assaults.

He was given a sixteen-year prison sentence.

After the conviction, Áine told the press that her Uncle Gerry had tried to prevent the public finding out about the allegations. In 2007, she said, Gerry Adams had heard that a local newspaper was planning to cover it and phoned his niece 'frantically' twenty times.

'He wanted to obtain a court injunction, with my help, to stop the story. He said he needed to make sure it didn't get into the press, to protect me. Looking back, he was buttering me up. It was all about PR and his own image,' she said at the time.

Seven days after the verdict, the Police Ombudsman's office announced it would be looking into a complaint it had received about the PSNI's handling of Gerry Adams's failure to mention his awareness of Liam Adams's abuse when he spoke to police in 2007.

Cliona O'Kane, who had been a candidate for the 2003 Assembly elections in East Derry, served on Sinn Féin's political directorate in Stormont at the time. She shared an office on the second floor with Leo Green.

Martin McGuinness was flustered. He had come into the office repeatedly looking for Green and one other person. He said he needed to talk to them urgently. O'Kane was around thirty at the time and had never seen McGuinness in such an agitated state. She told others: 'I dunno what the fuck's wrong with him but you better go find out.'

In a small room, McGuinness told his most trusted staffers: 'This Liam Adams stuff. Look at the papers, it's all Adams. We are taking on unbelievable damage on this. We can't do this. We can't let this go.'

According to a Sinn Féin staff member, McGuinness was a keen follower of the news aggregator website Newshound, and was 'demented' over the dominance of stories about Liam Adams among the top stories on the site.

The staff present lamented the circumstances they were in. They could not control Gerry Adams, and they did not believe Gerry Adams. To support Sinn Féin was to support Gerry Adams. Now it appeared that the leader of republicanism had turned a blind eye to child sexual abuse in his own family.

A month after Liam's conviction, McGuinness was called upon to defend Gerry Adams during Assembly Questions.

'Gerry Adams was fully in support of his niece, travelled to Buncrana, confronted his brother and supported his niece and her mother when she reported the abuse to the social services and to the RUC,' McGuinness said. He went on to mention that Gerry Adams Snr had been an abuser too, and that in many ways the entire family were victims. The narrative was to be repeated ad nauseam. But McGuinness wasn't happy about it.

Chronic dishonesty, and the general view that any atrocity could be excused by the righteousness of the party's cause, had brought Sinn Féin to this place. McGuinness and other republicans who were comfortable being associated with the acts of the IRA found themselves acutely uncomfortable being associated with Liam Adams. They had arrived at a moral quandary that any number of killings and any amount of lying for the cause had not brought them to.

One Sinn Féin staff member summarized a widespread view within Sinn Féin at the time: 'If you did wrong, and you were being castigated in the media for doing something wrong, which the party thinks is wrong, you shouldn't be the person who decides what the party says about it.'

Those present in the private meeting agreed with McGuinness. There was no way around it: Gerry Adams should step back from Sinn Féin until the official inquiries into his actions had been concluded. Martin McGuinness confided to his trusted staffers that 'a number of very senior people' within the party had told him they felt the same.

Green agreed. He told the group a number of staff had told him in previous weeks that the controversy had contaminated party development and that Gerry Adams's attitude towards the situation was making it worse.

Discussions began in earnest about who would replace Adams. To those involved, there was only one obvious answer: Martin McGuinness himself. McGuinness said he didn't want the job, but he was sure that the party could no longer weather the constant barrage of bad publicity linked to Liam and Gerry Adams.

The other issue was that no one in the party – including McGuinness – was brave enough to tell Gerry Adams that he should stand aside. The man had defined republicanism in his own image. And although the mantra was often repeated that no one was bigger than the cause, no one felt anyone really believed that when it came to Gerry Adams.

The exception was Leo Green, who volunteered to tell Adams that it was time for him to step aside.

McGuinness said he wished to speak to Adams about the issue alone first. He would allude to the fact that some within the party had been growing increasingly concerned and plant the idea that all was not well within the ranks.

The following Wednesday there was a meeting of the Coiste Seasta: the party's central committee of trusted decision makers who provide political oversight on big decisions. A number of members of the committee were asked to cancel their other plans and come to Dublin for a meeting with McGuinness and Adams in Dublin. Declan Kearney,

Marty 'Duckser' Lynch, Des Mackin, Sean Hughes, Dawn Doyle, Leo Green and Ted Howell would all be there. The inclusion of Leo Green alerted others that this was not a meeting organized by Gerry Adams, as the two did not get on well.

In advance of the meeting, Green made it clear to colleagues that he felt Gerry Adams had personally protected an abuser. For him, the issue was personal as well as political. Green's wife, Maggie, had been Liam Adams's line manager in a youth organization in Gerry Adams's constituency, the Blackie Centre in Beechmount. This was the second youth group in his brother's constituency Liam Adams had worked in after Gerry Adams had become aware that he was an abuser. Leo Green himself was on the management committee of the centre. In his position at the Blackie Centre, Liam Adams had ready access to young people.

Gerry Adams has claimed it was at his own direction that Liam left the position. Officially, Liam had left because he had a frozen shoulder.

Two weeks before the Coiste Seasta meeting, there was a celebratory event for republicans in a Belfast hotel, a fundraising dinner dance. At the fundraiser, Adams made a speech and received a standing ovation. Witnesses have confirmed that, after a delay, Leo Green eventually stood up to join the ovation. His wife Maggie never stood. Nor did one or two others who had been seated at their table and worked in community development. It was noted.

A number of Sinn Féin MLAs and staff members have told me that this snub of the party leader marked the beginning of the end of Leo Green's career in Sinn Féin.

Dawn Doyle was in Dublin when she received a message calling a meeting of Sinn Féin's senior leadership. Doyle, originally from Wexford, was a vital cog in the machine. She had become the Director of Political Operations in 2008, and in that role she was involved in every move Sinn Féin made.

She asked around to ascertain who else had been invited and what the meeting was about. The message had been vague, but only the most trusted individuals had been asked to attend.

Although none were certain, they assumed the meeting would be about Liam Adams. The affair had been hanging over the party in the months since the trial verdict, Green had made it clear he was unhappy, and the rank-and-file staff, especially the women, were pissed off at Adams's attitude and performance in the media. It couldn't be anything else, given the seniority of those invited.

The meeting was held in Sinn Féin head office in Dublin, in Parnell Square. The building is a converted Georgian house, with tall windows and high ceilings, facing the Rotunda Hospital. It has a number of rooms used for offices and media interviews.

McGuinness was already there when a senior Stormont staffer arrived and began to make himself a cup of tea, enquiring if McGuinness had had a chance to speak to Adams privately ahead of the meeting.

McGuinness said he planned to pull Adams aside privately before the meeting started, so as to not let him feel ambushed. The pair were whispering in the kitchen when Adams walked in.

Adams started making a cup of tea, and enquired about what room the meeting would be held in. The atmosphere was tense. McGuinness and his senior aide were keenly aware they had been caught out whispering, and worried that Adams had been listening outside the door beforehand.

They decided on the Ard Comhairle room. There was space for about twenty-five people to have a meeting around a number of tables pushed together.

McGuinness told Adams he'd like to have a word beforehand, but Adams refused, telling him: 'There's no need.'

McGuinness looked at his comrade and they exchanged a glance: *Gerry knows*.

'Gerry is now in control,' recalls the senior aide. 'We get into the room and Dawn is in a panic. I can see her face and she was looking at me for help, like, she didn't know what to do.'

Shortly before the meeting began, Richard McAuley, Marie Grogan and Seán Mac Brádaigh filed in.

McAuley, who hails from Andersonstown in west Belfast, was (and remains) Adams's most trusted advisor. A one-time trainee teacher, he spent five years in Long Kesh in the 1970s, working as the press officer for the prisoners while he was held there as a Special Category prisoner.

Upon release he worked for *An Phoblacht/Republican News* and became chair of Belfast Sinn Féin and stood for the Lagan Valley seat in 1983. In 1994, he became PA and press officer to Gerry Adams, a position which he still holds today.

Marie Grogan had been Adams's personal secretary both when he was an MP for Belfast West and when he was a TD for Louth. She had been trusted by the leader for decades.

Belfast native Mac Brádaigh was once described by the *Irish Times* as 'Gerry Adams's personal spokesman'.

Sean Hughes, a former IRA commander from Dromintee, Co. Armagh, also arrived. A former member of the IRA Army Council, he was now a senior Sinn Féin staffer.

The presence of the four, and its significance, was noted. 'Never had any of these people ever featured in critical decisions,' recalled one witness. 'They're staff, not political minds.'

Dawn Doyle volunteered to chair the meeting, asking who wanted to start. She made no reference to the reason why the meeting had been called. As the silence became deafening, she began desperately looking around for someone to begin speaking.

McGuinness, who was seated on Adams's right, shuffled in his chair and finally spoke: 'We're taking an awful lot of flak. Every day. It's hard to manage and measure the damage the party might be taking, but we just need to do something and I'm racking my brain about what we can do. Most of this is directed at Gerry and it's bad publicity . . . Nevertheless, the party's getting it in the neck and we're definitely losing support.'

McGuinness's senior aide remembers McGuinness pausing before going on to say: 'We need to be thinking about it . . . We shouldn't have anything off the table here and we should be thinking about the fact there are inquiries going on. There's a police investigation and a police ombudsman one.'

According to the senior aide, McGuinness referenced a recent scandal involving the wife of DUP leader Peter Robinson which led to Robinson stepping aside temporarily as First Minister.

'He got himself into a bit of a tangle a while ago and he stood down,' McGuinness said. 'So maybe, for example, I think Gerry could stand down for the course of one of these investigations. I'm only throwing that out, just a suggestion.'

It was a very uncomfortable speech for McGuinness to make. People present at the meeting say they felt McGuinness was intimidated by the presence of Adams.

According to the senior aide, Adams then made a long speech in which he insisted that he had done nothing wrong, and that standing aside was 'not on the table at all'. He acknowledged that he was 'taking flak', but argued that standing down would 'make it worse'.

Sean Hughes voiced agreement with Adams, and the rest of Adams's inner circle nodded their heads in agreement.

Leo Green replied that he felt the party needed to keep everything on the table. He said he actually disagreed with McGuinness on one point: the suggestion that Adams should step down for one of the inquiries.

'If we're considering Gerry stepping down for one of these inquiries, it needs to be all of them,' Green said.

Adams was livid. He refused to step down. Most of the others at the meeting were too afraid to speak up against him and little else was said.

The people who believed Adams should step down had no real plan, and lacked the guts to say it openly. McGuinness didn't want to be leader and was either too unsure or too intimidated to say that he definitively wanted Adams to go.

The meeting never fully got off the ground, and Adams remained in charge. Those who sat around the table walked away having received a lesson in how not to take on Gerry Adams.

6. The Disappeared and the Anointed

Gerry Adams decided who his successor as president of Sinn Féin would be years before he stepped down. Senior members of Sinn Féin have confirmed to me that both Adams and McGuinness spoke of Mary Lou McDonald taking over the party as far back as 2012.

When looking back at that year, it's perhaps not surprising that Adams was looking towards a successor, anticipating his expiry date in Irish politics.

In October 2011, Liam Adams had lost his bid to appeal against his extradition to Northern Ireland. This was the last significant obstacle to a trial of the Sinn Féin leader's brother on charges of raping his daughter.

In the summer of 2012, the case of Jean McConville came back to the fore.

On 6 July, the First Circuit Court of Appeals in Boston ruled in favour of the British government's request for the transcripts of the interviews conducted as part of Ed Moloney's oral history project on the Troubles, sponsored by Boston College. Former IRA combatants had spoken freely about their paramilitary careers under the assurance that the interviews wouldn't be made public until after they died.

The PSNI argued that the tapes included key evidence about the murder of Jean McConville.

When her husband died of cancer on 3 January 1972, Jean McConville went into a dark depression. She only left the family home to fetch groceries or visit her son, who had been interned. She did not associate much with her neighbours in the Divis flats. The high-rise block of flats was a tight-knit republican community with a strong IRA element, and surrounded by a heavy British Army presence. In the same year McConville became a widow, a gunfight broke out in the flat complex. Jean and her remaining children cowered on the floor. When the shooting stopped, a voice cried out outside their door: 'Please God, I don't want to die.' It was a British soldier who had been wounded and was lying in the public hallway of the flats. Jean brought a pillow for the man's head and said a prayer next to him, before returning to her home. Archie, the oldest son present, told Jean she was 'asking for trouble'. He was right.

The next day the words 'BRIT LOVER' were graffitied across their door.

Shortly after this, a group of men and women entered Jean McConville's home and, in front of her children, took her away. She screamed as she left, her daughter Agnes, who was thirteen at the time, recalled. Agnes remembered her mother was wearing red slippers. No one reported Jean missing and there is no record of any investigation by the RUC into her disappearance.

A week later a young boy came to their door with Jean's purse and three rings she had been wearing when she left. Her engagement ring, wedding ring and an eternity ring.

In the spring of 1999, the IRA acknowledged its role in Jean's murder but stated she had 'admitted being a British Army informer'. An investigation by the Police Ombudsman's Office, completed in 2006, found no evidence that Jean McConville had been an informer.

Adams had met with Jean's daughter Helen McConville in 1995. He had sympathized, but Helen later said he could not meet her eye. Adams said: 'For what it's worth, I apologize for what the Republican movement did to your mother.'

He also told the McConville children he had been in prison at the time of their mother's abduction. That was a lie. He had been released from Long Kesh in June 1972 on Ivor Bell's demand and flown to England for the negotiations. He was not rearrested until the following July. He has since said he was simply mixed up.

Jean McConville is not the only person who was abducted by republican paramilitaries, killed and secretly buried.

There are seventeen such people, collectively known as the 'Disappeared'. Their names (and ages at the time of their disappearance) are: Charlie Armstrong (54), Gerard (Gerry) Evans (24), Joseph Lynskey (45), John McClory (18), Jean McConville (38), Danny McIlhone (19), Kevin McKee (17), Brian McKinney (22), Columba McVeigh (19), Seamus Maguire (26), Brendan Megraw (23), Eamon Molloy (22), Captain Robert Nairac (29), Seamus Ruddy (33), Eugene Simons (26), Peter Wilson (21) and Seamus Wright (25). The remains of Lynskey, McVeigh, Nairac and Maguire have never been found.

Many of these people were taken from their families because the IRA believed, rightly or wrongly, that they had betrayed it in some way. Many were reported to be informers for the RUC or British Army, though the evidence for many of these claims is shaky at best.

From Sinn Féin's point of view, the 'Disappeared' are a liability and have been for decades. The Independent Commission for the Location of Victims' Remains was established following the Belfast Agreement to attempt to locate the Disappeared, often through painstaking searches of lonesome stretches of bog, forest or beach. The sight of families watching tractors pulling away earth in the hope it might uncover the abandoned corpse of their loved one has been a common experience for those who grew up in Ireland North and South. Every so often, the BBC and RTÉ beam pictures of the grief-stricken families and exhausted searchers into our homes and remind us who the IRA really were.

As the IRA's head of intelligence, Bobby Storey approached Ivor Bell and Dolours Price in 1998. Both were known to have been involved in the killing of Jean McConville. Storey wanted to know if they knew where her body had been buried. For his own part, Bell had said at the time that he felt McConville's body should be left in the street as a warning to others.

Dolours Price couldn't believe that Adams had sent someone to ask where McConville was. According to her testimony in the Boston College tapes, Price told Storey to 'go and see Gerry'. It appears that Dolours Price believed that Gerry Adams already knew the whereabouts of McConville's remains.

Within Sinn Féin, anyone who might possibly know anything about the whereabouts of McConville's remains was told to report what they knew to the leadership.

The way in which the IRA disappeared people contributed to the difficulty of locating their remains many years later. Those who were abducted were generally transported under cover of darkness to remote parts of the countryside. Memories fade, landscapes change. Many of those who were involved in the disappearances would not have been familiar with the areas where they left the dead bodies of their victims. Often, even members of the IRA disappearance teams didn't know where they were going with their victims, because they hadn't been told. Everything in the IRA was 'need to know', and they didn't need to know.

One former combatant who spoke to me was called a number of years ago by Padraic Wilson. Wilson had been released from the Maze prison in December 1999 after serving twenty-four years for possession of explosives and conspiracy to murder. Since his release he has been a key Sinn Féin advisor. He persuaded fellow inmates to back the party's political strategy and in May 1998 was given temporary parole to attend Sinn Féin's ruling council in Dublin to discuss the ratification of the Good Friday Agreement. He is not an elected representative, but has huge influence in the party.

Wilson was part of the Sinn Féin team trying to locate the bodies of the Disappeared. The former combatant met Wilson in a rural pub car park on a Saturday morning. Wilson quizzed the man, who had spent time living and serving much of his IRA career around the Donegal–Fermanagh border, where some of the Disappeared were believed to be buried.

'They came to me to see if I knew anybody who may have been involved,' the former combatant told me. 'There was one boy who was a bit of a maverick, [name redacted], who was about that area at the time . . .

'I was with him on a number of occasions . . . he had a bad streak in him. We were in Derrylin once, in a grocery shop and a post office, just a wee country place, we were doing a number of things, but we were planting a booby trap when the Brits arrived.

'We all ran and [name redacted] fuckin' shot the wee man in the shop in the leg for no reason with a fuckin' Armalite. There was no reason at all, he was a bad wee bastard. I said, "You may go ask [name redacted]. The last I heard he was living in Sweden."'

'Try and find some bad wee bastard who might live in

Sweden' is not evidence that one can hand over to a commission, and most of the information the leadership were receiving was of this nature.

There were meetings held with combatants all over the island of Ireland to try and jog memories and convince those who had them that it was safe to share them.

'There were extreme efforts made and resources and time and energy and meetings put in to trying to find those bodies at that point, because they just wanted all of them to go the fuck away,' one senior party staff member told me. 'It was horrible, politically horrible, morally horrible, it was just awkward really, you know, just like this scab couldn't heal.'

Many former combatants have told me they believe there are those within the republican movement who know where the final four bodies are and refuse to come forward.

Some have suggested fears of being implicated by DNA evidence, or killed by those they implicate if they do. Some believe that the Disappeared deserved it.

One senior figure in the party told me: 'Some of them were dirty jobs, and there were people that really shouldn't have been killed, or some shouldn't have been disappeared whether they deserved it or not, but the leadership didn't care until the politics became unpalatable.'

Those unpalatable politics may well have been on his mind when Adams started telling colleagues about the person who would be his successor: a young middle-class woman from Dublin with no links to the IRA.

Mary Louise McDonald – always known as Mary Lou – was born on May Day 1969, and raised in the leafy Dublin suburb of Rathgar.

She was the second of four children born to Patrick and

Joan McDonald. Patrick was a building contractor and a member of Fianna Fáil; Joan too was briefly a member of the party. Joan McDonald and Mary Lou's younger sister, Joanne, a scientist, who was once linked to the radical left-republican group Éirígí, remain Mary Lou's closest confidantes.

Although both parents were politically minded, McDonald has described her maternal grandmother, Molly Hayes, an 'old-style republican', as her political mentor.

Joan and Patrick McDonald separated when Mary Lou was nine.

She attended Notre Dame des Missions, a private Catholic girls' junior and secondary school. When she didn't gain the Leaving Certificate points she needed for the course she wanted, she did an additional year at Rathmines Senior College and repeated the exam. She went on to attend Trinity College, studying English literature. After a gap year in Spain teaching English, McDonald did a Master's degree in European Studies, later working as a researcher in a Dublin-based think-tank, the Institute of European Affairs. Then she began a PhD in Industrial Relations/Human Resource Management.

McDonald met Martin Lanigan in Peter's Pub in Dublin in the early 1990s, and they married in 1996.

Around the time of her wedding, McDonald joined the Irish National Congress, an organization of republicans and nationalists of all stripes who met to discuss their vision for the future of the island. McDonald was elected chair of the organization in March 2000. She quickly made a name for herself when protests against the Orange Order's plans to unveil a plaque on Dublin's Dawson Street took place. McDonald said the INC had 'strenuous objections' to the mayor of Dublin's engaging with the Orange Order.

Around this time she also joined Fianna Fáil, after being invited to come along to meetings by her friend Nora Comisky, a Fianna Fáil activist. Comisky was, as one former senior Fianna Fáil minister put it, very much part of the 'green wing of Fianna Fáil' – green in the sense of nationalist, rather than environmentalist.

She joined the Dublin West cumann and was a regular attender of meetings. Other members of the cumann told me that McDonald was 'obsessed' with the situation in Northern Ireland, and brought it up consistently. She spoke at the party's 1998 Ard Fheis on reform of the RUC, telling other attendees that the organization needed 'root and branch' reform.

'In fairness to Mary Lou, in the cumann at that time, they'd be on about the budget and legislation and she'd pipe up and say, "Did you see what happened in the North last week?" She was absolutely dedicated to the North,' the former Fianna Fáil minister told me.

McDonald has been open about the fact she did not feel her passion for the plight of her Northern cousins was widely shared or appreciated within Fianna Fáil.

She had been active in the parades issue, even visiting the Garvaghy Road at the time of the stand-off there, and later said that Fianna Fáil had a level of disengagement on the issue.

'I discovered I was just in the wrong party,' she later told TheJournal.ie.

She said that her former party were not as strong on social justice issues as she was. She maintains that she left the party of her own volition, and that the question of running for office never arose.

Another former Fianna Fáil minister says, however,

McDonald is being dishonest about the latter point. 'The true story is that Fianna Fáil wanted her to run but she wasn't interested and it was after that then we heard she had gone to Sinn Féin.'

McDonald told *An Phoblacht* about how she decided to join Sinn Féin:

I remember the first time that I saw Gerry and Martin speak. It was in the Mansion House, and I went along with a friend of mine. The place was packed and I remember saying to my friend on the way out, 'This is real; this isn't political rhetoric. This is history in the making . . .' At that point I decided not only that I would be politically active, but that Sinn Féin would be my political home.

McDonald did not specify in what year she heard Adams and McGuinness speak at the Mansion House, but she has claimed she joined Sinn Féin in 1999.

However, Shane Ross's book details the minutes of Fianna Fáil's Kevin Barry cumann, Porterstown, Castleknock, on 26 January 2000, showing that Mary Lou McDonald proposed another member, Edward McManus, as a delegate to the Fianna Fáil national executive during the meeting.

In any event, once she did make the switch to Sinn Féin, things began to move quickly.

In March 2001, she appeared at a commemoration for IRA volunteer Tom Smith, who was shot in 1975 trying to escape from Portlaoise prison. Councillor Nicky Kehoe, a convicted IRA member, was alongside her. The girl from Rathgar had no apparent objection to appearing with former paramilitaries to commemorate other paramilitaries.

'That was the thing about her, she knew who she had to

cosy up to,' one councillor who worked alongside McDonald told me.

'Then whenever she didn't need them, she just dropped them, because maybe she didn't feel that they were going to bring her where she needed. That's something that's quite common. I find when you're talking to people like Mary Lou, [the thing] is that, she's not a user, but she's very self-sufficient. Like she sees things a mile ahead.'

By 2001 she had joined the party Ard Comhairle, and she ran in the 2002 general election for Dublin West, coming seventh of nine candidates.

Her closeness to the leadership was remarked on from the start, as was her ability to pack a room in middle-class areas.

In that same year, Sinn Féin held a community meeting in a public hall in Dundrum – an upmarket suburb of south Dublin, not far from where McDonald was brought up. Adams was to speak at the meeting, but McDonald's presence – despite her very modest showing in the general election – was seen as crucial.

'It was obvious that this was Adams's plan from way, way, way back, to have Mary Lou take over and appeal to the middle classes,' the meeting organizer told me.

The meeting was packed out. The *Irish Times* wrote that 'a huge overflow attendance with the crowd in the hall spilled outside'.

'The meeting was billed as Mary Lou, the local girl who brought Gerry Adams,' the organizer said.

'I just remember thinking, "He has some fucking plans for her."

'Adams realized, what's the furthest you can get from an aggressive Belfast man with a war record? A south Dublin middle-class, private-schooled woman. That was it.'

There was a National Officer Board meeting afterwards. Witnesses said Adams was ecstatic about the packed Dundrum meeting.

After the 2002 election, McDonald took up a job in Leinster House as 'political strategy co-ordinator' for the party. And the party wasted no time in choosing her as its Dublin candidate for the European Parliament elections to be held in 2004.

Mary Lou McDonald was getting elected, if it was the last thing Sinn Féin ever did. And she was as dedicated as the party was. She gave birth to her first child, Iseult, on 8 June 2003 and appeared at a press conference six weeks later.

If she hadn't proved her dedication to the party by then, it could never be in doubt after what came next.

Seán Russell, born in Dublin in 1893, fought with the rebels in the Easter Rising. During the War of Independence, he was appointed Director of Munitions on the IRA General Headquarters Staff. When Irish nationalism split over the Treaty, he became Director of Munitions for the anti-Treaty IRA. During a brief period as IRA Chief of Staff in 1938–9, he presided over the S-Plan, a campaign of sabotage on British soil.

In early 1940, Russell travelled from the United States, where he had been doing propaganda work, to Berlin. He spent three months in Nazi Germany, meeting the Foreign Minister, Joachim von Ribbentrop, and training with the Abwehr. Russell wanted German weapons; the Germans thought the IRA could be part of a (never-realized) plan to hit the UK via Northern Ireland. Returning to Ireland in a U-boat, Russell died on 14 August 1940 and was buried at sea with full German military honours.

A statue in Russell's honour was erected in Dublin's Fairview Park in 1951 after a march and a ceremony attended by around 5,000 people. The statue has been vandalized repeatedly and there have been repeated calls to have it removed.

In September 2003, McDonald spoke at a commemoration at the Russell statue. We don't know who suggested that McDonald speak at the event, or exactly what the party was thinking. But if there was ever to be a moment when McDonald might have baulked at the republican movement's uncritical veneration of its dead, it surely would have been this one. Was it really necessary, the party's rising star might have wondered, for her to speak at a commemoration for a Nazi collaborator? There is no reason to believe that she saw Seán Russell as a model for the future of republicanism. But she must have understood that being a Sinn Féin politician requires regular demonstrations of fealty to the republican past, including some of its most unsavoury elements.

Fintan O'Toole wrote in the *Irish Times*: 'The bizarre Seán Russell event was presumably a kind of trial – McDonald's chance to prove that there was no aspect of the IRA's history that she would ever disown, even if it involved Nazis.'

The event caused outrage at the time, and there were further calls to have the statue removed from the park.

During the European Parliament campaign the following year, her opponents made an issue of McDonald's willingness to honour Seán Russell. Fianna Fáil candidate Eoin Ryan said she had 'stood shoulder to shoulder with a brutal IRA bomber less than nine months ago to honour a friend of the Holocaust . . . Shame on you Mary Lou and your warped principles.'

If the affair damaged McDonald in the eyes of Dublin voters, it was not enough to prevent her from coming fourth in the four-seat constituency and becoming Sinn Féin's first MEP in the Republic.

When her election had been confirmed, she was carried on the shoulders of her fellow party members in the RDS while the Everly Brothers' song 'Hello Mary Lou' was blasted from a speaker. When she returned to the ground, she called the staff around her for a huddle, where she told them that it was not her seat, but Sinn Féin's.

In January 2005, 33-year-old Robert McCartney was beaten and stabbed outside a Belfast pub after a row with senior republicans. McCartney later died from his injuries. There were seventy people in the pub, a number of whom were Sinn Féin members and representatives. Not a single eye-witness came forward to assist police.

When it emerged that Deirdre Hargey, a prospective election candidate for Sinn Féin, had been present in the pub the night the murder took place, she was temporarily suspended from the party. But she was soon brought back into the fold, and went on to become the Lord Mayor of Belfast.

A bizarre intervention which saw the IRA offer to murder the person or people who had taken McCartney's life further traumatized the McCartney family and soured the mood of the public.

McCartney's sisters embarked on a campaign to find the truth about who killed their brother. On 9 May 2005, the European Union voted on a motion condemning the murder and criticized Sinn Féin for its alleged failure to cooperate with the investigation. The motion condemned 'violence and criminality by the self-styled "Irish Republican Army" (IRA) in Northern Ireland, in particular the murder of Robert McCartney'. It urged the Sinn Féin leadership 'to insist that those responsible for the murder and witnesses to the murder co-operate directly with the Police Service of Northern Ireland and be free from the threat of reprisals from the IRA'.

The resolution also called for the unprecedented use of EU anti-terror funds to finance a civil legal action if Northern Ireland police failed to bring a criminal prosecution against the men who the sisters believed carried out the murder.

MEPs backed the resolution by 555–4, with 48 abstentions. McDonald and the other Sinn Féin MEP, Bairbre de Brún, were the only Irish representatives not to vote in favour and abstained.

The two Sinn Féin women backed a separate motion tabled by the Parliament's left-wing GUE/NGL grouping, of which Sinn Féin is a member. The motion noted that Sinn Féin had suspended seven members in connection with the episode, and claimed that the party backed the McCartneys' efforts for justice.

McDonald claimed that there was not a 'culture of fear' in Short Strand, preventing eyewitnesses coming forward.

I think there is a myth amongst certain sections of the media, perhaps a deliberately constructed one, around this business of fear in the community.

It is certainly not a fear of republicans in terms of bringing this information forward. We couldn't be more crystal clear, the IRA, Sinn Féin, republicans everywhere have called for people to bring the information forward [. . .].

No one bought it. The dogs in the street knew who killed McCartney and yet everyone remained silent. Gerard 'Jock'

Davison, a former IRA commander, was widely regarded as the man who gave the order to murder McCartney.

This was not a comfortable position for McDonald. In her first elected role, she was forced to comment on the horrific murder of an innocent man. A murder that had taken place where her fellow party members were present. A murder that went unsolved because information from republicans was not forthcoming. McDonald can't have had any first-hand knowledge of whether or not there was a 'culture of fear' in Short Strand. The working-class Catholic enclave in Belfast was a world away from Brussels and Rathgar. She was defending the indefensible.

In this, she was only doing what every party member was expected to do. One senior staff member summarizes the position thus:

'Whatever you think personally, you have to support it – the armed struggle. You can't ever say one particular thing was disgusting, you always have to say that the conflict was wrong and all people suffered, that's the line. You stick to the line.'

This staff member told me about a meeting at which the subject arose. 'I remember asking during the meeting if there was a place for people in Sinn Féin who don't support the armed struggle. Should we not have a situation where young people who join Sinn Féin feel free to say that what happened to Jean McConville was diabolical? I mean, what the fuck?

'They all just looked at me,' he said.

The staff member felt that the new generation of party members should not be bound by the movement's iron fealty to the acts of the IRA.

'Why should they have to defend what we defended? We know about it, we lived it, but that's why we were involved in all of this and we may have an instinct to defend it even if we're not totally on board. Young people shouldn't be shackled like us. Others should be able to go and say: "I wasn't even born, but by the way, what the fuck were those who did it thinking? It was wrong."'

The 2007 general election was to be held on 24 May, and Sinn Féin were certain that it would see Mary Lou McDonald elected to the Dáil. Everything in their electoral arsenal was thrown at Mary Lou's campaign, she *had* to get elected because of Adams's ambitions for her.

It was decided she would run in Dublin Central, the diverse inner-city constituency of the Taoiseach, Bertie Ahern. The previous general election had seen the Sinn Féin candidate for the area, former republican prisoner Nicky Kehoe, lose out on a seat by just fifty-seven votes. Everyone in the area assumed Kehoe would take another run at it, and rumours abounded of a rift within the party caused by McDonald's standing in Dublin Central despite having no previous connection to the constituency. But party sources insist that Kehoe did not wish to stand again, and, as one cumann member told me, 'It got to the point there didn't really seem like there was anyone else to do it anyway.'

'And once Dawn Doyle was on board, and talking her up, we knew she was the one who was going to be picked.' At this stage Doyle was head of publicity for Sinn Féin, and hugely influential in the party; she would be 26 County Director of Political Operations by the next year.

McDonald had no such issues with the people who some have referred to as 'old school' Sinn Féin, or 'army people'. These were people with known IRA histories, and it didn't faze McDonald – quite the contrary.

'She was clever enough to get in with the right people, the army people, so they really did push for her above any other woman in the party,' one campaign worker said.

'So because of that, she very quickly moved up the ranks, and it was decided she had to be put somewhere she could win.'

Teams of Sinn Féin people come in from Belfast and Armagh to canvass for McDonald in Dublin Central.

'There really was this feeling that Mary Lou was going to get it,' one local member said. 'We were all just kind of believing each other's hype.'

On the day, Mary Lou McDonald got just over 9 per cent of the first-preference vote – compared to 14.6 per cent for Nicky Keogh in 2002. The notion that Keogh's voters were Sinn Féin voters was soon put to bed. They belonged to Nicky and Sinn Féin had taken them for granted.

She did not win a seat. It was a dreadful performance, and yet her status as the party's next big thing remained intact.

The blame wasn't entirely McDonald's to carry. The party did badly everywhere, and despite being tipped to double their Dáil representation actually ended up losing a seat.

Henry McDonald wrote in the *Guardian*:

This weekend the knots of young Sinn Fein members gathered around the RDS, even the cadre from Northern Ireland, were subdued. Some were in shock as they realised the party's forward march had been halted. Sinn Fein seats were being lost; targeted constituencies were failing to return hotly tipped candidates; even the usually eloquent Gerry Adams was unable to explain what had happened.

Whisperings that McDonald is not 'a real republican' have followed her ever since she joined Sinn Féin and began her rise within the party. Her profile as a middle-class Dublin woman with a Fianna Fáil background has cast her as an interloper in the eyes of some hardline republicans: some say that she is play-acting 'for the boys' in order to further her political career. Her poor performance in Dublin Central in 2007 could very reasonably be viewed as evidence that she lacked the ability to connect with working-class voters.

But the fact that Mary Lou McDonald did not tick the traditional boxes was not an impediment to her rise within Sinn Féin. It was an advantage. The republican leadership had long understood that, if the party was to make real headway in the Republic, it needed a leader without IRA connections. It also helped that McDonald was well educated and intelligent, quick-witted and attractive. These were the things that made the party leadership feel she could help Sinn Féin achieve new levels of electoral success. But they were not enough. The electorate was not the only audience. McDonald also had to win over those within the movement who doubted she was a 'real republican'. From the start, she has gone about doing that – even when it has meant honouring a Nazi collaborator and IRA killers – with no apparent hesitation.

7. Shaking Hands with the Queen

In March 2011, shortly after it was announced that Queen Elizabeth would visit Ireland for the first time, Martin McAleese approached Gerry Adams.

Martin McAleese was the husband of Mary McAleese, the President of Ireland. During her fourteen-year presidency, he had played an active role in presidential initiatives, including a long-term programme of outreach to loyalist former paramilitaries. A Catholic who had grown up in a predominantly Protestant part of east Belfast, Martin McAleese also maintained a good working relationship with Sinn Féin.

Now, he was hoping to persuade Sinn Féin not to boycott the Queen's visit, but to take part in it. During his conversation with Adams, McAleese disclosed no details of the visit, except that it was expected the Queen would make a significant speech.

Queen Elizabeth had visited Northern Ireland over twenty times both as Princess and as Queen, but she had never visited the Republic. Indeed, no British monarch had ever visited independent Ireland. In 1993, the then President of Ireland, Mary Robinson, met the Queen in Buckingham Palace for tea, marking the first official meeting between the heads of state of Ireland and Britain. In 1995, the Prince of Wales (now King Charles III) visited Dublin. But even in the twelve years following the Good Friday Agreement, a visit from the Queen herself – who was seen by some in Ireland as embodying an entire painful colonial history, and whose cousin Lord Louis Mountbatten had been killed by the IRA in 1979 – seemed too fraught.

Now, finally, the President's invitation had been accepted. The Sinn Féin National Officer Board – which, within the byzantine structures of the party, is seen as more powerful than the Ard Comhairle – met to discuss the party's stance.

Gerry Adams started the meeting early by saying he had to be somewhere else. As members of the board were still filing in, he told the others that the Queen was coming to visit the twenty-six counties, and that the general view was that Sinn Féin should not attend. It was not clear when, or with whose input, this supposedly general view had been formed.

Adams was questioned on what kind of events the Queen was planning to attend.

He mentioned that the monarch would be attending a wreath-laying ceremony in honour of the Irish who had died fighting the British.

One senior staffer jumped in: 'The British Queen is coming down, she's going to lay a wreath at the grave of the republican dead, and Sinn Féin are not going to be there?'

'Well,' Adams said, backtracking, 'I'm not 100 per cent sure what she's doing, that's just a hypothetical.'

One staffer present said he felt it became obvious that senior IRA members within the Sinn Féin leadership had already decided that Sinn Féin would not participate in the Queen's visit.

'He was going through the motions of pretending to do a consultation, encouraging people to be negative,' one witness said.

Adams was giving the impression that he was interested in the Officer Board's view when, in reality, the decision had been made.

Many MLAs, TDs and staff knew there was a hierarchy above the formal leadership of the party. There were still men in rooms who had to be consulted about the big issues facing the party and with Adams in the middle, calling the shots, and who would ultimately decide what happened.

As the Queen's visit approached, Adams met senior staff and Martin McGuinness in the Deputy First Minister's office in Stormont. He said that although Sinn Féin would not participate in the Queen's visit, the party had been asked if there was anything they felt it might be useful for the Queen to say in the speech she was going to make at Dublin Castle.

Adams told McAleese he was concerned that the speech could cause embarrassment for Sinn Féin. However, there were things the Queen could say which would allow him to welcome the speech, even if the party were not present.

McGuinness – who had already privately told staff he thought it was a mistake to boycott the visit and had become exasperated with the media furore around the party's position – said, 'Maybe get her to say a few things might make it easier in the future.'

Leo Green, McGuinness and Adams composed several paragraphs, with Adams making final edits, and the document was sent it off to Martin McAleese.

One staffer who spoke to me took a dim view of this exercise. 'It is crazy hypocrisy: telling the party we're not doing it out of republican principles and then writing up speech notes for the Queen of England.' Equally, it could be argued that exactly this sort of 'hypocrisy' had characterized Sinn Féin's approach to the IRA's campaign and the peace process: it was part and parcel of how the party operated.

The Queen's visit was a roaring success. She stayed for four days, and her programme was heavily oriented towards peace and reconciliation. She laid a wreath at the Garden of Remembrance, and she visited Croke Park, site of the first Bloody Sunday massacre in 1920, when British forces opened fire on a GAA match.

On her fourth day, the Queen visited Cashel, Co. Tipperary. The town's Sinn Féin mayor, Michael Browne, met her and shook her hand.

Browne had been told by party headquarters to boycott the visit in keeping with party policy, but he disregarded the order. As Cllr Browne told *The Nationalist*:

> I just said 'I welcome you to Cashel your majesty and I hope you enjoy your stay' in Cashel. [. . .] She just said thanks very much. I am glad I met her. I can only see that her visit can do good. You could be protesting all your life. [. . .]
>
> We are in fierce hard economic times and the fact she has come here might encourage more tourists to visit. If the economy is to take off again that is the sort of money we have to get into the country [. . .].

For her speech at Dublin Castle, the Queen opened with a few words in Irish: 'A Uachtaráin agus a chairde,' she said. At her side, President McAleese – who had suggested some Irish phrases the Queen might use but assumed it wouldn't happen – gasped 'Wow', and spontaneous applause erupted among the crowd of 172 guests.

The visit had been a roaring success, and Sinn Féin had missed out on it. In the aftermath, speaking on BBC Radio 4's *Today* programme, Adams tried to defend the party's stance, while also hinting at an openness to future engagement:

Many people I have spoken to, particularly from the north, have expressed a disappointment that she did not apologise in a more direct and clear way for British involvement in Irish affairs. [. . .]

If there is to be more benefit out of this, it will be if it moves beyond these important gestures and remarks [. . .].

It's another step in the journey. It was the conditions created by the peace process which allowed this to happen.

It's a page in a book – and we need to write the next page and the next page and keep moving the process on.

Things moved on very quickly. Later that same year, as Sinn Féin's candidate for the Irish presidency, Martin McGuinness, said he was prepared to meet all heads of state without exception, including the Queen. The party knew it had been out of step with the rest of the island in its boycott of the Queen's visit, and wanted to ensure it wouldn't happen again.

In 2012, without consulting Sinn Féin, the Northern Ireland Office announced plans for a Queen's Jubilee party at Stormont. Far from writing briefing notes for Queen Elizabeth, now the party weren't even being told ahead of time.

McGuinness was in his office with a number of trusted advisors when, without prompting, he stated casually: 'Aye, I'm going to have to meet her.'

Those present in the Deputy First Minister's office knew what he meant, and got to work.

As with most things in Sinn Féin, a document had to be written on the decision.

A staffer pulled out a sheet of paper and immediately began drafting a briefing note. The note proposed that Sinn Féin should be a part of the Queen's visit, but it also included a list of pros and cons, for balance. The paper was given to the National Officer Board, which set up a discussion group, as was also par for the course.

It was agreed almost immediately within the party that McGuinness would not attend the Jubilee party, but would meet the Queen separately.

Hours of debate within the party were devoted to such issues as the location of the meeting, control of the photos, and whether it would be still photography only or live video. Live coverage could be a problem, the members agreed.

'Because you can be too friendly and you have no control over that and how it looks,' one person who was at the meeting told me. 'Whatever else about Martin, he has a friendly face, and he looks warm – what if he looks *too* warm?'

These debates were constant within the party, and only became more intense when it came to organizing the event with the other stakeholders.

The party's negotiator was running between the British and the DUP with any number of inane questions. He recalls their staff openly laughing, sometimes sympathetically.

Somebody raised the issue that if it happened at Stormont, there might be crowds of people waving Union Jacks. Martin McGuinness could not be seen standing in front of crowds waving Union Jacks. Stormont was out.

Peter Sheridan, the chief executive of Co-operation Ireland, proposed Belfast's Lyric Theatre as a possible location, saying it had 'a neutral, independent feel to it'. The Sinn Féin negotiator went to the theatre with staff from the NIO, the DUP and Buckingham Palace, and it was agreed that it would be a suitable venue.

Sinn Féin's Ard Comhairle voted on it, and accepted the Lyric Theatre, though not unanimously.

*

The story of Co-operation Ireland, its chief executive and Martin McGuinness is an interesting one in itself.

According to its website, 'Co-operation Ireland is an all-island peace-building organisation. We work to build a shared and cohesive society by addressing legacy issues of the conflict and facilitating contact and collaboration between people from different backgrounds across these islands.'

Peter Sheridan joined Co-operation Ireland in 2008 as its Chief Executive, after a career with the RUC and PSNI, during which he rose to the position of Assistant Chief Constable. Sheridan was responsible for the Crime Operations Department, which included investigations of organized crime and terrorism.

Sheridan believes the first time Martin McGuinness tried to have him killed was in March 1987. Sheridan had been called to the scene of an IRA murder in Derry when a booby-trapped car exploded. Two other detectives died instantly.

Two other attempts on his life were made in the 1990s. The Gardai uncovered an IRA plan to put a bomb under Sheridan's car while he was at Mass. The plan included details about his wife, children and his local church.

He first met McGuinness in Downing Street. Along with the then PSNI Chief Constable, Sir Hugh Orde, they met Gerry Adams, Gerry Kelly and Prime Minister Tony Blair, to try to convince Sinn Féin to support policing in Northern Ireland. Over the years the two men became close.

When asked about it later, Sheridan said: 'People have asked me did I like Martin. I think people who met him found it hard not to like him.'

McGuinness had told his closest confidants that he believed Co-operation Ireland was a front for MI5. He selected his old IRA comrade Terry Crossan, now a Sinn

Féin councillor in Donegal, to sit on the board. He wanted one of his men on the inside, to keep an eye on the organization. He wanted to ensure they never knew more than they needed to know about Sinn Féin and how the party operated.

McGuinness went on to develop a close relationship with Dr Christopher Moran, the chairman of Cooperation Ireland. Moran, who has described himself as 'astronomically wealthy', made his money through London real estate – he was a millionaire by the age of twenty-one – and has donated almost £300,000 to the Tories. In 1982, Lloyd's of London expelled him as an underwriter, for 'discreditable conduct'. Four years later he was censured by the Stock Exchange, and in 1992 he was fined $2 million in New York for insider dealing.

He owns the 48,000-acre Glenfiddich sporting estate in Scotland and bought the freehold to the fifteenth-century Tudor masterpiece Crosby Hall on the banks of the Thames in Chelsea's Cheyne Walk – the same street where McGuinness and Adams held their first talks with the British government back in 1972 – for just £100,000 in 1989. He displaced the tenants and has spent an estimated £25 million building a thirty-bedroom home.

Undercover investigations by the *Sunday Times* revealed that some of the buildings owned by Moran had been used as brothels. His Chelsea Cloisters block was described in the press as '10 floors of whores' despite Dr Moran's insistence he operated a 'zero-tolerance' policy to prostitution and had taken measures to crack down on the problem.

Upon McGuinness's death, the last person in the family home, apart from Adams and his immediate family, was Christopher Moran.

*

For the photo, Sinn Féin wanted McGuinness to stand next to the Irish President, Michael D. Higgins, with Peter Robinson next to the Queen. The party also wanted the photographs to be circulated to each office before being released to the media.

The negotiator was ticking off things from a sheet of paper that he had been sent with.

'They're saying to me; "Are you serious?" I *was* serious. I was here because these lunatics I'm representing sent me to be serious.

'I knew the idea that Martin had to be next to the President is just fucking nuts and the DUP knew I hadn't my heart in it, because I'm arguing the ridiculous, but everyone agreed with the request that Martin could stand next to the President.'

A new issue then arose. How would they leave the building? The DUP and Sinn Féin staffers stared blankly at the man from the palace. One of them said: 'Well, back the way we came.'

Impossible. The Queen doesn't retrace her steps.

'She doesn't go backwards,' the palace man said.

'I felt like I was losing my mind,' the Sinn Féin negotiator remembered, and things were about to get worse.

When he returned to Stormont and the party discussion group, he told them all their requests had been agreed.

He rattled off all they had been given – the choreography, the photographs, the stills – and then asked if it was acceptable.

Some of the group said they still felt Sinn Féin shouldn't be involved. It wasn't enough to guarantee the party could weather it. It would make some of the base turn on them. The debate began again, the pros and cons were trotted out.

The negotiator was at the end of his tether.

'Let me get this right, youse come up with a five or six things we need to make this acceptable, I'm going making a dickhead of myself during dozens of meeting with the DUP and the Brits. They agreed with every one of them. And I should go back and say, it's not acceptable? Fuck off.'

He left the room in search of McGuinness.

On his way to find the Deputy First Minister, the negotiator had a brief discussion with Gerry Adams.

He told him he had spent two weeks 'making a complete dickhead' of himself.

He laboured the point about McGuinness's impact with unionists. McGuinness had been seen as someone unionists could warm to, he had made some kind of amends with victims, he had been seen to be honest about some, but not all, of his IRA history.

'The story is Martin McGuinness and the Queen. Everything else is fluff,' the negotiator told Adams.

'It doesn't matter whether they're shaking hands, hugging or standing twenty feet away. Martin McGuinness and the Queen. That's the fucking story and that's a good story.

'This choreography about coming out of the lift in particular order – we're making ourselves out as complete and utter control freaks.' Adams nodded and walked off into the dark corridor.

The next day the same group was brought together in McGuinness's office, this time with McGuinness and Gerry Adams present.

Adams asked for a report of the outcome of the negotiations, and the negotiator rattled off the same presentation he had given the day before.

They canvassed the room.

'Every single fucking one of those same people who had doubts the day before now said we should do it,' the negotiator recalls.

As the group were leaving, the negotiator turned to one of those who had U-turned and said: 'Fair play to you, you held out for the whole ten hours before you got your instructions last night, well done.'

The negotiator believes the IRA had held a meeting the night before, and had made it clear to those with doubts that McGuinness could meet the Queen.

On 27 June 2012, in the Lyric Theatre's private McGrath suite, Martin McGuinness shook hands with Queen Elizabeth II, behind closed doors.

'Maidin mhaith,' he said: Good morning. And 'Céad míle fáilte': One hundred thousand welcomes.

For this first handshake, there were no cameras in the room. Along with the Queen, the First Minister and the Deputy First Minister, there were four other people in the room: the Duke of Edinburgh, President Higgins, his wife, Sabina Higgins, and the Queen's Private Secretary, Sir Christopher Geidt.

Cameras were allowed in later, when the group viewed an art exhibition organized by Co-operation Ireland, and they captured a second handshake that was staged for public consumption. The Queen, in 'apple green', as described by Buckingham Palace, worked her way down the longer receiving line. McGuinness did not bow his head while shaking the monarch's hand. The McGuinness handshake, according to the *Guardian* newspaper, 'lasted three times longer than the others'.

McGuinness told the Queen that her speech in Dublin the previous year had touched him, and he made clear he felt her conciliatory words were the catalyst for their historic meeting now in Belfast.

The choreography did not go according to Sinn Féin's plan: President Higgins was not visible in the most widely circulated photos. No one in Sinn Féin ever mentioned it afterwards.

As the Queen left, the two shook hands a third time, for the benefit of a single television cameraman and a photographer.

McGuinness said: 'Slan agus beannacht' – Goodbye and godspeed.

A day later, McGuinness said the handshake 'was in a very pointed, deliberate and symbolic way offering the hand of friendship to unionists through the person of Queen Elizabeth, for which many unionists have a deep affinity'.

'It is an offer I hope many will accept in the same spirit it was offered,' he said.

One palace handler told me: 'The Queen was satisfied with the outcome, and that's the only thing that could be said. She understood the symbolism of peace and reconciliation.'

8. The New Leaders

From the outside, Mary Lou McDonald's star appeared to be anything but on the rise when she became Sinn Féin vice-president in 2009, taking over from Pat Doherty under Adams's orders.

After the mess of the 2007 Irish general election, when Sinn Féin's representation in the Dáil dropped from five TDs to four, the party made some personnel changes. It was decided McDonald would be vice-president, Declan Kearney would be party chairman, Dawn Doyle the new general secretary, and Maurice Quinlivan and Rita O'Hare were joint party treasurers.

'For some time and for very obvious reasons Sinn Féin's main political strength has been in the North and the border counties,' Adams said when announcing McDonald's new role. 'For the last number of years there has been a consistent, ongoing project to make Sinn Féin fit for purpose everywhere on the island and to make republicanism relevant to people in their daily lives and this has, in my view, seen considerable progress.'

The announcement of McDonald's new job was all squared away well before the European elections that year, in which she would have to fight to keep her seat.

In 2008, the McDonald–Lanigan clan moved to the Dublin Central constituency, where Mary Lou was determined to win the seat. They rented 23 Ashington Heath, then 22A Villa Park Road, both in Cabra, before moving into 186 New

Cabra Road, where they converted a small bungalow into a large eleven-room house.

People might have had grounds to question how much she wanted to be in Brussels in the first place. In August 2008, the *Irish Examiner* reported MEPs' attendance from September 2007 to August 2008, a period in which McDonald had the worst attendance record of all 767 MEPs, the paper found.

The news of her attendance record can't have helped McDonald's re-election bid. In 2009, she lost her seat in Europe but her sights were clearly set on Dublin Central anyway.

Her presence around the constituency was conspicuous. Members of her cumann noticed an increase in meetings and productivity.

In January 2011, it was announced, to almost everyone's surprise, that Gerry Adams would be running in Louth for a seat in Dáil Éireann. He explained the decision in terms of the 'fightback' against the Fianna Fáil-led government that had led the country into the economic crash and was now implementing an austerity regime following an IMF–EU bailout.

It was an auspicious moment for Adams, who had always lived and stood for election in Northern Ireland, to enter Southern politics. Sinn Féin, which entered the election with five Dáil seats, emerged from it with fourteen. Adams topped the poll in Louth, and had the third-highest vote in the country.

In Dublin Central, McDonald benefited from both the economic climate and the absence of former Taoiseach Bertie Ahern from the ballot. She came third in first-preference votes and ultimately took the last seat in the four-seater. Finally, at the third attempt, she was a TD.

McDonald hit the ground running, and quickly earned a reputation as a skilful performer on the Public Accounts Committee.

Shane Ross, the former Independent TD and, more recently, McDonald's biographer, sat alongside McDonald on the committee. He wrote: 'She was excellent company, lively and amusing. As a performer in the sittings of the committee, she was second to none. She would go straight for the jugular. Witnesses feared her sharp tongue and her speedy ripostes. She was well briefed by the highly competent Sinn Féin back office, which was grooming her for greatness.'

After two uninspiring general election bids, and an indifferent performance in a Brussels seat she went on to lose, it would not have been entirely surprising if Adams had had second thoughts about McDonald. But there is no evidence that he ever lost faith. And now he must have felt more confident than ever that the long game he was playing with McDonald was going to bear fruit.

Unlike her comrade in Dublin, Michelle O'Neill's rise to the highest ranks of Sinn Féin was not plotted long in advance. It actually came as a shock to most people within her own party. O'Neill didn't immediately show star quality.

Born Michelle Doris in Fermoy, Co. Cork on 10 January 1977, Michelle O'Neill is steeped in republican tradition. Her grandmother Kathleen Doris was well known in east Tyrone as a civil rights campaigner, while her father, Brendan 'Basil' Doris, was a Provisional IRA prisoner as a member of the IRA's East Tyrone Brigade in the 1970s. He was arrested and spent time in Crumlin Road Jail, Armagh Jail, Long Kesh and Magilligan, where he earned a reputation for fighting with prison officers.

Released in 1976, he returned to IRA activities and married Kathleen, with whom he had two children, Michelle and Brian.

The family had moved from their homeland of Clonoe in Tyrone after what Michelle O'Neill has described as ongoing harassment of the family by British troops. They moved back to Clonoe when Michelle was four.

Basil Doris worked in construction. His brother Paul Doris is the former national president of the Irish Northern Aid Committee (NORAID), a republican fundraising group. A relative, Tony Doris, was one of three IRA members killed by the SAS in the Coagh ambush in 1991.

Another relative, Gareth Malachy Doris, was shot and wounded during the 1997 bomb attack on the army/RUC station in Coalisland. He was charged while recovering in hospital from gunshot wounds and jailed for ten years for possessing explosives, before being freed early in 2000 under the terms of the Good Friday Agreement. In 2017, he was convicted of fuel smuggling.

In 1992, aged fifteen, Michelle Doris became pregnant. Her family, although shocked, were supportive, and her mother gave up work so that Michelle could continue with her education at an all-girls Catholic grammar school.

'Certainly I had some very, very negative experiences when I was pregnant,' she later told the *Irish Times*.

I remember one particular day going to school, I was actually pregnant at the time. I was doing my GCSEs. I had to go in to do two practicals, but I was showing so I didn't fit in my school uniform. So I had to go in in my own clothes. And I remember getting on the bus and I forgot my bus pass because I wasn't in my uniform and

I didn't have it where I normally have it. And the bus driver fought with me that I actually wasn't a pupil at the school. And I didn't have money to pay for the bus or any of those things.

So I remember that being a particularly horrible start to the day and I actually got on the bus, got to school, and I remember being called in to be told I didn't inform them I was coming in, like I was a plague or something. I remember coming home that day and I walked through my front door and I fell on the floor and I collapsed and I cried. I'll never forget that experience and I thought nobody will ever treat me like this again.

Her daughter, Saoirse, was born in May of 1993. Michelle went back into school after the summer holidays, sitting her A levels in September.

'You were nearly put in a box – single mother, unmarried mother, nearly written off. But I was determined that I wasn't going to be written off, that I was going to work hard and make a good life for her,' O'Neill said.

She married Saoirse's father, Paddy O'Neill, two years later aged eighteen, and began her career in politics at twenty-one when she joined Sinn Féin.

When her father stepped down from Dungannon Borough Council in 2005 after first running in 1987, she won the seat he vacated. Gerry Adams delivered a graveside oration at her father's funeral after his sudden death of a heart attack, aged just fifty-four, in 2006.

Michelle O'Neill became a qualified welfare rights advisor, and started out in Stormont in 1998 as an assistant to former Sinn Féin Assembly member Francie Molloy.

She was first elected to Stormont as an MLA for Mid

Ulster in 2007, along with her former boss Molloy and Martin McGuinness.

She would later become the first woman to hold the post of mayor on the council in 2010, while politicians could still hold two elected roles at the same time.

As mayor, she unveiled a framed commemorative portrait of Martin McCaughey at a reception in the mayor's parlour.

Martin McCaughey was the youngest elected representative on the island of Ireland when he was elected Sinn Féin councillor for Dungannon and Tyrone Borough Council. He was shot ten times at a farm in Loughgall by the SAS in 1990, while on active service for the same IRA brigade O'Neill's father had belonged to.

When first elected to Stormont, O'Neill became Sinn Féin spokesperson for health and sat on the education committee.

By 2011, she got her first ministerial role in Stormont, being named the Minister for Agriculture and Rural Development. She raised eyebrows with some of her decisions, including a botched attempt to unilaterally reallocate over £100 million in European funding from a pot used for payments to farmers to schemes more favoured by environmental activists.

The DUP finance minister, Simon Hamilton, went to the high court to block the move. Lord Chief Justice Sir Declan Morgan ruled that by taking the decision without executive approval, O'Neill had broken the ministerial code.

'I conclude this matter should have been brought to the attention of the Executive Committee, and that the minister made the decision consequently in breach of the ministerial code.

'These findings are sufficient for me to conclude that she

had no authority to make the decision and in those circumstances I'm prepared to quash the decision.'

Following the 2016 election, she was appointed Minister
for Health, a role she clearly preferred to the agriculture
brief. Eight days after being appointed to the role, she
announced she would lift Northern Ireland's ban on gay men
donating blood.

It became obvious in late 2016 that McGuinness was seriously ill, and would have to stand down from politics.
Although many within Sinn Féin tipped Conor Murphy and
John O'Dowd for the role of Deputy First Minister/party
leader in Northern Ireland, McGuinness had decided on his
successor long before, and had told those closest to him,
including O'Neill. One aide of McGuinness's says he sensed
that she'd been tipped as early as 2013. Always conscientious,
now she was going above and beyond, asking for party
strategy documents to study at home, and appearing at
McGuinness's side constantly.

In other political parties, leaders do not choose their suc-
cessors: positions are filled by some sort of democratic
process. Sinn Féin is different. When Murphy was quizzed by
allies about why he didn't put himself forward for the job, he
said he had no interest in it.

It's not entirely clear if there was even a pathway available
to Murphy if he had wished to seek the position: no one had
ever challenged a nominee for president or vice-president
before.

Stormont was in chaos at the time, over a botched
renewable-energy scheme that cost the taxpayer around £500
million. In 2012, the Renewable Heat Incentive scheme was
managed and set up by the then Department of Enterprise,

Trade and Investment (DETI), overseen by the DUP's Arlene Foster as the department's minister.

The scheme encouraged the burning of wood pellets in biomass boilers and heat pumps to heat farms and businesses. But miscalculations and a lack of cost controls in the scheme meant that the subsidy more than covered the cost of the pellets, meaning that it was possible to make significant amounts of money at the state's expense simply by burning wood pellets. And, scandalously, the scheme was allowed to continue for years after whistleblowers pointed out its flaws.

Just before Christmas in 2016, Arlene Foster – now First Minister – survived a vote of no confidence and said she would not stand down from her post even temporarily while the matter was investigated.

Upon the announcement that Foster wouldn't resign, the Sinn Féin MLAs went to Stormont Castle. It was a Friday evening when they gathered in McGuinness's office.

'I distinctly remember him and Mark Mullan [McGuinness's special advisor] and a few others saying it was a case of keeping the show on the road, that we had to keep Stormont running,' one MLA present told me.

'They didn't see where the public mood was and I remember a group of us saying, for the public here the DUP screwed up massively, they fucking hate this and they fucking hate Arlene Foster, we could not be a mudguard for this.

'It was back and forward in this debate, and then it began to filter through.

'I wouldn't go as far as [saying] Martin wanted to stay, but he wasn't as angry as us. He was more reflective, he probably understood the consequences of it. We had also taken a decision strategically that following the 2016 election, that we just needed a different relationship with the DUP.

'We believed the wider nationalist community always understood Martin and Ian Paisley's relationship. But it damaged Paisley and the DUP . . . They always suffer more from compromising with us than vice versa. But it was clear senior party figures at the end of this meeting understood that we couldn't allow Arlene Foster to call the shots when the public were so angry. Arlene was different and we were worried we were starting to look stupid.'

Sinn Féin MLAs were openly hostile to Foster and the feeling was mutual. Gone were the days of the 'Chuckle Brothers', when McGuinness and Paisley enjoyed a convivial relationship. The mood was not the same with Peter Robinson, and by the time Arlene Foster took over, relations were awful.

In one instance, Sinn Féin infrastructure minister Chris Hazzard had complained to the party that Foster had summoned him to her office with a list of roads she wanted to be resurfaced in the run-up to the summer. When he asked if the demands were related to the upcoming marching season in her constituency, the pair got into a shouting match. Such instances were becoming more common.

Sinn Féin's National Officer Board met on Sunday, 8 January 2017, and agreed that Sinn Féin would dissolve Stormont.

The following day, a clearly frail and ill McGuinness resigned as Deputy First Minister of Northern Ireland.

Gerry Adams made the announcement that O'Neill would replace McGuinness in the Long Gallery of Parliament Buildings, Stormont, on 23 January 2017.

When the *Irish News* asked the party about the process involved in selecting O'Neill as McGuinness's successor, a spokesman said: 'The Sinn Féin president brought forward a recommendation that was ratified by the Ard Chomhairle on Saturday.'

There were doubts about O'Neill's qualities.

Fionnuala O Connor, a veteran observer of Northern politics, wrote in the *Irish News* upon her appointment:

And if she turns out to be a NOT very senior appointment, the handover is even more revealing. Though her public performances have a strong air of the stand-in, that could be misleading, nerves and painful circumstances combining to suggest the bearded senior beside her had marked her script with cues for his contributions.

O'Neill could turn out yet to be the new generation in action – no jail record, strong family and communal republican background, but an entire career in the service of republican politics rather than the last-stage management of IRA transition.

She may have her own way of doing things. But the choreography so far has suggested that she is meant to be more figurehead than real. It may indeed be that the 'wee girl from Clonoe' with the pleasant manner and open, almost theatrical awe of Adams and McGuinness, is perfectly content with her new role. Or, as she puts it, honoured, better than content.

Loyal activist and backroom worker for years, she may be exactly as she appears: no more than the female front for the northern branch of the collective leadership.

One month later, O'Neill was the main speaker at an event in Clonoe to mark the twenty-fifth anniversary of the deaths of four IRA men killed by the SAS. Arlene Foster denounced O'Neill's decision to attend, while the Ulster Unionist Party's

Mid Ulster candidate, Sandra Overend, said: 'It is only to be expected that republicans would wish to remember their dead, but Michelle O'Neill's presence at such an event is hardly sending a signal to the unionist community that she is some kind of new departure for Sinn Féin.'

O'Neill responded: 'I am a republican, that's not a secret.

'I did know these young fellas personally and I know their families and friends and I know the community they came from, so I don't think people should be surprised I was there.'

O'Neill's direct, informal manner is very different from that of McDonald, as is her background – and it's part of why McGuinness picked her to be the party's leading figure in the North. A privately educated woman who had previously been a member of another party would not have worked for the Sinn Féin base in Northern Ireland, which has a deep and abiding loyalty to the IRA.

McDonald's appearance at the event to honour Seán Russell had been widely seen as forced, symbolic – a blooding. O'Neill's presence at the event to honour the IRA dead at Clonoe was much more straightforward. And even as Sinn Féin modernized and a new generation of non-combatants took power in the party, a natural connection to the IRA like O'Neill's continued to be valued. McGuinness's successor had to have a connection to the IRA but no criminal record; had to be a proud republican but without any skeletons in the closet.

O'Neill got off to a rocky start as the party's leader at Stormont – and she was also the target of sexist jibes about her looks, her clothes, her eyebrows, the speed at which she spoke, her weight and rumours about her sex life. One *Daily Mail* story from the time was headlined: 'The beauty from a family drenched in blood'.

The story opened:

Glossy blonde hair. Bright lipstick. Curled eyelashes. Painted nails. Figure-hugging outfits. Michelle O'Neill certainly isn't what we expected. The glamorous mother-of-two was unveiled this week as the new face of Sinn Féin, the person chosen to succeed Martin McGuinness as leader [*sic*] of a party that numbers convicted IRA bombers and murderers in its ranks.

In May of that year, DUP leader Arlene Foster gave a wide-ranging interview to the *Sunday Independent* in which she was pressed to give a one-word judgement on O'Neill.

'I don't want to be sexist and I am not going to be sexist because I can't . . .' Foster said.

The interviewer replied: 'Ah go on, it's not sexist if it's true.'

'Blonde,' said Mrs Foster. Asked to expand, she went on: 'Michelle is very attractive. She presents herself very well and she always is – you know – her appearance is always "the same".'

One MLA told me that the early abuse brought about 'a crisis of confidence almost' in O'Neill. But party colleagues and civil servants alike heap praise on O'Neill, saying that she is over her brief, well intentioned and hard-working. She has been known to speak off the record to journalists, something McDonald never does.

In her first year, O'Neill oversaw Sinn Féin's two best electoral performances in Northern Ireland to that point. In March, Sinn Féin received just 1,200 votes fewer than the DUP in the Stormont election and won one fewer seat. And in the June general election, Sinn Féin picked off the SDLP's last two Westminster seats. The party now had seven abstentionist MPs.

*

On 18 November 2017, at the Sinn Féin Ard Fheis in Dublin, Gerry Adams announced his plans to retire after thirty-four years as president of the party.

He had seen off five British prime ministers, six taoisaigh and five US presidents, was shot in the neck, shoulder and arm and arrested, all while head of the party. Adams said it would take a year to put new leadership in place.

'I have always seen myself as a team player and a team builder. I have complete confidence in the leaders we elected this weekend and in the next generation of leaders . . .

'Leadership means knowing when it is time for change and that time is now.'

He said the party's national executive would agree a date in 2018 to elect the new Sinn Féin president. In truth, the election would be a formality. Mary Lou McDonald had already been anointed by the leader, and no one would argue.

There was no contest, just as there had been no contest for the election of Michelle O'Neill as the party's leader at Stormont. There had been no contest to elect Gerry Adams as president either.

McDonald's ascent to the top job in the party was confirmed on 20 January 2018. More than 2,000 Sinn Féin delegates attended a special Ard Fheis conference in Dublin's RDS arena to see McDonald confirmed as Adams's successor.

Her maiden speech as Sinn Féin leader on 10 February 2018 was a perfect example of how deftly McDonald plays to the Republican base and all that comes with it. She referred, of course, to the peace process.

'There would be no Good Friday Agreement, no peace process, without Gerry Adams. My political mentor. An inspirational leader. A great friend,' she said.

'When others said it was impossible, Gerry Adams, along with Martin McGuinness, John Hume and indeed others, bravely walked the path to peace.' But McDonald finished by raising her fist in the air and stating: 'So my friends of Sinn Féin. Let's get to work . . . Up the Republic, up the rebels, agus tiocfaidh ár lá.'

The text of her speech had been circulated to the media before she delivered it to the conference. The written version closed with a different form of words. It read: 'Let's get to work. Ar aghaidh linn le chéile! Up the Republic!' Her closing words – 'up the rebels, agus tiocfaidh ár lá' – had been added to the script at the last minute, or else improvised.

When challenged on RTÉ's *Late Late Show* about her choice of words, McDonald denied there was any issue with using a slogan associated with the Provisional IRA.

'For me to utter the words "Tiocfaidh ár lá" refers absolutely to that vision of a new Ireland. I know for some people that sounds like a harking to the past, yes; for me, it absolutely is not.'

Presenter Ryan Tubridy observed that 'there's a huge group of people who would find that quite disingenuous and might think that "tiocfaidh ár lá" means only one thing and that is a throwback to a very violent time and would find it very hard to comprehend maybe why you didn't think of saying something else, less sulphurous'.

McDonald claimed she believed that if language carries a negative connotation, 'you reclaim it'. Then, towards the end of the interview, McDonald seemed to say the quiet part out loud: 'I think you need to understand also that I am a republican leader. I'm speaking in the republican tradition. You're addressing a republican audience, and I'm doing that in a way that is very much about now and very modern.'

Even in 2018, even with a non-combatant leading the party, the Republican base's sense of itself had to be catered to. The party leadership was at pains to ensure it could never be credibly accused of selling out the IRA volunteers and the communities who backed them. Men and women in that room risked life, limb and future for the cause, some carried out heinous acts of violence in the name of what they believe to be Irish freedom. The notion that McDonald's words weren't directly referencing those people – 'the rebels' – is laughable to anyone who understands how republican politics work.

9. The Trials of Mairia Cahill

Mairia Cahill was born in Belfast in 1981. She is grand-niece of Joe Cahill, one of the founding members of the Provisional IRA, and a cousin of Siobhán O'Hanlon, one of Gerry Adams's closest confidants. She grew up in west Belfast, the heart of militant republicanism.

Young Mairia joined Ógra Shinn Féin, the party's youth movement, and was quickly tipped as a rising star. She told the journalist Malachi O'Doherty that she was elected National Secretary of Ógra without even knowing her name had been put forward for the position or attending the youth congress that selected her. She was approached by the IRA four times asking her to join, but she refused.

In the summer of 1997, while working in Ballymurphy with Sinn Féin, Mairia began staying in a house in Ballymurphy Drive with relatives. She was sixteen years old. Martin Morris, an IRA member and her uncle through marriage, was also staying there.

Cahill has alleged that Morris raped her several times for over a year. She would wake up to find him raping or groping her. Cahill told no one at first.

Morris was a member of the IRA's civil administration: the very group that was charged with maintaining law and order in nationalist neighbourhoods.

In 1998, Mairia Cahill had lost so much weight that she 'looked like something out of the famine'. She has said that she confided in her cousin Siobhán O'Hanlon. 'I told

Siobhán that [M] was raping me and I was worried I could be pregnant.'

She wasn't pregnant. But word spread in the republican movement about her allegations.

In 1999, the IRA began to question Cahill, who was still just a teenager, about her accusation. By March 2000, she has asserted, she was forced to face her abuser. Cahill claimed the IRA members involved in the investigation said they wanted to determine whether she or her alleged rapist was telling the truth.

Cahill has maintained that she was being questioned daily at some points, and that the interrogations could go on for hours. She was barred from telling her family. Eventually, she has claimed, the IRA accepted Morris's guilt, but not before Cahill was taken to a solicitor by an IRA handler who warned her against going to the police, on the grounds that a conviction was unlikely.

An offer was made to Mairia Cahill that, if she requested it, the IRA would kill her alleged abuser. She refused, and saw the offer as a way of putting responsibility back on her.

The entire episode almost broke Cahill. In 2006, she was admitted to the Royal Victoria Hospital after trying to kill herself.

In January 2010, Cahill went public with her allegations for the first time, giving an interview to Suzanne Breen in the *Sunday Tribune*.

Breen quoted Cahill describing the IRA's investigative methods:

I was only 18. M, the man who raped me, was nearly 40 and a prominent west Belfast IRA member. The IRA women drove me to the flat in Kenard Avenue in Andersonstown.

And then Seamie Finucane, the Belfast Brigade adjutant, walked in with M. I felt physically sick when I saw M.

Seamie sat down on the living room floor, took off his trainers and joked about having smelly feet. It was surreal. This was meant to be a serious investigation into sexual abuse.

M was handed the statement outlining the allegations I'd made. He said I was lying. 'You're a sick bastard claiming I did this to you,' he shouted. I yelled back that I was telling the truth. Seamie Finucane asked me to withdraw my statement but I wouldn't. I said I wasn't leaving the house until M admitted what he'd done. The IRA ended the meeting.

Breen went on to report:

In July 2000, five months after the IRA had closed its 'investigation', two of Cahill's cousins – then aged 17 and 14 – came forward and said M had sexually abused them two years earlier. People had seen M lifting one of the girls drunk from a social club into a taxi. Neighbours had then watched him carry her from a taxi into his home. The IRA reopened the investigation. 'I told them I wanted nothing to do with it,' Cahill says. 'I wanted to go to the Rape Crisis Centre. I said I needed professional help.'

The IRA said M was under 'house arrest' in Ardoyne. Days later, Cahill was told he had 'escaped'. Now she confided in her Uncle Joe (80) whom she had wanted to protect from hearing she'd been raped. 'He said, "If I'd known I'd have told you to go to the RUC. There has been a f**k up of the highest order in the movement."'

The word in Belfast was that the IRA had spirited M away to Donegal. 'I don't believe he escaped,' Cahill says. 'The IRA facilitated him leaving. I never wanted M killed. I wanted him tied to railings in Ballymurphy with a placard around his neck saying he was a rapist.'

A Sinn Féin figure recalls being present at a meeting in a hotel at which Gerry Adams handed out copies of the *Sunday Tribune* piece to a select group of staff. According to this witness, Adams said: 'She's made these accusations against someone in the IRA, but she's a bit mad.'

'I couldn't believe it,' the witness says. 'There was one woman who was there and I could tell by her face she was furious.'

By April 2010, Cahill had found the strength to speak to the PSNI about her allegations.

The legal process was complicated. As the *Irish Independent* later reported, 'It is understood that a large part of the prosecution case rested on the fact that Morris had used his position in the IRA to groom her, to intimidate her and frighten her into staying silent about what was happening.' In pretrial discussions, the defence successfully argued that in the absence of a conviction for IRA membership, it would oppose any reference to Morris being in the IRA. Because of this, prosecutors decided it was necessary to seek to convict Morris and the four alleged IRA interrogators of IRA membership before trying Morris for rape.

A meeting of senior Sinn Féin officials – including Marty Lynch, Declan Kearney, Leo Green, Gerry Adams, Gerry Kelly and Ted Howell – focused on the question of whether or not to argue for separate trials for the alleged interrogators and the alleged rapist. There were no women present at the meeting. 'I do think there was a belief in the room that Marty Morris was guilty, I do believe that they believed he raped this woman, but it just wasn't their main concern,' the senior staffer told me. The main concern of the others, the staffer felt, was that the alleged interrogators not be convicted of IRA membership.

When the senior staffer stated that the party should not do anything that would compromise Cahill's capacity to get Morris convicted, Gerry Kelly voiced agreement.

Morris was charged with IRA membership on the basis of an allegation by Cahill that Morris and Joe McCullough, Adams's one-time bodyguard, had asked her to move guns for the IRA. McCullough had not been spoken to by police, but on the day of the membership trial he turned up as a witness supporting Morris.

The prosecution team pulled the case after the emergence of McCullough, believing they had little chance at winning. They did not want Cahill to have to endure a cross-examination for nothing. Due to the collapse of the IRA membership case, the prospect of conviction in the other two trials, including the rape, was unlikely. Mairia Cahill walked away.

She signed a withdrawal statement, reiterating her claims against Morris of sexual abuse and against the four people accused of IRA interrogation. All five defendants were acquitted.

That was April 2014. In October, Cahill appeared on BBC Northern Ireland's *Spotlight* programme, laying out her allegations against the IRA. She detailed how she had initially described her experience of being raped to Siobhán O'Hanlon, Sinn Féin MLA Sue Ramsay, and her friend Rosa McLaughlin, who had been once convicted of spying for the IRA. She also repeated the claims about her interrogation. The claims were explosive. Many elected and non-elected Sinn Féin members had been accused of failing to help a vulnerable sexual abuse victim.

The following evening, Gerry Adams released a statement claiming that he had asked Joe Cahill to persuade his grand-niece to go to the RUC. Adams said: 'I met Mairia in good faith, at the behest of her cousin and my late friend Siobhán O'Hanlon who was concerned for Mairia's welfare following an episode of self-harming.'

In response, Mairia Cahill described Adams's statement as 'disgusting' and 'inaccurate'.

Both O'Hanlon and Joe Cahill were dead by the time Adams's statement was released, so the statement could not be verified.

Mary Lou McDonald said: 'If it were a thing that for anybody the IRA conducted an investigation into a matter of sexual abuse [sic], that is clearly wrong. It's reprehensible, it is entirely wrong, it is entirely inappropriate, it is absolutely not the way to deal with complaints of offences of this nature.'

Cahill met with political leaders across the spectrum in the North and South, including First Minister Peter Robinson and Taoiseach Enda Kenny. She had backing from almost all the political parties and huge public support.

One quote in particular had stuck in the minds of everyone who watched the programme.

Cahill detailed several meetings she had with Adams about the allegations:

> The most disturbing thing of that conversation for me was then he said: 'Well, you know, Mairia, abusers can be extremely manipulative.'
>
> And you know, he kind of put his hand on his chin and he sat forward a wee bit, and he said: 'Sometimes they're that manipulative, that the people who have been abused actually enjoy it.'
>
> I was absolutely horrified. And I, at that point, got very, very angry and said to him: 'Well I didn't enjoy it.'

And at that the meeting was over for me, there was no point.

Adams denied making the remarks attributed to him by Cahill and said he had contacted his solicitor.

Later that year, Adams said in the Dáil that 'All those from Sinn Fein who have met Mairia Cahill accept and acknowledge she was abused and traumatised. She then put a particular version of what occurred. These are not nameless, anonymous people. These are decent people.'

For many women in Sinn Féin, one female MLA told me, 'That was just a really awful time because so many of us had so much sympathy for [Cahill].'

The DUP brought a motion of no confidence in Sinn Féin MLA and junior minister Jennifer McCann, alleging that she had heard Mairia Cahill's allegations in 2005 and failed to report them to the authorities. McCann told the Assembly that 'at no time' did Cahill 'indicate to me that she wanted me to report this'.

'Jennifer was personally really upset about that,' recalls one MLA, noting that McCann had been crying in her office before and after the debate.

'She was just saying: "I remember that Mairia coming over to my house crying, and me getting my daughter out of bed and putting her into the bed and looking after her."

'She felt she had done everything right and looked after her, so she was really hurt [by Mairia's allegations].'

The party's female MLAs were furious when they were ordered to sit in the front row of the chamber.

'I was raging, it all just felt so obvious, there were so many of us who were considering not showing up and then just felt like puppets, like window dressing. It's so transparent,' says one former MLA. 'Mairia was sitting in the public gallery like directly facing down to us. She looked really distraught and it was horrendous really.'

During one party meeting, a draft statement by the leadership about the Cahill issue was circulated. Megan Fearon, the youngest MLA, was the first to speak up about it. She seemed a bit shaken to say it, according to someone in the room, but carried on: 'Listen, I don't think this was the intention but some of this language is quite victim-blaming.'

The comment was brushed off by one senior staffer before Gerry Kelly piped in that he agreed with Fearon. The statement was changed.

Mairia Cahill endured serious abuse for speaking out. In Ballymurphy, graffiti was painted in large letters facing the area where she says she was raped stating: 'Mairia Cahill bores me'. Cahill claims Sinn Féin called her a liar.

Guardian writer Roy Greenslade criticized the *Spotlight* documentary for failing to disclose that Ms Cahill joined a dissident group known as the Republican Network for Unity (RNU) after leaving Sinn Féin.

'The feeling lingers that the programme was flawed by being overly one-sided. Cahill's political stance should have been explored more fully,' Greenslade wrote.

Years later, in 2021, Greenslade wrote in the *British Journalism Review* that he had been a supporter of the Provisional IRA and that he had hidden this support while working as a journalist and editor.

February 7th, 1972, was the first day of my long silence. I knew that to own up to supporting Irish republicans would result in me losing my job. I could have taken that step myself by walking out on principle. But the idea of forsaking a Fleet Street career – indeed, a career of any kind in journalism – was unthinkable. [. . .] I needed a wage because I was on the verge of taking on a mortgage. Better, then, to button my lip and carry on.

Greenslade admitted he wrote for *An Phoblacht* for decades under the pseudonym George King, and was a member of Sinn Féin.

An article by an 'anonymous Republican' styled 'Ruaidrí Ua Conchobair' on the Belfast Child blog speculated Cahill had not been raped. Seamus Finucane, one of Cahill's alleged interrogators, 'liked' the blog on his Facebook page, as did a number of others within the party.

Cahill tweeted directly to deputy leader Mary Lou McDonald: 'Will you condemn Finucane for doing this and apologise now?'

McDonald responded: 'The assertion in that blog is shameful and cruel and should not be posted anywhere by anyone.'

Amidst the messy aftermath of the *Spotlight* programme, Bobby Storey, who was Sinn Féin's political director at Stormont at the time, instructed representatives not to engage with Cahill on social media:

At a wider level, party activists should refrain from making any comment on social media sites or in any other way around the issue of the sexual abuse of Mairia Cahill. Such comments are both inappropriate and elements of the media will attempt to misuse or misinterpret any comment – as has already happened.

He also warned that comments on social media 'should only be made if they are measured and rigorously accurate'.

When the memo was leaked, Cahill responded: 'If Bobby Storey and co were really concerned with child protection they'd have sent a memo calling on their members to come forward with information from within about child abusers.'

Meanwhile, Briege Wright, one of the four people accused of interrogating Cahill, released letters she said she received from Cahill in 2005 and 2008.

Wright in her statement said:

There has been a deluge of inaccurate, prejudiced and selective reporting of all aspects of this case, particularly my relationship with Mairia Cahill and in terms of the support that I offered her . . .

My intent was to try to help Mairia. I believe that these letters demonstrate that Mairia accepted and valued that support.

My legal team would have questioned her about these letters had there been a trial.

In the letter from 2005, Cahill told Wright that she was 'the only one from that time that I trusted and for me to trust anyone after everything that has happened to me is a major thing.

'You mean the world to me, you are kind, compassionate, committed and above all you gave me an ear when I needed it.'

Cahill concluded the letter: 'thanks a million Briege for helping me just by being you'.

Following the release of the letters, Cahill said it was 'grotesque' for people central to the allegations to be issuing a 'drip feed' of statements that was causing stress and confusion.

In 2014, Cahill made a complaint to the Police Ombudsman in relation to the PSNI's handling of her case. The sixty-five-page document of the Ombudsman's findings was given to Cahill in 2018.

Cahill revealed some of the findings, including that in 2000, she wrote, police had received reports 'that not only was my abuser abusing children, but that "the IRA were investigating it"'. However, no further action was taken.

In the aftermath of the report, Mary Lou McDonald commended the bravery of Mairia Cahill for waiving her anonymity.

'Sinn Féin has robust procedures in place for mandatory reporting of abuse. I deeply regret that these procedures were not in place at the time of Máiría Cahill's disclosure. For this I unreservedly apologise. I wish Máiría Cahill every best wish for the future.'

Cahill wrote on Twitter that this response was 'woefully inadequate'.

'They told everyone that I was a liar. Now, let's hear them admit I told the truth,' she wrote.

In May 2015, an independent review of the claims made by Mairia Cahill and other women, led by Keir Starmer, criticized the slow pace of the prosecutions. The report said that 'each case became weaker over time' as 'key witnesses pulled out' and 'evidential leads were not pursued'.

Given the 'failings in this case . . . it was almost inevitable' that the three women 'would pull out of the process', Starmer found.

Cahill met Starmer and Barra McGrory, the North's Director of Public Prosecutions. McGrory apologized directly to her.

The allegations of Mairia Cahill continued to hang over Sinn Féin. Eventually, following huge pressure from the public, media and Cahill herself, Mary Lou McDonald met Cahill in November 2018.

Directly after the meeting, Mairia Cahill told me she felt it had been 'potentially a waste of time' for both women:

> I don't feel like I have been treated with the respect I should have been afforded as a sexual abuse victim. She [Ms McDonald] has asserted that she can't admit there was an IRA investigation, so she said that she believed I was abused based on the strength of that there were three alleged victims that came forward.
>
> I asserted that if she believed that I was abused on the basis of other victims, she should also believe there was an IRA investigation as I was not the only person who said there was, but she didn't have an answer for that.

McDonald released a statement after the meeting in which she said:

> We had a lengthy and candid conversation. I listened carefully to what she had to say and I reiterated my unreserved apology and deep regret that procedures for the mandatory reporting of abuse allegations were not in place at the time.
>
> I acknowledged the hurt and pain that Mairia has been through and I stressed to her that robust procedures for the handling of abuse allegations are now in place . . . I reiterated to her that allegations of a criminal nature must be dealt with by the statutory authorities with responsibility for doing so.

Responding to Cahill's allegation that Martin Morris had been a member of Sinn Féin at the time of the abuse,

McDonald said that a lack of records meant she didn't know if this was true. She wasn't in a 'position' to answer allegations that he had been suspended from the party for abusing children, because she wasn't leader at the time, and the party did not have such paperwork to check. She claimed there was 'no cover-up in Sinn Fein' of the abuse.

To this day, the mention of Mairia Cahill's name sparks a visceral response from even some of the most progressive Sinn Féin members. One such member told me: 'We know what happened and we're all sorry, but what the fuck does she want?'

Mairia Cahill has not gone away. In February 2023, the publisher Head of Zeus announced plans to release her memoir. In a statement, Cahill said: 'I have to question how any political party can be trusted to treat its electorate properly when it treated an abuse victim so disgracefully.'

10. The Abortion Puzzle

Sarah Ewart was agitated and nervous as the car wound its way along the long road to Stormont Castle. Sarah wasn't into politics or public speaking. Born in loyalist east Belfast, she had voted, when she did vote, for unionist politicians all her life. Everyone she knew did. Today, Sarah Ewart wasn't going to Stormont to meet someone she had voted for, or supported, or even liked. She had a meeting with Martin McGuinness, the Deputy First Minister of Northern Ireland. The man she had known as the IRA commander, who had led men who terrorized her community, was waiting on the other side of a thick wooden door with an ornate handle. She held her breath as she walked into the office with her mother by her side. It was a large bright room with long windows and wooden panelling on the walls.

McGuinness sat at the end of a long wooden table. He smiled, so she did too. He stood up: 'It's lovely to meet you, Sarah.'

A few weeks after Sarah's wedding in 2013, the 23-year-old found out she was pregnant. She and her husband were delighted.

Nineteen weeks into the pregnancy, Sarah got a scan. The baby, a girl, could be seen on the screen. The ultrasound technician pointed out the baby's feet and legs. When she got to the baby's head, she paused. There was nothing above the baby's eyes: no skull or brain formation.

Sarah's baby had anencephaly, a birth defect which occurs in about six of every 10,000 births. There is no treatment, and babies who have the defect die before they're born, or shortly after birth, once the umbilical cord is severed.

Devastation turned to fear when Sarah was told that she would have to continue the pregnancy to term because of the law in Northern Ireland.

She asked for a medical termination and was refused. The laws in Northern Ireland, the healthcare provider told her, don't allow for it. 'You'll have to go across the water,' she said.

Unlike in the rest of the UK, the 1967 Abortion Act did not apply in Northern Ireland. Abortion was illegal except when a woman's life or her long-term physical and mental health were at risk.

Sarah told the *Irish News*: 'We asked where to go [for a termination] and they said they couldn't tell us.'

She thought of her bump showing. She thought of people asking when she was due, if she had a nursery, and the sex of the baby.

Sarah and her family were against abortion. They believed that life began at conception. But Sarah could not imagine having to carry her baby until it died in her womb, or until she gave birth to a child who would not survive the day.

At twenty-one weeks pregnant, Sarah travelled to London for an abortion. With flights and hotels, it cost more than £2,100. She had to take out a loan.

After she underwent the procedure, she named her baby daughter Ella and swore that something had to change.

Sarah embarked on a campaign that would take her to the highest court in the UK. During the campaign, she would come under sustained abuse and threats. She went on to have another child, Jacob, who also became the target of abuse online. She canvassed politicians, she met with Amnesty International, and she was paired up with a brilliant young human rights solicitor from Belfast, Darragh Mackin of Phoenix Law.

She contacted all 108 members of Stormont and every Northern Irish Westminster MP demanding their help in changing the law so that women carrying babies with a fatal foetal abnormality could access a termination. The Northern Ireland health minister, Jim Wells of the DUP, told her 'that I had destroyed a baby that would have survived, that the consultants get these diagnoses wrong'.

All this would bring her, in 2015, to an uncomfortable seat across the table from a man who everything in her background told her she should hate.

His IRA past was not the only thing that made Martin McGuinness an unlikely interlocutor for Sarah Ewart. McGuinness had made no secret of his devout Catholicism, or his aversion to a woman's right to choose abortion.

Sarah decided she would canvass Northern Ireland's politicians and tell them her story. She felt that once they had heard about the trauma she had gone through, they would have to help.

She felt she had the best chance with her own people, so she visited unionist politicians first. Meetings in constituency offices were organized by polite secretaries. One by one, each unionist politician she met made it clear they would not help her. Their parties and, they believed, the unionist electorate, with its strong background in right-wing Christian values, would not support any liberalizing of the abortion legislation in the North.

Sarah was dejected, but her mother decided they needed to broaden their efforts. They approached Alliance, but they only got a meeting with a spokesperson, and it was not productive.

In desperation Sarah and her mother approached Sinn Féin.

When the response came, it was to say that the party's leader in Stormont, Martin McGuinness, wanted to meet Sarah himself.

McGuinness listened intently as Sarah recalled the horror she had lived through.

While she was talking, the door opened, and Gerry Adams walked into the office. Sarah froze, and she sensed her mother's body stiffening beside her.

McGuinness looked at the women and back at Adams. Before Adams had time to speak, McGuinness said: 'Gerry, I'm having a private meeting here, could I come get you in a while?'

Adams left. McGuinness asked Sarah to continue.

Sarah told confidants afterwards that she sensed McGuinness knew instinctively that even being in the company of Gerry Adams was a step too far for these women. This was the moment Sarah knew she could deal with McGuinness.

In March 2015, shortly after the meeting, McGuinness told the press that political parties have a 'duty and responsibility' to address the issue of fatal foetal abnormality as the party prepared to debate the motion at the party Ard Fheis, that year being held in Derry.

The motion, from the James Connolly cumann in Ballyfermot, Dublin, called for legal frameworks to be introduced in the Republic and Northern Ireland to allow women access to abortion services under the 'limited circumstances' of fatal foetal abnormality.

Launching the agenda for the event, Mary Lou McDonald

said: 'I am personally very, very keen to see that motion accepted by the ard fheis.'

Ahead of the event, McGuinness held a press conference, where he said he had been moved by meeting Sarah. 'It was one of the most heartbreaking meetings I was ever at, alongside herself and her mother.'

At the Ard Fheis, the party voted in favour of the motion to support terminations in cases of fatal foetal abnormality.

If Sarah Ewart's campaign had been the spark for a change in Sinn Féin's abortion policy, it was not the first chink in the party's anti-choice armour. The party's general tendency was that it never wanted to be ahead of the tide of public opinion on the issue – but it also knew it couldn't afford to be significantly behind the tide either.

For many within Sinn Féin, your view on a woman's right to choose was strongly correlated with the number of years you had spent in prison. Prison offers up a lot of time for talking and education, and the IRA took education seriously. Women's studies was on the curriculum in Long Kesh, and many IRA prisoners came out of prison more left wing than they had been going in. Female prisoners in Maghaberry, too, sometimes lobbied for a change in the party's policy. Some in the party, though, remained conservative on abortion.

'They would send out a motion for the Ard Fheis and then someone would be sent in from head office for them to withdraw it,' one senior Sinn Féin official told me.

For a long time, the general view within Sinn Féin was that if they were attempting to build support in Catholic Ireland, a liberal policy on abortion would be counterproductive. Even to be seen debating the issue at an Ard Fheis felt like a lose–lose situation.

The 2013 law change in the South had not resolved the abortion issue there: a movement to repeal the Eighth Amendment to the constitution, which barred most abortions, was growing.

Before Sarah Ewart's intervention, the energies for change had come predominantly from the South. The case of Savita Halappanavar, who died of sepsis in a Galway hospital in October 2012 after being denied a potentially life-saving abortion, had horrified the county.

Shortly after Savita's death, Sinn Féin brought forward a Dáil motion demanding that the Government 'immediately introduce legislation to give effect to the 1992 judgment of the Supreme Court in the X case' – in other words, to allow for abortion when the mother's life was in danger. This was, by late 2012, an uncontroversial position, and the government passed legislation to that effect the following year.

The abortion regimes in both the Republic and Northern Ireland remained extremely strict, and anti-choice forces were becoming increasingly vocal. In January 2015, Archbishop Eamon Martin said that any Catholic politician who supported abortion would not be 'in communion with the church'. To this, McGuinness replied that he tried to be a 'good Catholic' and that although Sinn Féin was opposed to 'abortion on demand', he had been moved by meeting Sarah.

'I think, in the context of my responsibility as a government minister and other government ministers who have a duty to pass legislation, when we're faced with the case of Sarah Ewart, we have to deal with that in the most compassionate way possible.'

In the months and years afterwards, Sarah Ewart and Martin McGuinness developed a close friendship.

On one occasion, Sarah was meeting Alliance's David

Ford, who was at that time the Minister for Justice in the North. She was walking down Stormont's sloping hill back towards Belfast, when a sleek black ministerial car pulled up alongside her, slamming on the brakes.

McGuinness jumped out of the back seat and hugged Sarah, saying: 'Why didn't you tell me you were coming up? Sure I would've come and seen you.'

Their friendship endured, and after Sarah gave birth to a baby girl, she invited McGuinness to the christening.

McGuinness died in March 2017, before the baby was christened. Sarah was heartbroken at the loss of her friend and most ardent political supporter.

Weeks after he died, Sarah Ewart – from loyalist east Belfast, where Union flags line the street on which she lived – named her new baby girl Aoife. She chose the Irish name in tribute to Martin McGuinness. It derives from the Irish aoibh, which means 'beauty' or 'radiance'.

McGuinness had moved, so Sinn Féin would too.

By 2015, twelve Sinn Féin TDs told a Journal.ie survey of TDs that they supported repealing the Eighth Amendment. The twelve included the party leader, Gerry Adams, and the deputy leader, Mary Lou McDonald. Pearse Doherty said he was in favour of repealing the 8th, but would support abortion rights only in cases of rape, incest and fatal foetal abnormality.

The youngest MLA, Megan Fearon, helped to bring Sinn Féin's stance on abortion into line with the twenty-first century.

Fearon was made of strong stuff. In 2012, aged twenty-one, she was interrailing across Europe when Sean Hughes, her neighbour, called her and asked her if she would take Conor

Murphy's seat in Stormont. With the end of double-jobbing for politicians in Northern Ireland, Murphy was about to resign his seat in the Assembly while continuing as an abstentionist MP at Westminster. Fearon had been involved in Sinn Féin student politics since she was sixteen, when she joined the Jim Lochrie cumman, named after her mother's brother, an IRA volunteer who died at nineteen when a bomb he was bringing across the border with a comrade exploded prematurely.

She had made a name for herself as leadership material by encouraging the party to become more attractive to young people in rural areas.

The leadership had decided that Fearon would replace Murphy. She was seen as a guaranteed vote-getter. Intelligent, articulate, rural, feminist, barely in her twenties, and from a Republican background, she ticked all the boxes for the new generation Sinn Féin in the North wanted to put forward. Those in her local area who had dedicated their lives to republicanism were told not to bother expressing any interest in the position, or even thinking about putting themselves forward for selection.

Fearon answered the phone to Hughes, telling him she was in a bar in Poland. He asked her to come home from the holiday but she refused. She told her neighbour that if she was going to be an MLA, this would probably be the last holiday she'd have for a while.

Unbeknown to Fearon herself, hers was the only name to go to the selection convention for the seat. Fearon didn't attend her own selection and was selected to become an MLA *in absentia*.

She returned from her trip on a Sunday, started work as an MLA in Stormont on the Monday and graduated from university three days later.

Her first months were tough. Rape and death threats were called into her constituency office. She was sent home more than once to recuperate after the threats became more graphic and personal. One UUP MLA asked her who she had slept with to get her seat.

Fearon persevered, and was not afraid to speak up to the most senior figures in the party. She made it clear that she felt Sinn Féin was behind the curve on abortion. Others in the party would comment that they wouldn't have 'gotten away with' the same attitude in front of Adams and McGuinness.

At Sinn Féin awaydays and think-ins, Fearon would constantly bring up the abortion issue. She told others she never felt listened to, despite the party's insistence they wanted to listen to women and youth. One former MLA recalls Fearon going 'absolutely fucking mental' at seeing draft campaign material for Martin McGuinness that would state: 'I believe in the right to life.'

It was an Ard Comhairle meeting, and McGuinness wasn't present, which only served to make the others present more uncomfortable. A number of women in the party raged about the fact that McGuinness could state he was pro-life but they were unable to state publicly they were pro-choice.

One policy meeting for staff and representatives from Stormont and Leinster House was held in the City North Hotel, in 2017, at the Dublin–Meath county border. Sinn Féin had a slogan at the time: 'Equality, integrity and respect'.

Fearon spoke up: 'I'm so sick of hearing about equality and rights when we're just completely ignoring abortion. What about equality for women?'

Gerry Adams stopped the meeting: 'Okay, we need to talk about this. We can't keep ignoring it. Let's hear what people think.'

The dial had moved, those present felt comfortable to speak up.

Carál Ní Chuilín, Chris Hazzard and Gerry Kelly all spoke in favour of a change in policy. Francie Molloy was set against it.

In the Republic, a referendum to repeal the Eighth Amendment was set to be announced. Sinn Féin couldn't wait any longer: it needed a position.

At the time, Sinn Féin's policy supported abortion rights in cases of rape and incest, as well as fatal foetal abnormality and a threat to the life of the mother.

A group of Sinn Féin women, including MLAs Fearon and Ní Chuilín, TD Louise O'Reilly, MEP Lynn Boylan, and councillors such as Derry's Sandra Duffy, set about liberalizing the policy.

In one particular Ard Comhairle meeting it emerged that the party needed to update its briefing lines on what Sinn Féin representatives were allowed to say in public.

Martina Anderson lamented that Sinn Féin representatives were not allowed to even say they were pro-choice.

To which Mary Lou McDonald replied: 'I always say I'm pro-choice. Who told you that?'

McDonald told those present they were free to state their beliefs but they would vote as a party on any policy change.

One woman present recalled: 'We realized we just wasted the last few years not saying what we actually believe and getting grief for it . . . The fact is it was probably not ever said to us we couldn't, but it was just the general atmosphere. There is a lot of discipline, you don't speak out of turn in public.'

In the Republic, TDs Peadar Tóibín and Carol Nolan had begun to voice discontent.

Tóibín, who had been a respected member of the front

bench, had begun publicly stating that he was anti-choice around 2012.

It was around this time Gerry Adams asked Tóibín to join the party's National Officer Board. 'We'd love to have you,' he said, 'but you know, when you're on the Officer Board, we all have to speak with one voice.'

Tóibín declined the offer and knew that it had only been made in order to ensure he would stop speaking out publicly about the direction the party was going in.

Multiple sources have told me that Adams was always personally pro-choice but calculated that it wasn't in the party's best interests to change policy until the public was ready. Adams was seen as a supporter of Fearon. His influence would have no doubt brought others along with him, and he was determined to keep Tóibín and, to a lesser extent, Nolan in line.

In 2017, Tóibín began to put forward motions for an Ard Fheis vote on freedom of conscience on the issue of the 'right to life'.

'This is difficult for both sides of the argument,' he told the BBC's *The View* programme. 'This is a life-and-death issue.'

'There is no doubt that people feel very strongly around this, but I feel very strongly that if we approach this in a manner which allows people to express their views, there is no reason that this could create difficulties for the parties internally.'

He claimed he didn't want to change the party's policy but to allow for a broad church of Irish republicans, who could work together for the objective of a united Ireland while disagreeing on the abortion issue.

He told allies he had had over thirty local cumainn sign the motions to go forward to the Ard Fheis, until they started not showing up.

Reports allegedly started coming to Tóibín's camp that local secretaries were instructed to cancel upcoming local meetings so the motion couldn't be passed. One cumann reported back that they had passed the motion and given it to their local organizer, but it was never delivered to head office.

As the campaign to repeal the Eighth Amendment gathered steam in the Republic, Sinn Féin women and men began to throw their weight behind it, even though it was still technically against party policy.

In November 2017, Adams publicly revealed he had been at odds with Sinn Féin's policy on terminations for decades.

'My personal position is that it is up to women,' he told the *Irish Times*:

> Women have to have the right in all of these situations but as a party member I can only support the position which the party has worked out over a very, very long time, which as I say, I think reflects wider society [. . .] We are very much in support of the repeal of the amendment in the constitution, the repeal of the Eighth Amendment, we want to see that gone.
>
> It should never have been in the constitution in the first place and it should be replaced by legislation which reflects our party position.

The party's official policy on abortion had not yet changed, but the 'position' had. Adams had made it clear that Sinn Féin would be changing its stance. Sinn Féin would campaign in favour of overturning the Eighth Amendment.

In the referendum on 25 May 2018, voters in the Republic

of Ireland voted to overturn the abortion ban by 66.4 per cent to 33.6 per cent – a landslide. In the celebrating crowds at Dublin Castle, Mary Lou McDonald and Michelle O'Neill stood on the stage and held up a cardboard sign which read: 'The North is next.'

It wasn't to be that simple.

Galvanized by the referendum win in the Republic, Fearon and other pro-choice party figures offered to visit every single Comhairle Ceantair group in the North to drum up support for a new Sinn Féin abortion policy. The leadership was backing a motion that was to go before the party's 2018 Ard Fheis. The motion would bring Sinn Féin policy into line with the abortion regime that was shortly to be implemented in the Republic.

A timetable for such meetings notes that MLAs Colm Gildernew, Chris Hazzard, John O'Dowd, Caoimhe Archibald, Philip McGuigan, Karen Mullan, Gerry Kelly, Sinéad Ennis and Declan McAleer, along with MP Michelle Gildernew and TD Martin Kenny, took to almost every constituency in the North, armed with a six-page PowerPoint presentation and some speaking notes.

'We sat for hours sometimes answering every possible question that could be asked about the issue and the proposed policy change,' one member of the group told me.

'This was to make sure delegates at the Ard Fheis would vote with full knowledge and make sure it passed and so they would be equipped to answer questions themselves on doors in their communities.'

In Derry, local councillor Sandra Duffy conducted the meeting along with Karen Mullan MLA, and Paul Kavanagh, a former IRA man who was married to Martina Anderson.

The Derry meeting was well attended, and the South Armagh meeting in Mullaghbawn was standing room only.

In other instances, in other locations, some recall meeting rooms in Dungannon or North Antrim with only three people in attendance, but the group powered through and it worked.

Fearon and the others got Sinn Féin's policy change over the line with the Northern membership.

In June 2018, Sinn Féin delegates voted to change the party's position on abortion at the Ard Fheis in Belfast. Fittingly, perhaps, it was the first conference without Gerry Adams as the leader, with the new female leadership of Mary Lou McDonald and Michelle O'Neill bringing in the change.

More than twenty Sinn Féin branches had called for a free-conscience vote for Sinn Féin TDs taking part in the Dáil vote, but this was rejected. The same month, Offaly TD Carol Nolan left the party over the issue. In a statement, Nolan said she felt it was 'unethical to force TD's who were strongly opposed to abortion to vote against their conscience'.

One parliamentary assistant recalls another staff member bursting into their office exclaiming: 'Fuck, Carol's left!' before demanding they turn on the TV to find out what had happened in the room four doors down from them.

Nolan wasn't to be the last.

As the new Regulation of Termination of Pregnancy Bill, which will allow for unrestricted abortion in the first twelve weeks of pregnancy moved through the Houses of the Oireachtas, Peadar Tóibín became an issue once again.

The Meath West TD defied the party whip again and voted against the bill. He was suspended from Sinn Féin for six months. In a statement, Mr Tóibín said his suspension could be seen as a 'de facto expulsion' because of the prospect of a general election being held during the next six months.

Within two weeks, Tóibín had quit Sinn Féin after twenty-one years with 'a heavy heart' and formed his own anti-choice republican party, Aontú.

Sinn Féin came out of Repeal bruised but unbroken, a late-comer to the abortion issue to some. It had lost some older and more rural voters, two TDs and a small number of members, but had solidified its place as a party that understood the public and was willing to change its policy to accommodate new attitudes. The party is unlikely to have backed abortion had it not recognized the swell of public support for the Repeal campaign; this is true for other political parties in the Republic too.

All the major parties in Dublin were behind Repeal and Sinn Féin would not be the outlier if it wanted power. Sinn Féin probably gained more votes than it lost. Those who actively rejected abortion rights had nowhere else to go anyway.

The following April, two empty boxes were left in Tóibín's office. When he queried why they had been left there, a Sinn Féin official told him to 'Fuck off' out of the office within the party's area in the Leinster House complex 'before something happens'.

Sinn Féin released a statement which did not dispute Tóibín's account.

Peadar Tóibín has not been a member of Sinn Féin since November last year, yet he is still on the Sinn Féin floor in Leinster House.

A party official today asked him to move off the floor.

This was a private conversation.

This issue is not uncommon in other parties when members leave.

The party has no further comment to make.

In the North, change was driven not by the Assembly and Executive – which entered a three-year suspension in early 2017 over the Renewable Heating Initiative scandal – but by Westminster. In July 2019, MPs voted to decriminalize abortion in Northern Ireland and to introduce new regulations allowing for terminations in the first twelve weeks of a pregnancy in all circumstances, and at more advanced stages of gestation in limited circumstances.

The regime would be broadly similar to, but in some respects more liberal than, the post-referendum regime in the Republic.

The legislation set a deadline for the restoration of devolved government in Northern Ireland. When the deadline came and went, the decriminalization provisions of the legislation came into effect.

The devolved institutions resumed functioning in January 2020. The Westminster regulations remained the law of the land, and limited abortion services became available through some NHS trusts, but under UUP health minister Robin Swann the Executive failed to fully commission abortion services.

In 2021, the DUP introduced the Private Members' Severe Foetal Impairment Abortion (Amendment) Bill, which they said was designed to protect the lives of foetuses with non-fatal conditions such as Down syndrome. The new (but unimplemented) regulations for Northern Ireland allowed abortions beyond twelve weeks' gestation in cases of severe but non-fatal foetal abnormalities; the DUP bill would, in theory, change that. In reality, it was a purely performative bill: even if passed, it would have no binding effect. But in singling out one very specific provision of the Westminster regulations, it was teeing up an embarrassment for Sinn Féin.

Sinn Féin's policy, as ratified at the 2018 Ard Fheis, was in line with the abortion legislation in the Republic. This meant that party policy did not allow for an extension of the twelve-week gestation window for cases of severe (but non-fatal) abnormality. Rather than vote against the DUP bill – which would have put them at odds with their own policy – Sinn Féin abstained. The party then came in for heavy criticism for failing to oppose a DUP anti-abortion bill. Some critics, perhaps misunderstanding what was really at issue in the Stormont vote, accused Sinn Féin of having different abortion policies on each side of the border. The truth was exactly the opposite: the party was sticking to a clear all-Ireland policy, at the cost of significant political embarrassment.

11. 'When you're out, you're out'

After the abortive heave against Gerry Adams in late 2013, Adams identified the party's most senior Stormont staffer, Leo Green, as the instigator of the move. The two had, in fact, been at odds for some time.

Green complained that Adams had begun demanding answers and briefing papers at a moment's notice. The two bickered openly at meetings. In his capacity as chair of the cuige for the Six Counties, Green would often remind Adams that he was only allotted the same speaking time as other members — that Adams hated, and that some present saw as a power play.

Meanwhile, staff members surrounding Martin McGuinness kept him away from Parliament Buildings at Stormont, where the MLAs had their offices, as much as possible. McGuinness would come for his allotted question times, attend Sinn Féin team meetings, do a briefing and leave abruptly. As a result, says an MLA from the time, 'I don't think Martin realized the extent of morale being so bad.'

The MLAs and staff would meet every Monday morning to plan the week ahead. The atmosphere was constantly tense.

The former MLA recalls: 'I remember saying once, "I'm only new in this job and I barely speak to anyone", and someone replied: "You're an elected rep, you're not here for the craic." It was shite.'

The people I interviewed for this book who worked under Green and McMullan at Stormont in those days say it was dysfunctional at best, with new MLAs left to fend for themselves and often left feeling that they were being pitted against their colleagues.

Green would tell people he and others around him had had enough of the 'grey-haired men at the back of the room', a reference to local IRA groups in the North who attended Sinn Féin meetings to throw their weight around.

Adams felt that Green was too hard on people. Green rejected the assertion, and said the groups who had complained about the directorate's actions gave too much weight to the local IRA leadership and should do well to remember Sinn Féin was in charge now. This argument bore no weight with the elected reps like Chris Hazzard and Michelle Gildernew, who had no IRA history. Gildernew, an MLA, MP and one-time Good Friday Agreement negotiator, had complained to Adams about an exchange with Green during which she felt he had been insulting.

Seán Mac Brádaigh had informed the party that he wished to stand down as director of publicity. One of the problems the party identified in a review of the publicity operation – labelled 'a disaster' by one member of the review board – was that Mac Brádaigh didn't live in Dublin. He had moved to Leitrim and spent just one day a week in Dublin. Mac Brádaigh didn't want to move and didn't want the commute. He wanted out of the role.

Adams asked Green to take up the post. The offer did not make a lot of sense to people around Stormont. Green had no journalism background. McGuinness told one advisor he thought Adams's choice of Green for the role was an odd one.

The recommendation from the panel review was that

whoever took over the role needed to be based in Dublin. Green told those around him, including Jackie McMullan, that he felt Adams wanted him out of Stormont.

A meeting was set for Dundalk on a Friday in late 2013. Green told those closest to him before setting off to the meeting that he would be forced to resign afterwards.

After some general discussion of political issues and plans, Adams began a long speech about the publicity post, in which he accused Green of ignoring him and the needs of the party. The room became tense when Green cut across Adams mid-speech.

'Well, the answer is no,' Green said.

'Why?' Adams replied.

'The answer is no,' Green repeated. People present claim Leo Green told Adams he wouldn't be bullied.

'Well,' Adams said, 'I'm moving you.'

Referring to the fact that Green was expecting to be renominated as chair of the Northern cuige in the coming weeks, Adams continued: 'Oh and you shouldn't put your name forward for the chair of the Six Counties, you'll not be getting that.'

Green said he would be putting his name forward, as he had never received any complaints about his tenure.

Adams repeated that he wouldn't be getting the post, as leadership and most of the party wouldn't support him.

The room was silent when Green got up and left.

He wasn't seen by anyone from Sinn Féin for three days, and phoned in sick on the Monday.

Panicked about where the situation was headed, Martin McGuinness phoned Green. McGuinness tried to resolve the situation, sources say, telling Green he could work for him exclusively.

On Tuesday morning, Green arrived in Stormont. He emailed his resignation from his position as Sinn Féin's political director in the North after almost three decades of service to republican politics.

He met with McGuinness and McMullan, and told them that he had been to see a solicitor and that he would be suing Sinn Féin. The men sat opposite Green in shock. McGuinness pleaded with Green to see sense.

McGuinness said the situation was 'madness'. He talked about the party sticking together and argued that Green and Adams should call a truce.

He asked Green to meet with him and Adams privately.

Eventually, Green agreed. He brought McMullan as a witness. The four men met in a Drogheda hotel.

Adams suggested Green had indicated he would take the director of publicity job initially, and that he'd left the party stranded now he had changed his mind.

Green said that Adams was a liar.

McGuinness stared at McMullan before interjecting something about 'crossed wires'.

McGuinness proposed that Green could remain in Stormont, not as a special advisor paid by the civil service, but as an advisor to the Deputy First Minister, working in Stormont alongside McGuinness full time, paid by the party.

Green refused, stating that the issue wasn't about the job and that they all knew it. The issue was Adams. McGuinness then mumbled something about 'publicity' if Green left in such a way.

Green and McMullan stood up and left.

A meeting of the political directorate was due the following day. Green met Spike Murray and a number of other colleagues beforehand. He told them he was leaving. Murray was a previous chair of the Northern cuige himself, and knew Sinn Féin politics like the back of his hand. He had served twelve years for IRA offences, and had been named as a one-time commander of Northern Command.

Murray didn't seem shocked by the turn of events. There had been a split brewing and everyone expected that it would be Green who would have to go. Some present told Green that they were sad to see him go, that they had no part in his exit.

Derry MLA and former hunger-striker Raymond McCartney chose a different tack: 'You know Dodie McGuinness took a case against us in Derry, and now no one talks to her.'

This was a clear warning: once you take a case against Sinn Féin, you're a pariah to your comrades.

Anne 'Dodie' Harkin McGuinness was a Sinn Féin stalwart.

In 1985, she was elected to Derry City Council for Sinn Féin and retained the seat until 1993. She married Martin McGuinness's brother Paul and was elected to the Ard Comhairle in 1994, where she would remain until 2005.

In 1996, she was elected to the Northern Ireland Forum, the precursor to the Stormont Assembly, as one of four Sinn Féin representatives. In 1997, she was director of elections for Northern Ireland.

By 2003, she was the head of the Sinn Féin Bureau in England and by 2005 deputy head of the party's International Department.

She was made redundant from her job in Sinn Féin's Westminster office in November 2007. She later sued Sinn Féin over claims the party discriminated against her on grounds of age and gender in not giving her an opportunity to apply for two other jobs, which were given to men, both younger than her. She was awarded £15,000.

Sinn Féin agreed to pay out without admission of liability, and the party said it 'regretted any perception that she was put at a disadvantage'.

Despite her service to the party, and her connection to McGuinness, Dodie was cast out: shunned by some of her friends and colleagues in the party. Raymond McCartney's warning was that the same thing would be coming for Leo Green.

There were fifteen people at the meeting of the political directorate, but only Adams and Green spoke. It was a showdown.

Adams repeated his claim that Green had left him in the lurch. Green stated calmly: 'I want everybody just to hear me say this: Gerry, you're a liar.'

The other attendees stared at each other in stunned silence.

Green continued: 'You are lying to the leadership of the party in the North.'

Raymond McCartney interjected with what one witness called 'the stupidest thing I've ever heard'. McCartney referred back to the Belfast dinner dance at which Green's wife, Maggie, had not joined the standing ovation for Adams. 'You know, that's just terrible, showing no respect,' McCartney said.

The room stared at him blankly. Green got up and left.

In the days following, Sinn Féin received notification that Green was suing the party on a number of grounds, through the Fair Employment Tribunal. Green claimed discrimination for holding a political opinion, unfair dismissal and breach of contract. The party settled the case with Green on 'amicable' and 'confidential' terms.

Green left the North and moved to the Republic. He is seen now and again at republican funerals, where he is friendly with his former comrades, except Adams. At McGuinness's funeral, he was seen speaking with Bobby Storey, who replaced him as the chair of the Northern cuige and took over running the Stormont operation.

The narrative that Sinn Féin circulated in the aftermath – and as the Áine Adams controversy occupied the party – was that Green and to a lesser extent McMullan had tried to move against Adams. They had planned a takeover of the party and were turning representatives against the leader. Narrative is the most important thing to Sinn Féin. Once you're gone, they get to decide the story.

Many people who spoke to me for this book said the same thing: with Sinn Féin, 'When you're out, you're out.' It does not matter how many years you have given to the party, how many elections you have contested, how many prison sentences you have endured: if you leave the party, it's like you never existed. For those who speak out publicly against the party it can be even worse.

Every political party has internal rows and problematic members, but Sinn Féin is particularly bad at weeding out local issues and bullying early on. The party's intensely hierarchical structure makes it hard to complain if the ones you wish to complain about reside higher on the totem pole. The result is that local problems are likely to escalate and, despite the party's instinctive secrecy, enter the public domain.

From 2015 onwards, Sinn Féin's operation in the Republic of Ireland was rocked by resignations, suspensions and rumours of bullying both at Leinster House and in local cumainn.

In June of that year, after a confidential internal party review chaired by Cork North Central TD Jonathan O'Brien,

Cork councillor Kieran McCarthy was expelled from the party. McCarthy was a former member of the Irish Defence Forces who joined the IRA after he and his army colleagues were humiliated by the British Army at gunpoint in front of locals while in South Armagh. He was arrested in Belgium for his IRA activity before joining Sinn Féin and being elected a local representative.

Sinn Féin figures claimed at the time that McCarthy was formally warned about his conduct towards Cork East TD Sandra McLellan and his alleged refusal to invite McLellan to public events. McCarthy denied that he'd received any warning before being expelled.

Another Cork councillor, Melissa Mullane, was suspended for twelve months, accused of 'uncomradely behaviour' towards McLellan.

When Mullane was reinstated to the party, Fermoy-based councillor June Murphy, who was a close confidante of McLellan, stepped down, citing the effects of the bitter local row. 'I have found my time in the party to be an increasingly negative experience,' said Murphy.

Sandra McLellan, for her part, decided not to run in the 2016 general election, citing 'vicious' efforts to 'undermine and malign' her.

In April 2017, just three years after joining the party, Kildare councillor Sorcha O'Neill resigned, claiming she had been a victim of 'bullying, hostility, and aggression'. Four other local Sinn Féin activists quit the party at the same time.

That same year, Eugene Greenan, the youngest member of Cavan County Council, stepped down from his position on the local authority, and subsequently resigned from the party. Greenan said in a statement: 'I cannot be a member of an organisation that treats its members so poorly and that effortlessly disregards its mantra of fairness and equality.'

In July 2017, Paul Hogan, a member of Westmeath County Council, quit Sinn Féin after claiming that he had been subject to an 'unrelenting campaign' by colleagues.

'[. . .] I have highlighted a number of issues internally within Sinn Féin dating back some years,' he told the *Athlone Advertiser*. 'I am continuing to seek justice in this regard. I have also indicated that there is a significant cohort of listed members who should not be members of Sinn Féin. It would therefore be hypocritical of me to align myself with these individuals.'

He claimed that he had been 'intimidated, received a death threat, was subjected to an anonymous hate mail campaign, and had to appear before a Sinn Féin "kangaroo court" to deny allegations against him'.

Sinn Féin said that its National Investigations Committee had dealt with Hogan's complaints properly.

In September 2017, Sinn Féin expelled three Wicklow councillors following a row. Gerry O'Neill, Oliver O'Brien and John Snell were expelled from the party after objecting to the selection of a relatively new councillor, Nicola Lawless, to lead the Sinn Féin group on the council. Sinn Féin put out a statement alleging that the three men had failed to attend council team meetings for the previous eighteen months. Gerry O'Neill told TheJournal.ie:

Bit of a surprise that I get a phone call from RTÉ saying that I have been expelled from the party. I've seen the email [sent by the party to the press] and it's a barrage of lies that say I didn't attend meetings – codology. None of the issues that we had raised were referred to.

In November 2017, Tipperary councillor Seamus Morris resigned, telling the *Tipperary Star* that there was a 'nasty culture in the party who believed in dictating to councillors from darkened rooms'.

In the previous September, Morris said he had considered taking his own life after he was expelled from his local party branch in Tipperary after 'an intense nine-month hate campaign of harassment and slander'.

In his resignation letter, he wrote: 'These unaddressed allegations have had a desperate impact on my family and myself over the last number of months.

'Due process has not been followed to resolve the situation to a point now, where for the sake of my family and my own health, I am leaving the party.'

Sinn Féin said: 'The party found no evidence of a smear campaign against Councillor Morris.

'As part of that process, complaints were made against Councillor Morris regarding his behaviour towards fellow party members in the constituency.

'The party had been looking into these complaints.'

In the same month, Trevor Ó Clochartaigh, who had been a Sinn Féin senator since 2011, left the party citing concerns about 'serious breaches' of conduct and 'unacceptable behaviour' in Galway West.

Sinn Féin issued a statement stating Ó Clochartaigh was motivated by a concern he would not win the party's Galway West selection convention to run again for the Dáil after failing to get elected as a TD in 2016. This time the convention would see him run against Galway city-based councillor Mairéad Farrell, a niece of the IRA woman Mairéad Farrell who was shot by the SAS in Gibraltar in 1988.

The party claimed Ó Clochartaigh had been making a case for a two-candidate strategy in the constituency.

'Given the party didn't make the quota or elected a TD in the last election we were going with a one-candidate strategy on this occasion,' the statement said. 'It is clear that Trevor was worried that a democratic vote of party members in the constituency would not select him to contest the election.'

Ó Clochartaigh denied this in the *Irish Times*, stating that the conduct of party members was the main reason for his resignation.

'We have had serious breaches of the Sinn Féin code of conduct in Galway West going unpunished and unacceptable behaviour against me and a number of other members locally, from a small number of ruthless, unscrupulous and ambitious individuals going back a number of years now.'

Days later, Galway councillor Gabe Cronnelly announced his resignation too.

The Athenry–Oranmore area councillor said: 'I am awfully disappointed at the way Sinn Féin leadership have refused to address the concerns of so many decent members here in Galway, in relation to unacceptable behaviour by a small group of people.'

One Sinn Féin TD attributes the wave of bullying allegations to the unexpected bounce the party received in the local elections in 2014.

'We had a pretty significant number of people who weren't cut out for the job and we probably didn't expect them to get elected,' the TD told me. 'That's the problem with political parties when you're not prepared. And if you're not organizationally strong, local issues fester. We have weak organizations all over the country.'

'In most cases, when I look back, people felt some weren't doing their job and it's this tension that builds a lot of cases. So I think in some cases, in terms of local candidates, we could have done more to support them. Leadership didn't have the time or energy to look into it.'

At one time, Noeleen Reilly looked like a rising star in Sinn Féin.

Born in Cavan, to a republican family, she joined Sinn Féin at a young age. Upon moving to Ballymun in Dublin in 2006, she began helping out with the local Sinn Féin cumann while doing community work. Reilly was smart, articulate and attractive, and she rose through the ranks quickly. She became Mary Lou McDonald's director of finance for her 2007 election campaign.

Reilly ran in the 2014 local elections for Ballymun, and topped the poll. Her career in Sinn Féin appeared to be going from strength to strength. In reality, her relationship with a number of her local party colleagues had broken down by this stage, and in the count centre local party members lifted her running mate, Cathleen Carney Boud, in celebration, while Reilly stood beside them, unlifted.

Reilly began making complaints to the party with allegations that some local members had been spreading false rumours about her sex life.

In March 2016, the situation reached fever pitch at an Easter Commemoration at a GAA club in Cabra. A woman known to Sinn Féin's TD for Dublin North-West, Dessie Ellis, allegedly assaulted Reilly, grabbing her by the hair from behind and assaulting her repeatedly.

Reilly was told to stay quiet about the incident to protect the party, and that leadership would help straighten things out. Reilly said later that she did not contact the gardaí for this reason.

She sent an email to a Sinn Féin head office staffer days after the assault, asking for a meeting with Gerry Adams. She wrote that the person who assaulted her was not a Sinn Féin member, but did attend party events. 'How can I feel safe going to anything again?' she said.

Later, she sent another email complaining that she felt compelled to leave the party's Ard Fheis because the person she said attacked her was there.

She sent Adams the photos of her injuries, to no avail. She was told by another member that Gerry didn't get involved in 'local issues'.

In the weeks after the alleged attack, rumours continued about Reilly and she continued to ask for help.

'I feel my personal safety is now at risk,' she wrote in an email to party headquarters. 'Given that I was told nothing could be done within the party about my assault as she is not a member, I find it hypocritical that she is now invited to our ard fheis.'

In early February 2018, Sinn Féin suspended Reilly for six months, accusing her of 'orchestrating a vicious bullying campaign' against Cathleen Carney Boud on social media. The party also censured Dessie Ellis, the local TD, for comments he made suggesting Reilly was not fit to serve in Sinn Féin.

For her part, Cathleen Carney Boud released a statement welcoming the move: 'Having been the victim of an orchestrated online bullying campaign I made a complaint to Sinn Féin against Councillor Noeleen Reilly who I believed to be behind the campaign.'

Reilly took to social media, writing on Facebook to McDonald and Adams: 'Assuming it's OK now to defend myself considering I was told to stay quiet to protect the party.'

There were a number of photographs showing severe bruises to her legs.

Finally, on 5 February, she left Sinn Féin.

In a statement Reilly said she had been left with 'very little choice' but to leave.

She alleged 'physical assaults, verbal abuse, total isolation, smear campaigns' by members of Sinn Féin, dating back to February 2014, and said that she had asked for help repeatedly.

'Every time I did so it was either ignored or an angle was found to blame me for their treatment. I was always told to keep these matters internal and I did so for four years hoping that justice would take place at some time.'

Reilly said she was 'up against the wrong people and this was never a battle I was going to win'.

Reilly remains an independent councillor, winning her seat again in 2019. On the doors in Ballymun she had heard that local Sinn Féin members had further spread sexist rumours.

'You can't vote for her, she's a whore and a cokehead,' one neighbour was told.

On social media, one account called her the 'bike of Ballymun'. Reilly was repeatedly told that running again was a fool's errand. That she wasn't going to be re-elected, that it was 'a Sinn Féin seat' and they'd be taking it back from her on polling day.

Reilly came second in the 2019 local elections, and remains an independent councillor on Dublin City Council.

Much like Adams and McGuinness before her, staff and TDs say McDonald does not get involved in local issues, and it would be unrealistic to expect her to do so. However, when local issues become national, as they frequently have, the party are left facing uncomfortable questions in the media and public. Local structures were continually either keeping issues from head office or being left to sort them out themselves, with McDonald at the helm.

Allegations of bullying have haunted Sinn Féin. The old adage that Sinn Féin is 'not a normal party' is one they completely reject, but the number of messy internal disputes that have come to public attention – despite the party's secrecy – is on a different scale from other parties. As we will see, problems with candidate vetting and selection, and a failure to manage disputes within the party, would continue to haunt Sinn Féin, even as its electoral fortunes hit new heights.

12. Dark Days in Derry

In January 2017, when announcing his resignation as Deputy First Minister and collapsing Stormont over the 'cash for ash' scandal, Martin McGuinness looked frail. Three months later, he was dead.

He was just sixty-six, and had become ill from a genetic disorder. Amyloidosis is a condition that attacks the vital organs. McGuinness's mother hailed from Donegal, where there is a notable cluster of those carrying the genetic mutation that causes the disorder.

Many of the sitting MLAs did not feel able to return to work in the week of McGuinness's death. People queued for hours outside his Bogside home to visit his body during the wake. The funeral was attended by thousands. The eulogy was given by former US President Bill Clinton, who said McGuinness had 'risked the wrath of his comrades and the rejection of his enemies'.

Even before McGuinness's death Sinn Féin's operation in Derry had been in a poor state.

'Martin didn't know the half of it,' says one close friend of McGuinness. 'It was kept from him, he didn't know the extent of the developing culture. It was horrendous to watch it. There was a core group of people there who just didn't want to listen, despite all the warning signs.'

In every part of Northern Ireland where the IRA had a presence, the 'volunteers' dinner dance' is a fixture of the social calendar. These are generally ticketed functions, with the money raised used to support republican causes, including the upkeep of the graves of the local IRA dead.

In 2018, the volunteers' dinner dance in Derry was held in the function room of a bar in the city centre, close to the Bogside. A number of younger Sinn Féin members, staff and an elected representative sloped off to a room that one of the group had booked for the night. The friends were drinking and snorting cocaine from the table in the room. One of the group took a number of videos and posted them to their social media. In the background of the videos, which showed friends laughing and dancing, it was clear that there were drugs being used. The videos and images were quickly shared through WhatsApp, forwarded hundreds of times.

Republican areas had been mostly devoid of hard drugs in the 1970s and '80s due to the IRA's vigilante policing of the neighbourhoods. Anyone pushing anything stronger than cannabis was painting a target on their own back. Graffiti would tag walls in these areas: 'Drug dealers will be shot'.

Even in the South, where the IRA did not make any organized attempt to usurp local policing, republicans became active in anti-drugs vigilantism during the 1980s, infiltrating an organization called Concerned Parents Against Drugs. In the North following the IRA ceasefire, an organization called Direct Action Against Drugs, which was believed to be linked to the IRA, was responsible for a number of killings. The IRA worried about drug use in their communities because they feared addicts and petty criminals were vulnerable to being recruited as informers. Aside from the security risks, the IRA and many of those in Sinn Féin have historically held extremely conservative views on drug use.

Following the emergence of the videos from the Derry dinner dance, a republican splinter group in Derry, Saoradh, which was mostly made up of former combatants who were against the peace process, posted the images on their Facebook page with a long spiel about the lack of discipline and respect for fallen heroes.

I submitted a query to the Sinn Féin press office in Belfast seeking comment. Minutes later, my phone rang. It was Caolan McGinley, a young Sinn Féin press officer from Derry who had been working in Stormont for years. He and I had a friendly rapport: we were the same age, and knew each other previously from McGinley's side career as a DJ in our hometown.

McGinley said he was giving me a warning 'as a friend' that the party were prepared to sue any outlet that accused Sinn Féin members of using drugs at the event. He said that other outlets had enquired and been told the same thing.

Rumours were rife. Some of the people pictured in the video were suspended from the party – but not all.

Belfast MLA Alex Maskey was sent to investigate what was happening with Sinn Féin in Derry in the aftermath. Alex Maskey is a lifelong republican, a long-time MLA and a key ally of Gerry Adams.

In the early 1970s, at the start of the Troubles, he was twice interned after becoming involved with the IRA. His wife, Liz, was the first woman to be interned in Northern Ireland. Maskey had become a figure of hate for loyalists when, in 1983, he was the first Sinn Féin councillor to be elected to Belfast City Hall. The unionists were horrified to have an IRA supporter in their midst and made it known. One Unionist councillor tried to spray Maskey with disinfectant to 'sanitize' the chamber of his presence. That same year, Maskey survived a shotgun blast to the abdomen when the UDA attacked him.

He went to the Channel Islands to recover. On his journey back to Belfast, he was detained at London's Heathrow Airport under the Prevention of Terrorism Act.

Six years later, his friend Alan Lundy, a father of five, was murdered by the UDA as he helped secure Maskey's house against further attacks.

Maskey has a stocky build, signature beard and bald head. His amateur boxing record lists seventy-five fights and only four losses.

He was Sinn Féin's whip in Stormont and it was in this capacity that he travelled to Derry to find out what was happening.

The city's local organization had come to be seen as a 'basket case', according to one Sinn Féin MP. For years, two families had dominated. The Andersons included Martina Anderson, her nephew Mickey Anderson and her niece Elisha McCallion, among a number of other prominent party members. The McCartneys were headed by the then MLA and former hunger-striker Raymond McCartney. Their late father, Liam McCartney, had been an election agent for Martin McGuinness. Raymond McCartney's brother Andrew also held different leadership roles over the years for the party in Derry.

Word had got out that Maskey was in town to hear people's concerns. One sister of a slain IRA man made an appointment to see him in the party's Rath Mor offices in Creggan.

The office was small and adorned with framed pictures of the hunger-strikers and volunteers who had died on IRA duty. Maskey sat at one side of the desk when the woman began speaking.

'How fucking dare they?' she said.

Maskey stared back in silence. He didn't ask her who or what she was referring to.

She continued: 'Those girls got dressed up, they got their hair done, makeup done, swanky dresses, the men were suited and booted and to me they may as well have put a picture down of my dead brother and poured the cocaine out on his head.

'It was an event to remember volunteers, young men who died in Derry, and they disgraced the entire thing.'

Maskey listened, nodded, but said little. The woman left the office by saying: 'I hope you're the pied piper and you take the rats away with you.'

She never heard from Sinn Féin or Alex Maskey again.

In 2020, when it emerged that the former Foyle MP and then senator Elisha McCallion had received, along with two other party officials, payments from a Stormont Covid-19 grant scheme, the Sinn Féin messaging machine went into overdrive.

Rumblings had begun in the north when BBC Radio Ulster host Stephen Nolan revealed on 28 October that three Sinn Féin offices had received £10,000 in payments set aside for businesses struggling in the pandemic. The offices had not requested the grants, but they were not eligible to receive them and the money had not been returned. The party had paid the money back on 27 October, after the BBC had come looking for answers.

McCallion had been selected for the Seanad after spectacularly losing her seat in Westminster by a massive 17,110 votes to the SDLP leader, Colum Eastwood. She was widely regarded as a disappointing if not slightly embarrassing MP for her home city. She made a number of gaffes during her tenure and seemed annoyed that she had to travel to London at all when she wasn't even taking her seat in the Commons.

In 2017, she faced criticism after she took to social media to complain about the size of her London hotel room, stating: 'Don't let anyone fool you that a life of a Sinn Fein MP is lavish!! Never stayed in a smaller hotel room in all my life, literally my bathroom at home is bigger lol xx.'

After she lost, McCallion was selected for the Seanad, where she had made very little impact by the time the scandal had come knocking.

In a statement, McCallion said she had not applied for the grant nor received any correspondence about it from the Department of the Economy. She said that the £10,000 payment had been lodged in a joint account she shared with her husband:

> I fully accept that as a named signature on the account that I should have taken steps to verify this situation, before it was brought to my attention on Monday.
>
> The money was repaid in full on Tuesday.
>
> I apologise unreservedly for the poor judgement I showed in relation to this and therefore, last night I spoke to the party leader and tendered my resignation as a member of Seanad Éireann with immediate effect.

The press went wild on both sides of the border and everyone wanted to know what had happened. When I began enquiring with Sinn Féin representatives and staff, I was given explanations that are not publishable, and that I have reason to believe were concocted to shift the focus away from the party's role in the affair.

The question being asked by the public and the media was: how would you not notice if someone put ten grand in your bank account?

One former MLA, who was not echoing the party line, told me that the explanation was obvious: 'Because you have no fucking control over your account.

'That wasn't her on her own account. I would bet everything I own, that was a directive, "Let it [the pandemic payment] sit. If they were stupid enough to put it into our account, leave it." That's how they think.

'The week it happened and they were panicking, someone in Belfast rang me and said: "There's still an account open in your name."

'I said: "Get it to fuck, there better not be ten grand lying in it." [. . .] I don't know if my signature was on it, I never saw a bank statement. I went down the same week and closed the account.

'She [McCallion] might not actually have seen it, but I know what happened was that somebody somewhere said: "Fuck it, leave it sitting here."'

I don't know if the MLA's theory is true. But the fact that it *could* have been true, as late as 2020, is telling. Why was Sinn Féin the only party with members who received erroneous pandemic payments and failed to flag them up? Perhaps because it was the only party that had opened bank accounts to receive the salaries of elected officials, and kept them open even when salaries were no longer being paid into them.

Elisha McCallion, like almost everyone else in Derry Sinn Féin, refused to comment or respond to my requests for interview.

*

The McCallion affair and the videos that emerged from the volunteers' dinner dance were embarrassments for Sinn Féin in Derry, but the party's malaise in the city ran far deeper.

More than two decades on from the last, permanent IRA ceasefire, a group of Sinn Féin figures in Derry took the view that their ideas and policies were the right ones because they were former combatants.

'Derry was run like an armed support unit as opposed to a political organization,' one former MLA told me.

Word was sent back to the leadership in Dublin that some canvassers for the party had been told by former blanket protesters and other IRA prisoners in Derry that they would be voting for the SDLP, so bad was the level of support for the party in the wake of McGuinness's death and an impression of total arrogance and disregard of the community's needs.

This wasn't just another case of local squabbling: it was having electoral consequences. In the local elections in 2019, Sinn Féin lost five seats on Derry and Strabane council and surrendered its position as the council's biggest party. McDonald decided in the aftermath that something had to be done about Derry.

Senior party officials were dispatched to the city to interview those in the community sector, a traditional wellspring of Sinn Féin support and candidates.

What they found was worse than they had expected. The cocaine story was told and retold. The traditional republican anti-drugs stance and local cultural conservatism about the issue were factors, but what seemed to bother people I spoke to most was the fact that the party did not apologize to volunteers' families. The incident, they felt, crystallized what Derry Sinn Féin had become: arrogant and secretive, taking their electoral base for granted and closing ranks to protect those important to them.

There was also a widespread feeling that Sinn Féin members exerted undue influence in community groups in Derry, ensuring that members, relatives and friends were given plum jobs. There were widespread claims of nepotism and poor governance. Many who had got into the community sector to help their underfunded and neglected communities felt they were working for proxy Sinn Féin outlets. Many community organizations in republican areas in Derry had always had Sinn Féin links, but something had shifted in the way the party was viewed locally. It became clear to some that those who were affiliated with Sinn Féin were favoured for positions and funding, while those who took issue with the party felt undermined or cast out.

The Sinn Féin review of the situation in Derry canvassed activists past and present, including those who worked in community groups. It did not seem that there was any saving grace. The same deeply unpopular names were repeated over and over.

It was decided there was only one chance to save the party in the city. Everyone had to go: not just the entire Comhairle Ceantair, but also the party's two Foyle MLAs, Martina Anderson and Karen Mullan.

I broke the story – or a version of it – in the *Irish Examiner* on 27 April 2021, after an odd intervention.

I was working at home when I got a message from a distant acquaintance in Derry. This man owns a successful business in the city. He messaged me on social media looking for my number, and called me right away when I passed it on.

'Listen, I have a story for you,' he said. 'A wee birdie told me that everyone who runs Derry Sinn Féin has been sacked. Belfast came down and told them they'd run the place into the ground and they had to go.'

The entire situation was strange. I had never even spoken to this person on the phone before. He wasn't a member of Sinn Féin. It seemed unlikely that, if the entire leadership of the party in Derry had been sacked, I would be hearing about it first from him.

I probed further but he said that was all he knew. Next, I phoned one of my best Sinn Féin contacts: a former IRA prisoner, now an elected representative and adjacent to the Army Council.

When I asked him outright if the story was true, he lied. He was bad at it.

'Naw, never heard that,' he said gingerly.

'You're lying, aren't you?' I replied. He heard everything, even the untrue rumours.

'Okay, aye, but no one is supposed to know, so you didn't hear it from me.'

I poked and prodded at him for another ten minutes before I managed to get enough out of him to start calling other representatives.

The day moved so fast thereafter, I did not stop to think about why or how I had gotten the story. The story was all I wanted. The *Irish Examiner* broke the exclusive: the entire Comhairle Ceantair in Derry had been removed.

The next day, the Sinn Féin source phoned back: 'Hi, you've missed a bit. Martina and Karen are gone too.'

The entire day was spent on the phone. The Sinn Féin

press office refused to confirm. The press officers refused my calls, as did Mullan and Anderson and every other member of the Comhairle Ceantair. Eventually I managed to get a number of Derry Sinn Féin members to confirm it off the record.

I approached the paper's political editor, Daniel McConnell, an energetic Dub with a tough exterior who was like a dog with a bone when he got a good story.

I explained that Sinn Féin wouldn't confirm but I had at least five elected representatives confirming, as well as someone close to Anderson.

He trusted me and *Irish Examiner* released the story at 18:10 on Wednesday, 28 April 2021. It was seismic. Martina Anderson, a bomber who had given everything to the republican cause, had been sacked by her own.

I spent the next few hours waiting for Sinn Féin to deny the story. For the press office to come out and say it was nonsense. The denial never came, but I wouldn't sleep until they confirmed the story was true.

A senior source in the party said that the party's operation in Derry would need 'a generation' to recover.

'This has been coming a long time. There's a clique that has run the place into the ground effectively,' they said.

'There are people on the leadership who aren't responsible, and that's unfair if they've been forced to stand aside, but it needed a clear-out in order to bring about the change that's needed to build up confidence and trust locally, and it'll take a considerable amount of time.

'There was a core group making decisions about controlling power as opposed to progressive politics.'

The next morning on BBC Radio, Sinn Féin finance minister Conor Murphy confirmed the truth of the story I'd written.

He said:

What it means is that the party, like any sensible party, in a specific geographical area where you are having poorer election results and that's in contrast to better results right across Ireland then has to recognise that there are issues there that the party needs to examine internally, in terms of the local organisation, and see how they can put together solutions to fix those and to get ready for upcoming elections.

That's simply what the party is doing. It's an internal matter.

I spent the following days calling sources to follow up on the story; Martina Anderson was the main target of people's ire. Her behaviour was described as 'erratic' and 'embarrassing'. Her statements in the European Parliament had become more and more outlandish. In 2017, rejecting any kind of border in Ireland after Brexit, she directly addressed Prime Minister Theresa May: 'Theresa, your notion of a border, hard and soft, stick it where the sun doesn't shine 'cos you're not putting it in Ireland.'

After the abolition of the UK's seats in Brussels in early 2020, Raymond McCartney resigned his seat as MLA for Foyle and Anderson was co-opted into the seat.

In August, during ongoing negotiations over a 'Troubles pension' which would see compensation paid to those wounded in the conflict, Anderson tweeted:

£800 MILLION 4 Pensions mainly for those who fought Britain's dirty war in Ireland
£800 MILLION mainly 4 those involved in Collusion

£800 MILLION mainly 4 British Troops like Paras who
murdered ppl on Bloody Sunday & Ballymurphy
£800 MILLION mainly to discriminate, criminalise and
exclude

The post caused uproar. Innocent people who had been
maimed in the conflict were furious. Political opponents
called for the PSNI to investigate the tweet. The Sinn Féin
leadership went into overdrive.

In a short and frank phone call, Michelle O'Neill told
Anderson to delete her tweet immediately. One MLA told
me that the tension between O'Neill and Anderson had by
this point turned into a power struggle. McDonald spoke to
Anderson too.

Anderson deleted the tweet and apologized.

In the aftermath of the Derry upheaval, the briefing against
Martina Anderson by Sinn Féin colleagues was fierce. Anderson's misadventures took place largely in Brussels and Stormont,
and while her family was clearly very influential in Derry, no
single figure could be held responsible for Sinn Féin's dysfunc-
tion there. But the briefing against her following the sacking of
the Comhairle Ceantair was characteristic of a party that has an
instinct for creating simple narratives out of complex failures.

It was also suggested to me that it was not an accident
that the story of the Derry upheavals had fallen into my
lap through an unlikely source, who was not even a party
member, as part of a complex strategy to make it harder
for Anderson to resist pressure to resign her Stormont
seat.

I don't know if it's true or not. With Sinn Féin, the line
between cock-up and conspiracy can be a very fine one.

*

In a drab meeting room in the Sinn Féin office in the Rath Mór shopping centre in Derry, a young woman sat down across from Michelle O'Neill. It was July 2021.

The young Derry woman who had come to see the Deputy First Minister had been working for Sinn Féin for less than a year when she was asked if she would consider putting herself forward for the selection convention to replace Martina Anderson and Karen Mullan as MLAs. She had no real interest in the role. She had no public-facing experience, no real knowledge of how Stormont worked on a day-to-day basis. She felt pressured into going to the meeting, and was keen not to appear rude. She had canvassed her friends and family about the offer. Almost all of them said it was her decision and they would support her but advised her against it.

O'Neill warned her that if she went forward, her appearance, background and personal life would all come under heavy scrutiny. She said that the abuse would be constant, that she would have to develop a thick skin and that the job was not for everyone.

The others in the room, all male, promised her she'd be looked after in Stormont. They said she would not be burdened with the ongoing local issues: the party would see they were sorted out. This was a new Sinn Féin, they said; don't pay attention to the media or anyone else who said that the party was run by anyone other than those paid to do so.

She was starting to feel stifled when the door opened. Gerry Adams, wearing jeans and with his hair down to his shoulders, walked in and greeted her by name. The Covid pandemic was still a worry, and he produced his elbow so they could avoid spreading germs. She sat quietly, surprised. Those who invited her had promised a no-pressure chat about what the job would entail. Now she found herself in front of Gerry Adams and Michelle O'Neill, and she knew she didn't want the job.

She wrapped up the conversation and left the office. She would phone them later and tell them no.

There were numerous meetings like this after the removal of Martina Anderson and Karen Mullan: dozens of people were canvassed to replace the MLAs. The common notable characteristic among all of them was their lack of a criminal record or connection to the IRA. Those entrusted with finding candidates wanted to shed the image of a nepotistic organization that was stuck in the paramilitary past. Fresh faces, hard workers, and good public speakers were what was needed.

At the selection convention held at Derry's Everglades Hotel in September, Ciara Ferguson, a community worker from nearby Strabane, and Padraig Delargy, a schoolteacher, were selected to assume the vacant Stormont seats. Anderson and Mullan did not attend the convention. Nor did former MLA Raymond McCartney, or any of the removed Comhairle Ceantair.

The constitution of Sinn Féin specifies that a prospective candidate has to have been a member of the party for at least six months before selection. Ciara Ferguson did not meet this criterion, but was chosen anyway. The party did not respond to my query about this.

At the front row of the convention sat Gerry Kelly. He sat with his arms folded and spoke little to anyone.

'We all got it,' one member present told me. 'Gerry was there to represent the leadership, to say, "Anyone who has a fucking problem with this can come to me", and no one did. No one would.'

13. Structure and Chaos

In 2013, Sinn Féin organized a conference aimed at reaching out to unionists, loyalists and those whose family members had been murdered by the IRA. The conference, to be held in June at the Europa Hotel in Belfast, was titled 'A City of Equals on an Island of Equals'.

'It was billed as a place for unionists to come speak to Sinn Féin, as opposed to Sinn Féin explaining that the union is rather stupid and they really should support a United Ireland,' one organizer told me.

The keynote addresses were to be given by Martin McGuinness and a scholar specializing in 'conflict transformation', Peter Shirlow. The person chosen to chair the conference was Brian Rowan, whose family had been intimidated out of their home by loyalists and who had gone on to a distinguished career as BBC Northern Ireland's security correspondent. Over the decades, Rowan had watched McGuinness morph from one of the most feared men in the North into the Sinn Féin representative most willing to extend a hand of friendship to the unionist community. In his work with the BBC, Rowan had had any number of rows and arguments with Sinn Féin members, but he had remained on cordial terms with the party leadership and backroom team in the years since his retirement.

Among those who were to attend the conference were Alan McBride, whose wife and father-in-law were killed in the IRA's notorious Shankill Road bombing of 1993; the

Reverend Harold Good, former Moderator of the Method-
ist Church; and the Chief Constable of the PSNI, Matt
Baggott.

For Sinn Féin, there was just one problem. 'Gerry was
peeved as fuck that Martin was speaking as keynote,' the
organizer told me. It had been made clear to Adams that he
could not front any effort to speak to unionist people or
victims of IRA violence. Although it was never directly said
to the Sinn Féin president, there was a sense that because
McGuinness had admitted to his IRA membership and to
some of his crimes, he was capable of making – and of being
seen to make – an honest attempt at reconciliation. No victim
of IRA violence would be prepared to listen to anything
Adams had to say on the matter, given that he couldn't even
be honest about being a member of the IRA, let alone his
role in causing death and destruction.

It was put to McGuinness that it would be tough to drum
up any press attention to the event, which was likely to be
seen as self-promotional for Sinn Féin. Party staff told
McGuinness that he would have to say something new at the
conference: the same old platitudes wouldn't cut it. They
knew whatever McGuinness said would have to be about the
legacy of the violence.

One speechwriter and advisor said: 'What would you think
about you saying; "I don't think anyone should go to prison
for any conflict-related offences, whether it's a Brit, or army
[IRA]"?'

McGuinness replied: 'Well, that is my position. Write the
speech.'

The speech was written. The speechwriter told me the
draft noted the tragedy of violence on all sides and the imprint
it had left on the North. The call for a general amnesty would

put all victims on a level footing. More importantly, perhaps, it would put IRA violence on an equal footing with that carried out by state forces.

Along with families of the slain and victims' groups, Sinn Féin had long pushed for prosecutions of British soldiers, intelligence operatives and RUC men who had committed crimes during the Troubles. In practice, though, this approach had borne minimal fruit.

At the time, only four British military personnel had been convicted of murder for their duties during the Troubles. Families trying to fight for justice for those killed at the hands of British forces had run up against long delays and legal obstruction. The speech McGuinness planned to make would involve the abandonment of those campaigns in favour of an amnesty that would also, of course, apply to paramilitaries.

Sinn Féin communications officers told Rowan that he should be aware that McGuinness had an important speech to make.

Four days before the event, as the press release was sent out to the newsrooms, Adams hastily called a meeting. The usual squad were in attendance: McGuinness, Ted Howell, Duckser Lynch, Leo Green and Jackie McMullan.

Adams, now a TD for Louth, had travelled north in a fluster.

He told the group in no uncertain terms that McGuinness could not call for an amnesty.

'It's not our position,' he said. 'Now we will get crucified for this. We'll be crucified by the victims' groups.'

Green replied: 'We tell them [the victims' groups] what to say anyway, and Jackie works with victims' groups for people who have been injured in the past and have teased that out, and they're not totally against it.'

Adams replied: 'That's not how our people think.'

A person who was at the meeting remembers thinking, 'Who the fuck are "our people"? I kept hearing everyone saying that. It was like these people had no free thought, we gave them no credit, as if they couldn't make up their own minds.'

Éamon de Valera once said: 'Whenever I wanted to know what the Irish people wanted, I had only to examine my own heart and it told me straight off what the Irish people wanted.'

This, according to past and present party members who have spoken to me, is how Gerry Adams feels about Irish republicans. He believes he knows intuitively what they will and won't stomach, and his view in 2013 was that they would not stomach letting British soldiers and loyalist gangs off the hook for the chaos they had caused to their friends, family and neighbours.

'Take that paragraph out,' Adams said curtly. McGuinness' eyes darted from Adams to the advisor who had written the speech, who sighed loudly. The order had come down. The paragraph was out.

The conference went ahead with little fanfare. The news stories from the day focused mainly on the loyalist protests outside.

When the conference came to an end, Rowan approached the senior Sinn Féin man who had written McGuinness's address.

'I thought Martin was gonna make a big speech?'

'He was.'

Steering the party in a new policy direction, without going through party channels, was very much not the done thing in Sinn Féin, as McGuinness knew well. Adams was an exceptionally powerful party leader for a long time, but his power did not derive entirely from his personal stature within the party. It was buttressed by structures that appear byzantine and democratic, but that are intended to centralize power.

Local Sinn Féin groups are organized into cumainn, usually named after slain IRA volunteers or other Irish historical figures. The cumainn are overseen by a more senior local group, known as the Comhairle Ceantair. Local cumainn discuss community issues and their thoughts on wider Sinn Féin policy and pass these on to their Comhairle Ceantair.

The local Comhairle Ceantair groups report to a larger group known as a cuige, who represent entire regions.

Motions to change policy can originate with a cumann, Comhairle Ceantair or cuige. Such motions must be submitted to the Ard Comhairle.

The Ard Comhairle is made up of around fifty people, who according to some within Sinn Féin discuss 'mundane' matters and put meat on the bones of policy.

Six men and six women are elected from the floor of the Ard Fheis to the group; the rest are selected by leadership. Groupings within the party will have delegates selected to attend the Ard Fheis (national conference) from each cuige: groups such as TDs and councillors and different local organizers will all be represented.

The Ard Fheis conference delegates are the representative body of the everyday members.

Cuige representatives in particular are not always in line with leadership, members say, although 'Six County' representatives always are.

When issues are considered at the Ard Fheis, Ard Comhairle

and National Officer Board members sit at the head of many tables, representing the party leadership.

Another thread of power within Sinn Féin consists of the party organizers. Until 2011, these were volunteer positions: a member of the local Comhairle Ceantair would be elected by the local group into that representative position. Now organizers are selected by the party in each constituency, and they are paid. Their job, as one local organizer put it, is to 'do a lot of the donkey work': attracting new members, scouting for potential candidates and ensuring head office is kept aware of any local issues which could create difficulties.

Members say this change weakens the Comhairle Ceantair, because the local organization is now more dependent on a paid organizer appointed centrally.

A review of the policy written by a local organizer from 2017 notes:

> An unforeseen consequence of their work is that the Comhairle Ceantair has weakened significantly.
>
> Instead of being responsible to the Comhairle Ceantair the Organisers have taken on the role of directing the actions of the Comhairle Ceantair. They hold significant power without democratic overview, which in a minority of cases can be used in favour of certain individuals or policies. They are also seen as management enforcers.

One former TD recalls that when Dublin West TD Eoin Ó Broin ran against Dawn Doyle for the position of party general secretary at the Ard Fheis in 2018, their local paid organizer told the members to vote for Dawn Doyle.

'So, what you had was a centralized decision being spread

right around the country to a paid kind of civil service within the organization that this is the decision that leadership wanted. It's not democratic at all,' the former TD said.

The National Officer Board is the most powerful grouping within Sinn Féin. The board is elected by the delegates at the Ard Fheis and 'meets monthly with responsibility for national political co-ordination, strategic planning and oversight and accountability', according to Sinn Féin.

The Ard Comhairle is ostensibly the most powerful grouping, and meets once a month, but in practice the National Officer Board has more clout.

The Coiste Seasta meets fortnightly and is responsible for the day-to-day business of the party between Ard Comhairle meetings. All internal departments are accountable to the Ard Comhairle through the Coiste Seasta.

As of the summer of 2023, the National Officer Board consisted of:

President: Mary Lou McDonald
Vice-president: Michelle O'Neill
General secretary: Ken O'Connell
Chairperson: Declan Kearney
Treasurers: Pearse Doherty and Conor Murphy

At local level, the Comhairle Ceantair officer board of local groups meet in advance of the cumann meeting to discuss policy implementation for their local area and usually dictate this to the members.

As we have seen, senior former IRA figures continue to be consulted informally about party policy. They are no longer referred to as the Army Council. Their influence has gradually diminished over time, but remains significant.

'We don't sit around talking about policies or legislation,' one senior IRA figure told me, 'but we're consulted and kept in the know for certain things around political strategy.'

Sometimes, the consultation is not so informal. During the official inquiry into the cash-for-ash scandal, it emerged that in 2017 the Sinn Féin minister for finance at Stormont, Máirtín Ó Muilleoir, had sent an email seeking the blessing of Ted Howell – a former IRA man and Gerry Adams's closest political confidant – for the implementation of a plan to reduce the cost of the RHI scheme.

For many of the older members of Sinn Féin, such consultations are how things have always been done. For newer staff, it's an uncomfortable reality. It's rarely discussed openly, but it is how the party operates, whether they like it or not.

The party's byzantine structures and systems create an impression of internal democracy and grass-roots empowerment. In reality, Sinn Féin is a radically top-down party. It is unheard of for a policy change to be driven by the grass roots. Loose talk and deviations from policy are not tolerated.

A former independent politician who joined Sinn Féin in the early 2000s and served as a councillor for the party gave me an insight into how the party operates.

'I realized afterwards that probably the only reason they wanted me to join was it neutralized me as a threat to the party dominance,' the former councillor told me, 'and it was all downhill from there.'

'It was fucking mental. I only lasted a couple of years.'

He told me that the party targeted their own people that they didn't want in certain positions and 'went after them', undermining their abilities and intimidating them. Known local IRA men would attend Comhairle Ceantair meetings, sitting at the back of the hall and not speaking.

'They would never really say anything. The atmosphere was fucking brutal.'

In this area where this councillor worked, the CO of the local branch of the IRA was on the Comhairle Ceantair.

'That information was always coming in, it was very intertwined. I really wouldn't have a problem with that though to be honest – who runs Fianna Fáil? At least we know who the Shinners are.

'The way that they do their business, that's the problem I would have with it. When you sign up for Sinn Féin, you know the IRA are involved. We took orders from the NOB [National Officer Board], and they were getting orders from wherever, you didn't ask.'

When this councillor decided he had had enough, he called a meeting and read out a statement in which he listed the litany of issues he had with the party. The local leadership listened, and then called for an adjournment. They told the representative they would solve his problems. The local chairman tore up the written statement the representative had submitted and dumped it in a wastepaper bin.

A few months later, in 2005, the councillor was approached by a local IRA member and asked to join the army – this at a time when the IRA was close to completing the decommissioning of its weapons.

'I knew then that I was fucked,' he told me. 'If I was in the army, then I wouldn't leave the party. And plus, I could have been ordered not to do anything. I knew this was it.'

In order to sort out the local issues, which included the councillor's continued complaints of being undermined and ignored, a number of meetings were to be held in the area.

The first meeting was with the complaining councillor. He sat across the table from the local chairman and the head of the cuige. The chairman began unfolding the document that had been torn to pieces and thrown in the bin. Apparently, someone had retrieved it and sellotaped it back together in order to quiz him on his allegations. It was laid out on the table in front of him.

'I remember thinking: these people are fucking mad. I felt like there's no point in continuing on with this. They're mad enough to pick things out of the bin, they're fucking crazy.'

Until 2019, the party staff had as much clout within the party as elected representatives. Within the party, this could be framed as democratic: valuing the views of all party members, whether or not they held elective office. But in relation to the public, it could seem undemocratic. Elected officials put themselves before the public and receive a mandate from voters. In other parties, this gives elected officials the biggest voice. That was not the case in Sinn Féin.

In the Dáil there was no weekly parliamentary party meeting of elected representatives, as is regular for other parties. There was instead a team meeting. An elected TD representing 10,000 people had the same input as a staff member who did not represent anyone.

A number of TDs and senators, past and present, have confirmed that they saw the parliamentary party as a focus group for the leadership. Elected representatives never make a decision on anything, but feed into a wider debate.

All of that changed, rather dramatically, as a result of an electoral disaster.

In the 2019 local elections in the Republic, Sinn Féin lost nearly half its seats on local councils, taking under 10 per cent of the first-preference vote. Two of the three Sinn Féin MEPs – Lynn Boylan in Dublin and Liadh Ní Riada in

Ireland South – also lost their seats. Only Monaghan's Matt Carthy survived, with a much-reduced vote.

Party members and representatives were furious.

McDonald said at the time that 'We'll dust ourselves down' and that Sinn Féin 'aren't cry-babies'; later, she revealed she was 'past crying' by the time the counting was done.

This was Sinn Féin's second election campaign since McDonald had become president of Sinn Féin. The first, the presidential election in 2018, had gone badly. This one had been a complete fiasco.

A review found defects in the party's approach to canvassing. Sinn Féin had also underestimated the strength of locally based independent candidates who were identified as champions for their respective areas. Party branding made very little difference: voters opted for people who they identified as fighting for their part of the constituency. This was especially true in the cities, where the Sinn Féin vote plummeted.

The review also concluded that the party had become too negative. Many felt that Sinn Féin had been sucked into a dynamic of 'giving out all the time', as one TD put it. 'We were highlighting the problems all the time. We were criticizing the government all the time, and that's fine. But at the macro level, at the front door level, people just want stuff fixed.'

A message went back to leadership that people who were frustrated and fed up with the government didn't feel that was any reason to come out and vote for Sinn Féin: they hadn't given them any positive alternative.

In the aftermath, Dublin Mid-West TD and housing spokesperson Eoin Ó Broin said:

We need to have a very quick but very honest review of what happened. We are going to have to make changes in how the party does its business, how we communicate, how we campaign, how we work in the Oireachtas.

One of the things we were hearing on some of the doors was criticism that we are a bit too negative as a party. The people we are trying to represent want to hear constructive solutions.

Between now and General Election, [what] our target voters will want to hear is how we are going to do things differently.

The first parliamentary party meeting in the aftermath was tense.

'People were really upset,' one staffer told me. 'And it really sank in for everyone. [. . .] Everyone knew their seat was in danger in the general election the year after. They were in danger, the staff that they hire were in danger, the party was in danger, everything that they'd worked towards.

'Staff ourselves, we were making our exit plans and all this happened over a weekend.'

McDonald was at pains to assert that she was open to hearing people's grievances.

'People wanted to know what the hell happened and why didn't we catch this and what are we going to do now? That's what was kind of the main crux of it, Mary Lou was very calm but everyone was rattled,' the staffer told me.

At the top table sat McDonald, Brian Keane, Ken O'Connell and the senior press officer, Joe Lynch. People had things to get off their chest.

Eoin Ó Broin and Louise O'Reilly had a lot to say.

'There's a few people who were trying to influence things and there are a few people that would just want to be heard,' a staffer said, mentioning Mayo TD Rose Conway-Walsh as being in the latter category.

O'Reilly, a confident operator who often spoke her mind, took the party to task but was constructive in her contribution.

Carlow-Kilkenny TD Kathleen Funchion was very upset, because the Sinn Féin representation on her council had been almost wiped out.

The 2019 local elections were 'like a bomb went off', one Leinster House staffer recalled. 'It was an absolute catastrophe in terms of just the mood in those offices and in those corridors.'

'Following that, there was a noticeable shift that the party did not really want to hear more from staff and then staff kicked off a bit and it was clear the leadership had gotten very sick of us and there were a few tense meetings,' the staffer said.

Brian Keane, Pearse Doherty, Ken O'Connell and Mary Lou McDonald had all been drafted in to tell staff that their status was about to change. Since the changes that followed the 2019 local elections, there is not even a meeting for staff to get together and discuss matters of policy or current affairs as a group.

Every Wednesday evening, Sinn Féin TDs meet McDonald, Doyle and O'Connell in the Sinn Féin party room in Leinster House, and staff are kept in the background. Staff refer to the process as leadership keeping it 'tight at the top'.

No political party in Ireland works harder to control its members, and to centralize power, than Sinn Féin. But political parties are made up of human beings, and, as we have seen, human beings can be hard to control. In the North, there is of course another factor: the legacies of decades of violence and trauma.

In 2017, Peter Sheridan, who had been the most senior Catholic within the PSNI as Assistant Chief Constable, was in his office in his new role as the chief executive of Co-operation Ireland.

Just before the Christmas holiday, Sheridan left his office and found a senior IRA man sitting in reception.

Sheridan did a double take. There had been numerous plots to kill Sheridan as a senior Catholic in the police, but those days were over. He had come toe to toe with killers before, but had no idea why one had turned up in his new civilian place of work.

Sheridan brought the IRA man into his office and closed the door. The man was sheepish and stumbled over his words, but eventually managed to explain to Sheridan that he wanted to talk to the widow of a police officer he had murdered. He hoped Sheridan could help put them in touch.

Sheridan told the man that the murder had taken place before he had even joined the police, so he didn't know the woman or if she was even alive.

The IRA man was persistent. He told Sheridan he wanted to apologize. Sheridan was frank: he said his worry was that they would re-traumatize this now elderly woman.

Sheridan eventually found the woman through contacts within the PSNI, and reached out. The woman said she would like to meet her husband's murderer, but she did not want him in her house and she did not want her family to find out. She told Sheridan that she would not be telling her nearest and dearest.

Sheridan secured a location for the pair to meet. On a Monday morning, he accompanied the IRA man there.

When they got into the room, he said he would leave, so that the pair could speak privately. But the woman asked Sheridan to stay.

The first two hours were mostly made up of the IRA man explaining his background, where he grew up and how he got involved with paramilitaries. The man was at pains to explain that he was not trying to justify his life choices; he just wanted her to understand where he came from.

Towards the end of the meeting, the man said: 'Peter, would you mind giving us a couple of minutes?'

The woman nodded. The former police officer left the room.

In their time alone, the man told others afterwards, he wept as he said he did not expect her forgiveness and asked the woman if he could give her a hug. She wept as she said yes. The pair leaned across in their chairs and embraced each other.

The IRA man had not initially set out to approach Sheridan to set up the meeting. He was an active member of Sinn Féin, and he told the party he wished to make contact with the widow of the man he'd killed. The party figures he approached told him they would come back with an answer when they had discussed it with their superiors. The answer eventually came: no.

One senior party member told me that the ruling was consistent with Sinn Féin's general approach to such matters. A former IRA volunteer may have committed an act, but 'It's not your memory to know, irrespective of how this affects people. The movement has made a decision there'll be a story told around this. And it's not your story.'

14. 'Something is going on'

Following the disasters of 2019, Sinn Féin created a Strategic Policy Unit to make more systematic use of polling data and local research.

'Instead of basing your analysis on who Mary saw at a funeral, or what your neighbour told you in the supermarket, which is literally what we were doing, mad stuff, we would be using data to inform our analysis of public feeling,' a senior TD told me.

McDonald, the TD says, 'has to take credit for what happened after 2019. She personally drove the turnaround. As leader the buck stops with her, when it worked and [when] it didn't.'

One early finding of the party's new analysis was that voters felt the party 'had moved away from [a] united Ireland. We were suffering because our message was falling on deaf ears, they didn't really hear us. In terms of how we delivered our message, that changed. We were blessed too. We were very lucky, we had Pearse [Doherty] and Mary Lou, formidable communicators, so we pushed them.'

Born in Glasgow, before moving to the Gaeltacht in Donegal, Pearse Doherty was spotted as a rising star from his early days in Sinn Féin, when he was a founder of Sinn Féin Republican Youth after joining the party in 1996.

Doherty was elected to the Dáil in November 2010, when he won a by-election in Donegal South-West with 13,719 first-preference votes, 6,000 more than the Fianna Fáil candidate. Since then he has moved swiftly through the ranks, becoming the party's finance spokesperson and, in 2018, deputy leader of the party in the Republic. His performances holding officials to account during committee appearances and fiery exchanges in the Dáil have earned him a reputation for being fierce, though outside Leinster House he is reserved.

If McDonald and Doherty have been the two most senior Sinn Féin figures in Leinster House for the past several years, the person most often described by party members as deserving of credit for Sinn Féin's rise in popularity after 2019 is Eoin Ó Broin.

Born in 1972, Ó Broin grew up in the middle-class south Dublin suburb of Cabinteely and was educated at one of the country's most prestigious private schools, Blackrock College. He has a degree in cultural studies from the University of East London and a master's in Irish politics from Queen's University Belfast.

He was national organizer of Ógra Shinn Féin, and was elected to Belfast City Council in 2001, serving until 2004. He is considered with Sinn Féin to be the party's ticket to government in the Republic because of his specialist knowledge and passion for housing policy, at a time when an escalating housing crisis has become the defining issue in Irish politics.

The first signal that things were looking up for Sinn Féin electorally was a by-election in Ó Broin's constituency, Dublin Mid-West, in November 2019. Sinn Féin's Mark Ward won the by-election, giving the party two TDs in the constituency. The party also performed respectably in the Cork North-Central by-election the same day, with its candidate, Thomas Gould, coming second. In retrospect, the

November 2019 by-elections look like a turning point, but at the time the party's confidence was still so damaged that it was not seen in those terms. And the party's position in national polls remained modest.

On 14 January 2020, the Taoiseach, Leo Varadkar, called an election to be held on 8 February. The day after the election was called, Ó Broin was canvassing in Palmerstown, west Dublin. The group handing out leaflets noticed straightaway there was an uptick in support.

Ó Broin phoned Sinn Féin head office immediately after the canvass and said: 'Something is going on.'

As soon as the election was called, Sinn Féin started to perform better in opinion polls. On 18 January, IPSOS, which had had the party on 14 per cent in October, showed Sinn Féin on 21 per cent – only narrowly behind Fianna Fáil and Fine Gael. A week before the election, the same pollster published a survey that would prove eerily accurate, showing Sinn Féin on 25 per cent, narrowly in front.

Sinn Féin's performance on election day was historic. Having never finished higher than third in an Irish general election, the party won 24.5 per cent of the first-preference vote, making it the most popular party in the Republic by that metric, ahead of Fianna Fáil (22.1 per cent) and Fine Gael (20.8 per cent). Because Sinn Féin had not anticipated its dramatic rise in support, and because of difficulties in the candidate selection pipeline, the party had not stood enough candidates to reap the full benefit of its vote. In a number of constituencies, Sinn Féin's lone candidate doubled the quota needed for election. As a consequence, the party won fewer seats than Fianna Fáil; and with both Fianna Fáil and Fine Gael unwilling to contemplate going into government with Sinn Féin, they had no route to forming a governing coalition.

After extensive wrangling, Fianna Fáil, Fine Gael and the Green Party formed a three-party coalition, and Sinn Féin became the main opposition party. One TD told me they now 'feel lucky' they didn't take power. The events of the coming weeks and months would help explain why.

In the months leading up to the election, Sinn Féin had struggled in a number of constituencies with candidate selection. The issue ran deep in the political pipeline. Sinn Féin expects its councillors to work full-time, unlike the other parties, which treat the role of councillor as a part-time role. Councillors for other parties usually hold another job. Sinn Féin councillors generally don't. This makes it harder for Sinn Féin to recruit suitable candidates for council elections – and that has implications when general elections come around.

The candidates chosen for the 2020 general election were a mixed bag. Martin Browne was selected to stand in Tipperary, and went on to win a seat. It later emerged that when Browne was a councillor he had suggested on Facebook that a hologram of a plane was used to fake the attacks on 11 September 2001. In another post from 2014, he shared a link to a story from *Russia Today* in which the late Cuban president Fidel Castro was quoted comparing NATO to the Nazi SS, and criticizing the US and Israel for creating ISIS. Mr Browne wrote: 'He may not be wrong.'

Patricia Ryan, a candidate for Kildare South, went on holiday with her family during the election campaign. It didn't stop her getting elected.

Following a messy selection process in Clare, Sinn Féin's

candidate there was Violet-Anne Wynne. In the 2019 local elections, Wynne had secured just 4.2 per cent of the vote in Kilrush, finishing eighth of nine candidates. Nine months later, the people of Clare chose her to serve in Dáil Éireann. Wynne's rise was amongst the clearest indications of the transformation of the Sinn Féin brand.

Speaking to the *Clare Echo* after she was elected, Wynne spoke about why she had persisted with her political career: 'I have been pushed by anger towards my own circumstances, just feeling hardship every day that I decided to put myself forward and I wasn't going to change my mind on that most definitely but I had no idea I was going to actually be the candidate in this election and I had no idea that it was going to transpire to this kind of result.'

At one point during the candidate selection process, Wynne told me, she had been asked to remove herself from the nomination because the cumann 'had changed their mind'.

'I refused,' she said, 'and it got worse from there.'

When she was elected, she says, a local party member told her: 'You're head office's problem now.'

At the time of her election, Wynne was thirty-two years old, receiving social welfare, and raising five young children with her partner. The couple had moved from Dublin to Kilrush in 2011, and lived in social housing provided by the agency Rural Resettlement Ireland.

Within a week of the general election, it emerged that Rural Resettlement Ireland (RRI) had secured a judgment against Wynne and her partner in 2016 in the sum of €12,126, representing three years' arrears owed on a social house. As of Wynne's election to the Dáil in February 2020, the sum had not been repaid. Wynne claimed the rent had gone unpaid owing to a dispute over leaking pipes and to her partner's illness, which kept him out of work.

Because Rural Resettlement Ireland had ceased operating by the time the story broke, Wynne was called up by party headquarters and told she would have to make a donation to charity in the amount of the rent arrears owing. She didn't have the money, so the party gave Wynne a loan.

Then the Covid pandemic struck. With her children unable to attend school, Wynne's attendance in Dáil Éireann fell short of the 120-day minimum required to claim the full Oireachtas travel and accommodation allowance. When she had to repay part of the allowance, her loan repayments to Sinn Féin stopped, and the party noticed.

Wynne told me that Sinn Féin's finance officer, Des Mackin, called her, saying that because she wasn't making repayments at that point, the party was going to have to write the loan off as a donation. He also suggested, she claimed, that she might be 'unseated' because she had not declared the donation.

Wynne resumed making small repayments immediately, terrified she would be humiliated in the press again, and that she would lose her seat.

On her first day in Leinster House, the *Irish Independent* reported that Wynne had criticised the HPV vaccine in August 2017. Wynne said:

> Parents that have spoken out with concern are not scaremongering but are speaking out with the experiences they have witnessed suffered by their daughters. The fact is the truth hurts.
>
> It does have side-effects and I think people should be aware and there are many families out there not being heard.
> [. . .]

You like your coffee, right? So the place you usually go to is shut, would the coffee be the same in the other shop? [. . .]

It should be, it is coffee, the same label same ingredients, but there is something different. Just like the vaccines.

Wynne claimed she was not anti-vaccine, but was concerned at how parents of children who had had adverse reactions to the vaccine were accused of spreading misinformation.

She missed the induction for new TDs with the Oireachtas staff due to the overwhelming media attention. She claimed she was 'lectured' on the party policy on vaccines for five minutes with no further follow-up.

It's clear in retrospect that the Sinn Féin leadership had decided that Wynne was to be kept away from the media and the public in the aftermath of the two stories about her that broke after the election. They assigned her staff who were given strict instructions to keep a lid on her. One was moved from Limerick TD Maurice Quinlivan's office. Wynne told me that she was not allowed to interview candidates.

In Leinster House, Wynne says, she was told by one of her staff she should 'only aim for one speaking slot per week'.

'I was being told to stay at home, was being told what questions I'd be asking, wasn't being proposed for anything.' Things weren't much better back home. Wynne says she was not invited to events in her constituency, was not kept informed of council matters, and was undermined by local members, who spoke about her disparagingly.

'I almost feel like they were trying to almost mentally break me down,' she said.

'It was as if I was being punished, it was actually said to me, "Well, this is what you wanted, wasn't it? You wanted to be the candidate. So you're getting what you're asked for.'''

Things were about to get worse: Wynne found out she was pregnant. She told me that she sought support from the party, to allow her to work more from home during her pregnancy, but did not receive it.

A party spokesperson denied this, telling me that 'significant supports, mentoring and training was put in place to assist Violet-Anne and her staff, including full support measures to support her during her maternity leave'.

Wynne announced her resignation from Sinn Féin in February 2022. She alleged she had been the victim of a campaign of 'psychological warfare'.

She added: 'I learned very fast that the party do not take kindly to autonomy and those who do not follow their plans.'

Wynne's sad story reflects the strange duality of Sinn Féin, between the leadership's tight control of the party's direction and the climate of disorganization and conflict that often prevails at constituency level. It also reflects the party's difficulties with candidate recruitment, vetting and selection – problems that were dragged into unforgiving light when apparent no-hoper candidates ended up in Leinster House.

'I have no doubt some people were probably assholes to [Wynne],' one TD told me. 'But she wasn't cut out for it and it was obvious to everyone she was overwhelmed. [. . .] What happened was she was out of her depth. She's not a bad person, but we couldn't save her from drowning.'

Sinn Féin has had a remarkably good election. It has also been badly caught out: completely failing to anticipate its own popularity and thus missing out on a chance to lead a government. The leadership were determined that they would not make the same mistake again, and got to work right away preparing the ground for the next election. Candidate selection protocols would be put in place and there would be a focus on diversity.

Former TDs Jonathan O'Brien and Martin Ferris were tasked with 'shaking up' constituencies. The next general election in the Republic will see Sinn Féin operate a 40 per cent quota for female candidates. Three areas that failed to elect a TD for Sinn Féin in 2020 have been designated as female-only: Limerick County, Cork North-West and Cork South-West.

In March 2021, Limerick's Séighin Ó Ceallaigh, the Sinn Féin candidate for the county in 2020, who narrowly missed taking the third seat in the constituency, was told he would not be selected for the next election.

When I put it to a Sinn Féin press officer that Ó Ceallaigh felt shafted, I was urged to google his background. In 2019, as a councillor in his area, Ó Ceallaigh objected to the theme of a St Patrick's Day parade because it centred on the anniversary of the first man on the moon, something he claims is 'fake news', describing the moon landing itself as 'much-disputed'. Ó Ceallaigh went on to say that he would prefer to see the funding allocated to events commemorating the 100th anniversary of the Limerick Soviet, as the moon landing had nothing to do with Limerick.

Sinn Féin was keen to distance itself from such views, but the problem remained: how to assemble a slate of candidates commensurate with the party's electoral strength? In 2022, I spoke to one person involved in Sinn Féin candidate selection who lamented the quality of some proposed representatives and quipped: 'Moon landing guy might make the cut at this stage.'

*

In the North, too, something was shifting, and Brexit was an enormous factor. The province voted 56:44 in favour of staying in the EU in the June 2016 referendum, but was forced to leave with the rest of the UK.

In the aftermath of the referendum, Sinn Féin called a leadership meeting. McGuinness asked Stephen McGlade to flesh out a position. McGlade had been a civil servant before being hired by Sinn Féin to work for MLA Conor Murphy. He has a degree in International Relations from Queen's University, and his dissertation was on EU integration.

'I need you to give me something to say, argue for something, not against things,' McGuinness told McGlade. 'I need something in the affirmative.'

Despite its long history of being critical of the EU, the Sinn Féin Brexit policy that emerged was, apart from a few quirks, broadly in keeping with the consensus in Dublin and Brussels. The DUP, meanwhile, having supported Brexit, struggled badly to cope with its consequences. When the EU refused to countenance the reintroduction of border infrastructure on the island of Ireland, UK Prime Minister Boris Johnson did the only thing he could plausibly have done, signing up to a Brexit deal that would mean different trading arrangements for Northern Ireland from the rest of the UK. Johnson had promised the DUP he would do no such thing; now they had been punished for being foolish enough to believe him. DUP leader Arlene Foster was accused of poor judgement, and meanwhile the cash-for-ash scandal increasingly centred on what she knew and when she knew it.

With loyalist communities up in arms about the Brexit protocol, the heave against Foster came in April 2021. The chaotic period that followed – in which Edwin Poots, a Young Earth creationist, won the DUP leadership and then resigned within three weeks – suggested a party increasingly out of touch with political realities.

In the Northern Ireland Assembly election of May 2022, Sinn Féin won 29 per cent of the first-preference vote, up 1.1 per cent from 2017. With the DUP's support significantly down, Sinn Féin was now comfortably the most popular party in Northern Ireland, and – with twenty-seven seats (twelve of them held by women) to the DUP's twenty-five – the biggest at Stormont. The ground had shifted in Northern Ireland. The unionists had lost their pre-eminence in a province that, as the BBC's Lewis Goodall put it on election day, 'was literally designed, its borders were designed, so that wouldn't happen'.

Three months before the election, Stormont had collapsed again. The ostensible cause was the DUP's opposition to the Brexit protocol, but it appears that the DUP was also anticipating Sinn Féin's electoral victory. The spectre of a Sinn Féin First Minister was hardly going to encourage the DUP to soften its stance on the protocol and allow devolved government to be restored, and so even following the adjustments and compromises of the Windsor Framework announced in February 2023, the institutions remained in suspension.

Even as Sinn Féin's electoral position in the North grew stronger, even as its positions on non-constitutional issues grew closer to the mainstream of public opinion (while the DUP went in the other direction), the party remained susceptible to the kind of controversies that simply didn't affect other parties.

On 20 June 2021, Bobby Storey died after an unsuccessful lung transplant in a hospital in England. He was sixty-four.

'Big Bobby', as his best friend, Gerry Adams, called him, was beloved in the republican movement. In the research for this book I have been unable to find one former or current representative or staff member with anything negative to say about Storey. He was seen as a gentle giant and a mentor to younger representatives.

At the funeral, Adams said he did not know anyone who knew Storey 'who didn't like him – except for MI5, MI6, the old RUC, the British army, and prison governors'.

The pandemic regulations in place at the time forbade outdoor gatherings of more than thirty people. The regulations appear to have been ignored. Buses were organized from around the North to bring mourners to Belfast for the funeral. One text message sent from a local Sinn Féin group warned members to be in proper dress, with no smoking, no drinking and no gum-chewing. Nearly 1,800 people, dressed in black trousers and suit trousers, white shirts and black ties, lined up along the Andersonstown and Falls roads, decorated in black flags, to give Storey a hero's send-off in republican west Belfast.

Storey's coffin was draped in a tricolour and driven from his home in west Belfast to St Agnes's Church on the Andersonstown Road.

Most funerals involve a single cemetery. Storey's pandemic funeral involved two. Storey's remains were taken to Milltown Cemetery, where Adams made his speech. The body was then taken to Roselawn Cemetery in east Belfast, where it was cremated.

O'Neill, Adams, McDonald, MP Chris Hazzard and Pearse Doherty were all photographed as part of the funeral cortège. Photos show little to no social distancing in the crowds.

The BBC reported that the Requiem Mass in St Agnes's church was attended by about 120 people, including O'Neill. At Milltown cemetery, O'Neill posed for a photograph with a man who had his arm around her shoulders. She subsequently said this incident took place 'in the blink of an eye' and 'shouldn't have happened'.

Immediately after, the party maintained they acted within the guidelines at all times and broke no rules, claiming that the funeral cortège itself had consisted of fewer than thirty people. It didn't make a difference: the public, North and South, was furious.

O'Neill later issued a statement expressing concern for families of those who had died in the pandemic, but continuing to insist that she had done nothing wrong.

McDonald told RTÉ: 'I do understand that looking at the images of very busy pathways in west Belfast and taking all of that in obviously has jolted and has caused some hurt among some of those families, and for that I am very sorry.

'That certainly would never have been my intention, or Michelle's intention, or the intention of the Storey family as they laid Bobby to rest.'

The truth is, Sinn Féin knew exactly what a big republican funeral, attended by all the top party leaders, would look like in the middle of a pandemic that had been dramatically limiting people's lives for over a year. The party's decision to attend the funeral was risk-assessed. They decided it was worth it.

'There was an understanding that we were going to get in bother for it,' one senior figure told me. 'Then disappointment in certain people posing for photographs: that was stupid.'

The decision was not second-guessed afterwards.

'We had to go. We play to the base. We liked Bobby. He was one of the best people in there. So we went. We took the hit. The press ended up annoying people for not letting the family grieve because they kept bringing it up. It was worth the heat.'

Following the announcement in March 2021 that nobody would be prosecuted in relation to the funeral, O'Neill apologized again 'for the hurt that has been caused to so many, including to Bobby Storey's own family, who have been thrust into the headlines at a time of immense grief'.

Sinn Féin's victory in local elections in the North in May 2023 confirmed its position as the largest party in the North. In the South, it is universally expected to top the polls comfortably at the next general election. The party is preparing for government on both sides of the border.

A gap remains between the party's popularity and its political capacity. In the South, Sinn Féin has just eighty-one sitting councillors (of a total of 949): a reminder that as recently as May 2019 the party was strikingly unpopular. It also narrows the candidate selection pool for the general election that is expected in 2024 or, at the latest, early 2025.

'Organizationally, we still have a long way to go,' one senior TD told me. 'A massively important thing is the local elections [in May 2024], to get to as many elected as possible.' The TD said the party was targeting 'over 200' council seats: a huge increase on 2019, but a modest enough goal given the party's national standing. The TD told me that Sinn Féin would prefer the next general election to happen after the May 2024 local elections, so that a larger slate of councillors would be *in situ*.

Since the 2020 general election, Sinn Féin has consistently

polled over 30 per cent in the Republic, comfortably ahead of Fianna Fáil and Fine Gael. The party fully expects to be in government after the next general election, and to a remarkable degree the same is true of the other political parties, the media and the public. In Leinster House, Sinn Féin frontbenchers are meeting trade unions, employer groups and chambers of commerce in preparation for government. They are also meeting secretaries-general of departments and other civil servants to build relationships and gauge who will be a help and who will be a hindrance.

'There's no doubt our mentality is prepared because if you think about how many of us have been around a few years, this is our one big chance at it,' the TD told me. 'But we'll need two years: the country is a mess.'

15. Next, Nigh, Near

In 2014, TheJournal.ie ran a story under the headline 'Another election poster is blocking a traffic light in Dublin'. The poster advertised a Sinn Féin candidate for Dublin City Council. When approached about the poster, a Sinn Féin spokesperson said: 'We're going to get it down immediately.'

The candidate was a young local businessman called Jonathan Dowdall.

Jonathan Dowdall grew up in working-class Ballybough in Dublin's inner city. He founded a successful electrical business, ABCO Electrical, in 2007, when still in his twenties. By the time he stood for Sinn Féin in the 2014 council election, he was married with four children, and drove a white BMW. He lived on the Navan Road in Cabra, where he was a neighbour of Mary Lou McDonald. ABCO sponsored a number of local football teams, as well as Peter Carr, a champion kick-boxer.

Dowdall gave a €1,000 donation to McDonald in 2011. He also purchased tickets for party fundraisers, and was pictured with McDonald and Gerry Adams at one such fundraiser in the Gresham Hotel in 2013.

Thus it was not merely as a successful local businessman but as a Sinn Féin donor that Dowdall joined the party in 2013, and became an area representative that year. He was quickly in the frame as a potential candidate for the North Inner City ward in the May 2014 council elections.

Interestingly, the Social Democrats TD Gary Gannon told me that he was interviewed as a potential Sinn Féin candidate for that same election in North Inner City. Gannon was never a member of the party, but at the time he was interning in the office of Sinn Féin senator – and later TD – David Cullinane as part of a master's degree he was completing. Gannon spoke at length with Brian Keane and Alan Donnelly, but he made it clear that he could not stand by the party's restrictive abortion policy at the time, and there was no second meeting. Gannon would be elected as an independent councillor for North Inner City in the 2014 election, and joined the Social Democrats shortly after the party's formation the following year. Gannon went on to become a respected TD. Dowdall went on to become a notorious criminal and a massive embarrassment for Sinn Féin. If Sinn Féin had been a bit quicker to reform its abortion policy, might things have gone very differently?

The vetting of Jonathan Dowdall as a potential council candidate in 2014 would become an extremely sore point for Sinn Féin in 2022. As we shall see, concerns within the party went well beyond what Sinn Féin has publicly acknowledged. But Dowdall passed muster and was selected as a candidate.

One member of Dowdall's campaign team told me he went missing the day before the election. No one could get a hold of him. Dowdall threatened one of his campaign organizers the morning the votes were cast, paranoid that the organizer was working against him.

Dowdall was elected on the thirteenth count to represent Inner City North on Dublin City Council in May 2014. His running mate, Janice Boylan, topped the poll.

Just four months later, Dowdall resigned from the council, citing health issues.

McDonald made a statement in which she described Dowdall as 'a hard worker who will be missed in his elected role by local constituents' and added:

> It is with much regret that we accept Jonathan's decision to step down. I fully accept his decision and the reasons behind it.
>
> Jonathan is a very popular and respected member of his community and he will be missed in his elected role by me, the local party organisation and by local constituents.
>
> I want to thank Jonathan for all his hard work for the party and for the local community. I wish him, his wife Trish and his family all the best and look forward to working with him in the future.
>
> I would ask to the media to respect Jonathan and his family's privacy at this time.

Just days after the announcement, it emerged that Dowdall had not officially resigned from Dublin City Council, though he had quit Sinn Féin. Dowdall said he had left Sinn Féin after a 'small element' in the party in his area had spread negative rumours about him.

Speaking to TheJournal.ie, the 34-year-old was mostly very positive about the party: 'Sinn Féin itself is an absolutely super party and I strongly believe in Sinn Féin's politics. The councillors in Sinn Féin I believe are the best councillors out there. Mary Lou I have the height of respect for.'

His claims at the time about the actions of the 'small element' who had caused him to leave the party were vague. According to TheJournal.ie:

[. . .] Dowdall said that he had heard comments from people saying they heard that Sinn Féin didn't want him and that they wanted another candidate.

He also said family members and some members of other political parties had told him they had heard negative things about him from others in social situations.

He thought that the rumours would end after the elections, but said that they didn't.

He said that between these stories he was hearing, and the 'trying to get back and forth to get to hospitals and rear a young family and run a company', he thought 'what is the point?'.

He later claimed that when he was ill, Sinn Fein staff called three or four times a day ordering him to return to work or give up the council seat, and that he had been barred from visiting certain areas of his constituency as it would upset other members of the party.

By October, Dowdall was back in Sinn Féin. All had been forgiven, it seemed. Dowdall told TheJournal.ie that he was 'delighted' to be back in the fold and that McDonald had been a 'total support'.

One associate of Dowdall told me that the sequence of events – quitting the party, then coming back – was par for the course.

'That was Jonathan – he was impulsive and paranoid. He'd make rash decisions based on nothing.'

One councillor from the time told me when Dowdall appeared back in the fold, he told his fellow councillors that McDonald had visited his home to ask him to stay. He had bragged that McDonald had appeared at his family door in the evening in her pyjamas.

'Now remember, Jonathan said this, so it doesn't mean it's true,' the councillor told me. 'He lied about everything. We knew he was dodgy.' McDonald has denied visiting Dowdall to convince him to stay in the party.

The councillor adds that locals including cumann leader Peter Lynch (a brother of former IRA prisoner and MLA Sean Lynch), Janice Boylan and Séamas McGrattan all made it very clear to their colleagues that Dowdall should not be in Sinn Fein before he was elected to the council. There was concern about his links to the Hutch crime family, and a suspicion that he had been the perpetrator of a gun attack on the home of his uncle.

'Janice and Dowdall didn't speak,' the councillor told me. 'Everyone knew how she felt. They could barely be in the same room together running for election, certainly not at each other's fundraisers or anything.'

Another thing a number of knowledgeable people told me about Jonathan Dowdall is that he had a cocaine problem. His tendency to paranoia and rash decision-making were seen as linked to his use of cocaine. When he wasn't using, his personality was very different, people told me.

Shortly after resigning from and then rejoining Sinn Féin in 2014, Dowdall advertised a BMW motorcycle on the website DoneDeal. A man called Alexander Hurley agreed to buy the motorcycle. In January 2015, while still a Sinn Féin councillor in Mary Lou McDonald's neighbourhood, Dowdall lured Hurley to his home.

What happened next was recorded on a mobile phone. The footage showed Jonathan Dowdall, in a balaclava, holding a tea towel to Hurley's face and pouring water over his head, while boasting that he was a member of the IRA. His father, Patrick Dowdall, could be heard threatening to rip off Hurley's fingers with pliers.

After being tortured, Hurley was abandoned in a remote part of Dublin. Having been threatened, he didn't tell his family what had happened, and lived in fear until gardaí approached him a year later.

By 13 February 2015, weeks after he had carried out the torture, Dowdall resigned again. This time he quit the council entirely, and he gave the seat back to Sinn Féin to fill in his place.

In a statement, Sinn Féin group leader Séamas McGrattan said:

> We wish Jonathan the best in the future and his contribution to the Dublin Sinn Féin council team will be greatly missed.
>
> I would like to acknowledge his commitment to the party and I am sorry to lose such a valuable member of the group.
>
> I enjoyed working with Jonathan and I would like to offer him a sincere thanks on behalf of all the team. I hope Jonathan will remain involved with Sinn Féin in the North Inner City.

The good feeling didn't last long. By June, Dowdall was back in the media claiming he'd quit the party because of bullying: 'There were numerous attacks on myself from a certain element within Sinn Fein, and there were attacks on my team members. [. . .] I could no longer stand over and watch certain attacks from certain elements within the party [. . .].'

Dowdall's associate told me: 'That was all complete bullshit. Jonathan was from around here, he ran with the Hutches, he wasn't going to be bullied or kept out of any part of this area. He was no wilting flower.'

On 5 February 2016, David Byrne, an associate of the Kinahan crime cartel, was shot by armed men who stormed Dublin's Regency Hotel at a boxing weigh-in. The intended victim was Daniel Kinahan, the head of the cartel, who fled to Dubai in the aftermath. The attack was understood to be a retaliation for the murder of 34-year-old Gary Hutch, son of Patsy Hutch and nephew of Gerry Hutch, in 2015. The feud that ensued between the two families would leave sixteen people dead.

In March 2016, as part of their investigation into the gangland feud, gardaí searched Dowdall's home. A day after news of the search emerged publicly, Dowdall called the RTÉ Radio call-in show *Liveline*. He said his home had been raided by armed officers, and that the Garda sub-aqua team had searched a pond on his property where Dowdall kept koi. Dowdall's fifteen minutes on the air were rambling and bizarre. At one point he spoke about the care taken by the gardaí to protect the exotic fish. Dowdall was at pains to deny he had any connection to criminality. He had no criminal record apart from a twenty-year-old breach of the peace. 'I do know the Hutch family, some I'm very proud to know and some I don't know,' he said. 'I'm friends with Patsy since I was a child.' He chastized the media for how they treated Sinn Féin, adding: 'I was friends with Mary Lou for years.'

During the raid, a USB pen with the footage of the torture on it was found. The news was shocking, but many in the inner city weren't shocked. One person who spoke to me claims Jonathan Dowdall showed him and others the video before he was arrested. 'That's the kind of person he was, having people up to the house and showing them the video. We told him to delete it, he'd get caught. He was a fucking idiot. The public didn't know but loads around here knew, we were in shock. He thought it was funny because your man pissed his pants and all that.'

Dowdall and his father were arrested. They both pleaded guilty to falsely imprisoning and threatening to kill Hurley. In June 2017, Jonathan Dowdall – who had been described by Mary Lou McDonald less than three years earlier as 'a very popular and respected member of his community' – was jailed for twelve years.

In April 2021, after a lengthy investigation, three men – Jason Bonney, Paul Murphy and Patrick Dowdall, the father of Jonathan Dowdall – were charged in the Special Criminal Court with having knowledge of a criminal organization and helping the Hutch crime gang to commit the murder of David Byrne at the Regency Hotel. A week later, Jonathan Dowdall was charged with murder. And in September 2021, Gerry Hutch was extradited from Spain, following a filmed arrest by Spanish police, and charged with murder.

The following autumn, Jonathan Dowdall pleaded guilty to a lesser charge of facilitating the murder of David Byrne by booking a room in the Regency Hotel for the use of the killers. And then it was announced that Jonathan Dowdall would give evidence for the state in the trial of Gerry Hutch, Jason Bonney and Paul Murphy. The murder charge against the former Sinn Féin councillor was dropped.

At trial, Dowdall testified that Gerry Hutch had collected key cards for a room in the hotel the evening before the attack. He also claimed that, a few days after the attack, Hutch had confessed to him that he had been one of the gunmen.

The gardaí bugged a car used by Hutch and Dowdall for a trip to Northern Ireland – for the purpose, according to Dowdall, of getting dissident republicans to intervene as peacekeepers in the Hutch–Kinahan feud. Gardaí were aware of four previous trips Dowdall had made to see republicans in Northern Ireland and Donegal: twice before the Regency attack and twice after it. Gerry Hutch was with him on two of those trips – once before the Regency attack and once afterwards. It was by no means clear that the sole purpose of the trips was peacekeeping.

The true extent of Dowdall's involvement or connections with dissident republicans and the remnants of the Provisional IRA remains unclear. At the trial, it emerged that Dowdall had made fourteen visits to Pearse McAuley in prison between February 2015 and January 2016, according to prison visitor logs. Dowdall, who had told the court he'd visited McAuley two or three times, had been caught in another lie.

McAuley was a member of the Provisional IRA when he took part in the killing of Det. Garda Jerry McCabe in 1996. He was released from prison in 2009, then returned after repeatedly stabbing his estranged wife, Pauline Tully, in the home where she lived with their children. Tully is now a Sinn Féin TD.

It appeared that McAuley helped put Dowdall in contact with the republicans he visited in the North before and after the Regency attack.

The tapes of the conversations between Hutch and Dowdall on their trip north on 7 March – a month after the Regency attack – were at the heart of the prosecution case against Hutch, and became the biggest talking point of the trial.

At one point, Dowdall criticized McDonald for not attending the funeral of Edward Hutch, Gerry's brother, after he was murdered.

Dowdall said: 'But ya's were good enough to use, Gerard, for votes, ya's were good enough to use for money.'

The suggestion was clear: that McDonald had been happy to accept money and political support from the Hutches. But Dowdall withdrew the claim under cross-examination. 'I made a comment about Mary Lou [McDonald] which was very unfair on a personal level.'

He added: 'What I done is being used to drag down a political party. I think that's very unfair.'

Dowdall was a terrible witness. He admitted he had lied to the Special Criminal Court in his trial for the false imprisonment of Alexander Hurley. When he was called on to explain the lies he'd told on *Liveline*, he said his life was 'upside down' at that time, that he was taking medication, that he 'wasn't thinking' and that he should never have gone on the programme.

It was clear that nothing Dowdall said could be taken at face value. McDonald would have clear grounds for dismissing his insinuations about her in the bugged conversation with Hutch. But as this kidnapper, torturer, accessory to murder and chronic liar dominated the news agenda during the days of his testimony, it was impossible for Sinn Féin and its leader to hide from the fact that Dowdall had been a councillor in McDonald's home ward, and that upon both of his resignations he had left with the praise of the party ringing in his ears.

While the trial was going on, another headache cropped up for McDonald and the Cabra cumann.

On 6 December 2022, councillor Janice Boylan posted a cryptic message to her Facebook page claiming she was preparing to make an announcement to reveal her 'experience, facts and lived truths'.

Boylan said if she had advice for anyone it would be to 'know your worth, stay in circles that respect and support you, don't stay anywhere you don't feel supported or valued'. She added: 'Remember this . . . If you make it to the top, don't draw the ladder up once you've done so build steps to make it easier for others to follow.'

She said she sometimes had a lot to say but felt the need to 'go quiet' until she found the 'right words'. And she seemed to be building up to an announcement: 'Finding the right words doesn't only mean thinking about what you want to say but figuring out how you'll say it, what you'll say and what you won't say too.'

Boylan said someone had told her a long time ago to 'play the long grass game . . . That has stuck with me to this day. I'm still not fully ready to speak my truths but they are coming, there will be a lot of changes too.'

The post was screenshotted and quickly made its way around WhatsApp until it reached the media. Boylan refused to take any calls. One councillor told me at the time: 'She's in a very bad way and calling it a day. She told us during the week.'

On 15 December, McDonald's close ally announced that she was quitting Sinn Féin.

Her letter, sent to Sinn Féin councillors, said that she had been 'humiliated numerous times', adding: 'I can not stay where I am not supported, valued or even really respected.'

Boylan said her decision was 'based on [. . .] numerous times I have been humiliated and numerous times the party has failed to support me therefore made my role as a councillor harder than it ever needed to be.'

It emerged that Boylan, who was once considered to be the natural choice as the second Dáil candidate in McDonald's Dublin Central constituency – where the party would be confident of taking a second seat at the next election – had been turned down for that. However, Boylan said she had 'accepted last year that this wasn't likely going to be me' and that it wasn't the reason she was quitting.

Almost immediately, Sinn Féin was claiming that Boylan was still in the fold and that, her resignation statement notwithstanding, 'At no point did she resign from the party.'

There were rumours that Boylan had been offered a Seanad seat in return for staying put. Sinn Féin denied this too.

Days after the resignation story broke, McDonald tweeted a photo of herself and Boylan out for a walk, in a blatant attempt to convince the public that everything had been resolved in the constituency.

Days later, Boylan, speaking through the Sinn Féin press office, said: 'I am very proud to serve as a Sinn Féin Dublin City councillor and I am focused entirely on delivering for workers and families in the north inner city as part of the Sinn Féin team in Dublin Central.'

After a trial that ran fifty-two days, and a period of nearly three months during which the judges of the Special Criminal Court considered their verdict, Jason Bonney and Paul Murphy were convicted, but Gerry Hutch was found not guilty of murder. In its 140-page judgement, the Special Criminal Court was scathing about Jonathan Dowdall and his evidence.

For observers of Sinn Féin, the main question thrown up by the trial was: how on earth did Dowdall become a candidate for the party, right under the watchful eye of Mary Lou McDonald?

Before the council elections in 2014, Sinn Féin officials Brian Keane and Stephen McCormick quizzed Dowdall about the gun attack on Dowdall's uncle's home in Raheny, north Dublin, on 31 March 2011. No one was ever charged for the offence.

On the car journey Dowdall took with Gerry Hutch on 7 March 2016, Dowdall was recorded speaking about the inquiries the party made into the 2011 shooting incident at his uncle's house. Dowdall said that Brian Keane, the party's director of elections in Dublin, was 'after ringing me non-stop, he arrived at my gaff three times'. During the meetings, Dowdall told Hutch, 'Brian Keane is doing all the talking.' According to Dowdall, Keane said: 'ya riddled your uncle's house', and 'this is my job to ask this in case it comes out in the media'.

Sinn Féin put out a statement claiming that it was Dowdall who brought the incident to their attention:

> The party's director of elections in Dublin met with all candidates on a regular basis. At one of these meetings with Jonathan Dowdall, Jonathan Dowdall raised an incident at his uncle's house in case it became an issue in the campaign.
>
> Jonathan Dowdall said that he did not know who was involved. There was no suggestion that Jonathan Dowdall was involved in any form of criminality at this stage.

The vetting of Jonathan Dowdall was not restricted to the meetings between Dowdall and Brian Keane.

An inner-city IRA veteran told me that at some point

between Dowdall's entry to the party and his selection as a council candidate, he got a call from a member of the Sinn Féin Ard Comhairle who had a bad feeling about Dowdall. The Ard Comhairle member asked the IRA veteran to 'check him out'.

'He was a wee bit apprehensive about him, but I'd never heard of Dowdall so I called a pal I know from the local boxing club. Literally the first person I called, he couldn't believe Sinn Féin were even considering him,' the inner-city IRA veteran told me.

The IRA veteran met Dowdall a week before the selection of candidates for the council election. 'He was a bit of a Walter Mitty character. He was hyper and never stopped talking. He seemed very impulsive and distracted.

'I sent word back to someone on the Ard Comhairle that this was not someone they wanted. That he was a known associate of Patsy Hutch and generally capable of anything. They were told and they did know.'

Following the verdict, McDonald put out a statement:

In relation to false and deeply offensive comments made about me during the course of this trial, I want to set out the facts.

I have never met Gerard Hutch. I have never received money or electoral support from Gerard Hutch. The record shows that I have stood resolutely on the side of the community in the fight against criminal gangs, drug dealers and antisocial elements, and I will continue to do so [. . .]

Jonathan Dowdall should never have been a member of Sinn Féin. Had I known what he would become involved in he would not have been a party member for one minute, never mind running for public office – I would not tolerate that [. . .]

McDonald later told RTÉ's *Six One News* that if she had known what Dowdall would go on to do, Dowdall would not have been 'next, nigh or near us'.

By sticking firmly to narrow formulations relating to things Dowdall did after leaving Sinn Féin, McDonald avoided the issue of what she and the party might have done differently with the information they had in 2014. McDonald's discomfort over the Dowdall connection had also been evident in November 2022, shortly before the Regency trial began, when she claimed that Dowdall's €1,000 donation to her in 2011 had in fact been a donation 'to the Dublin Central constituency'. McDonald was eventually forced to concede that the donation had been made to her personally, as her declaration from the time had made clear. Her attempt to distance herself from the donation was an unforced error that only drew more attention to it.

One Cabra cumann member told me: 'Jonathan was very good at the game. He'd have you eating out of his hand.' The cumann member was also scathing about McDonald, saying that she 'seriously lacks judgement. She's not learned from this entire shambles at all. She surrounds herself with people who are subpar, in a constituency like this [. . .] that's a foolish game. Look at Gerry Adams – he had serious heads around him. Mary Lou hasn't a clue.'

As an overall judgement on McDonald, it seems excessively harsh. But given the concerns about Dowdall that members of the party had, and actively investigated, before his candidacy for Dublin City Council, it is hard not to agree with the Cabra cumann member's view that the Dowdall affair exposed a significant weakness in the party leader's judgement.

If the Dowdall affair had been invented for a TV series or a novel, it would probably have seemed too on the nose. Sinn Féin had spent decades gradually taking control of the republican movement, and the gunmen – some of whom had been involved in kidnapping, torture, murder – were receding into history. Then, the country watched a bizarre and riveting trial centred on a recent party councillor, in the party leader's own ward, who had been involved in kidnapping, torture and murder.

It remains to be seen how damaging the Dowdall affair will be for Sinn Féin. Opinion polling suggests it has not significantly affected the party's popularity. It may be that the whiff of sulphur that continues to hang around Sinn Féin has been completely priced in by the electorate. Sinn Féin's mixture of nationalism and left-ish economic policy is perfectly suited to the political dynamics of the moment, North and South. And the party is lucky in its main opponents: the DUP in the North, which appears out of touch with the realities of Brexit and the changing electorate, and the civil war parties in the South, which have, through chronic neglect, allowed a housing crisis to reach catastrophic proportions.

In the North, the structures of power-sharing – which allow a single party to effectively hand the devolved powers back to Westminster if it doesn't feel like sharing them – mean that Sinn Féin's path to the First Minister's office remains uncertain at the time of writing. And even if and when Michelle O'Neill takes office, Sinn Féin will have to share power with unionists. Equally, while Brexit sparked a surge of interest in the possibility of Irish unity, opinion polling suggests that the people of Northern Ireland are nowhere near ready to vote for it. Sinn Féin, understanding this, will continue to act as though unity is a pressing necessity, while knowing that a unity campaign is, at best, a medium-term priority.

In the South, the party's path to real power is clearer than in the North – but here, too, uncertainties and complications abound. If Sinn Féin's support holds steady, the party will emerge as the clear winner of the next general election, but it will need to form a coalition. A left coalition, on the current numbers, looks unlikely; and an alliance with Fine Gael is all but unthinkable. That leaves Fianna Fáil. The current Fianna Fáil leader, Micheál Martin, ruled out going into government with Sinn Féin in 2020. It remains to be seen whether or not Martin will lead Fianna Fáil into the next election, and whether or not he or his successor will change the party's stance on Sinn Féin.

If Mary Lou McDonald emerges as the next Taoiseach, it will be arguably the crowning achievement of the party's long game. Sinn Féin people will, of course, insist that unity is the ultimate objective, as it has always been. But there is reason to doubt that, if and when the people of Ireland eventually vote for unity, they will have been led to that position by Sinn Féin. In any event, long before unity becomes a live political question, Sinn Féin, a party with its roots in militant republicanism in Northern Ireland, will need to face the challenge of housing the people of the twenty-six-county Republic.

Source Notes

Some of the sources that have informed this book are referred to in the text. Here, I credit the other human and written sources that I drew upon.

Prologue

Regarding the killing of Charles Love and its aftermath, I interviewed IRA members, relatives of Bloody Sunday victims, and people who were present in the home of Mitchel McLaughlin after the killing.

Details of the life of Charles Love are from Joe Duffy and Freya McClements, *Children of the Troubles* (Hachette, 2019), and *An Phoblacht*. For the death of Charles Love, I drew upon newspaper reports in the *Belfast News Letter* and by Mary Holland in the *Irish Times*.

Details of the aftermath of Love's killing are from reports by AP News and the *Irish Times*. Eamonn McCann's article about the meaning of the tragedy was published in *Hot Press*.

Regarding the killing of Patsy Gillespie and its aftermath, I interviewed senior IRA operatives in Derry and Belfast, and drew on reports in the *Irish Times*, the *Irish News*, Sky News and the 'Peace by Piece' podcast.

1. 'The IRA will decide'

Regarding Albert, Dolours and Marian Price, I drew upon, as well as an interview with an IRA comrade of Dolours Price: Patrick Radden Keefe, *Say Nothing: A True Story of Murder and Memory in Northern Ireland* (William Collins, 2018), and the documentary film *I, Dolours,* directed by Maurice Sweeney.

For my account of the hunger strike and subsequent elections, I interviewed IRA men in Belfast and Derry, including a former cellmate of Bobby Sands and negotiator for the prisoners, as well as non-affiliated campaigners for Sands and a former MLA.

This chapter was also informed by Brian Feeney, *Sinn Féin: A Hundred Turbulent Years* (O'Brien Press, 2002); Patrick Radden Keefe, *Say Nothing*; Gerry Kelly, *Playing My Part* (G&M Publications, 2019); Ed Moloney, *A Secret History of the IRA* (Allen Lane, 2002); Peter Taylor, *Provos: The IRA and Sinn Fein* (Bloomsbury, 1997); David Beresford, *Ten Men Dead* (Grafton, 1987); and Gerry Adams, *Hope and History: Making Peace in Ireland* (Brandon, 2003). I also drew upon reporting from the *Irish Times*, the *New York Times* and *An Phoblacht*, as well as the CAIN archive.

2. The Ends of Violence and the Purposes of Peace

Close confidants of Martin McGuinness, both inside and outside the IRA, provided background and quotes for the profile of McGuinness. I also interviewed a member of the British security services, a member of the Hegarty family, journalist Nell McCafferty and former RUC assistant chief constable Peter Sheridan.

Interviews with former IRA members, Sinn Féin staffers and one relative of Gerry Adams informed the profile of the former Sinn Féin president.

Details on the back channel between the IRA and the British were provided by people in Derry with knowledge of the operation.

Regarding the peace process, I interviewed Sinn Féin staff and negotiators from the period, senior ministers in the Irish government and officials from the Irish Department of Foreign Affairs, as well as representatives from the other Northern Ireland political parties. I also made use of news reports from the BBC, the *Guardian*, *The Times*, the *Evening Standard* and *An Phoblacht*, and the CAIN archive.

A number of books informed my account: Ed Moloney, *A Secret History of the IRA*; Ed Moloney, *Voices from the Grave: Two Men's War in Ireland* (Faber and Faber, 2010); Patrick Radden Keefe, *Say Nothing*; Peter Taylor, *Operation Chiffon: The Secret Story of MI5 and MI6 and the Road to Peace in Ireland* (Bloomsbury, 2023); Peter Taylor, *Loyalists: War and Peace in Northern Ireland* (Bloomsbury, 2000); Gerry Adams, *Hope and History*; Seán Mac Stíofáin, *Memoirs of a Revolutionary* (Gordon & Cremonesi, 1975); and Jonathan Powell, *Great Hatred, Little Room: Making Peace in Northern Ireland* (Vintage, 2009).

3. Sink or Swim

Interviews with a number of former and current Sinn Féin MLAs, MPs and councillors informed my account of the inner workings of Sinn Féin in Stormont. Regarding the party's operation in Leinster House, I interviewed a number of Sinn Féin staff and senior leadership figures from the time. I am grateful to the journalist Brian Rowan and to a former member of the PSNI for background for the Stormontgate allegations.

For my account of the welfare reform controversy, I drew upon interviews with MLAs, MPs and staff from the time.

I also drew upon Jude Collins, *Martin McGuinness: The Man I Knew* (Mercier Press, 2018), and on news reports from the BBC, the *Irish Times*, *The Detail*, TheJournal.ie, the *Belfast Telegraph*, *An Phoblacht*, the *Irish Independent*, the *Guardian*, the *Irish Examiner* and the *News Letter*.

4. Wrapping It Up

Interviews for this chapter were conducted with a number of people who were present for the meetings held across the country to discuss decommissioning, as well as those in the IRA tasked with giving the briefings. My account of the decommissioning process is also indebted to Brian Rowan, to security service personnel and to IRA members who left the movement after decommissioning.

Stories about Gerry Kelly are from a former comrade of Kelly's in the Belfast Brigade of the IRA. Stories about Anderson are from a close friend of Adams's.

I drew upon Gerry Kelly, *Playing My Part*; Evelyn Brady, *In the Footsteps of Anne: Stories of Women Republican Ex-Prisoners* (Shanway, 2011); Brian Rowan, *The Armed Peace: Life and Death after the Ceasefires* (Mainstream, 2004); Ed Moloney, *A Secret History of the IRA*; and Jonathan Powell, *Great Hatred, Little Room*. The chapter is also informed by news reports from the BBC, the *Irish Times*, *An Phoblacht*, the *Irish Independent*, the *Guardian*, the *Sydney Morning Herald* and Danny Morrison's article about Kieran Nugent on dannymorrison.com, as well as the CAIN archive and the documentary *Martina Anderson: Mná an IRA*, directed by Martina Durac.

5. *Crime and Punishment*

Regarding domestic violence in republican communities, I interviewed Derry Sinn Féin and IRA members from the 1970s and '80s.

For my account of the story of Áine Adams, I interviewed Sinn Féin MLAs, MPs and staff who were present at the time.

I drew upon Malachi O'Doherty, *Gerry Adams: An Unauthorised Life* (Faber & Faber, 2017), and Joan McKiernan and Monica McWilliams, 'The Impact of Political Conflict on Domestic Violence in Northern Ireland', in *Gender Relations in Public and Private: New Research Perspectives*, ed. Lydia Morris and E. Stina Lyon (Macmillan, 1996); on news reports from the *New York Times*, the BBC, the *Irish Independent*, the *Irish Times*, the *Sunday Tribune*, the *Belfast Telegraph*, *An Phoblacht* and the *Guardian*; and from Ed Moloney's blog 'The Broken Elbow' and Joe Austin's interview with Richard McAuley on the Scéalta podcast

6. *The Disappeared and the Anointed*

For my account of Gerry Adams's thinking around the choosing of Mary Lou McDonald as his successor, I drew upon interviews with senior Sinn Féin staff.

For the section on the Disappeared, I interviewed senior Sinn Féin staff, including some who had been in the IRA, and a former IRA man in Donegal who was quizzed by Padraic Wilson.

For the section on Mary Lou McDonald, I talked to staff from her past election campaigns and to former Leinster House staff. Fianna Fáil ministers and members offered information on McDonald's stint as a member of their party.

Regarding Robert McCartney's murder, I drew on interviews with a staffer for Martin McGuinness and a former IRA member who worked in Stormont.

Books that informed this chapter are Patrick Radden Keefe, *Say Nothing*; Shane Ross, *Mary Lou McDonald: A Republican Riddle* (Atlantic, 2022); and Deaglán de Bréadún, *Power Play: The Rise of Modern Sinn Féin* (Merrion Press, 2015). I also drew upon news reports from the BBC, the *Belfast Telegraph*, the *Irish Independent*, TheJournal.ie, the *Guardian* and the *Irish Times*, and on the CAIN archive.

7. Shaking Hands with the Queen

For the account of Sinn Féin's handling of the two visits of Queen Elizabeth II, I interviewed a number of senior staff in Stormont and a Buckingham Palace official from the time. I am grateful to Martin McAleese and Áras An Uachtaráin for help with fact-checking.

The section on Co-operation Ireland was informed by interviews with allies of Martin McGuinness and members of the board of the organization.

Books consulted for this chapter include: Mary McAleese, *Here's the Story: A Memoir* (Sandycove, 2020), Patrick Radden Keefe, *Say Nothing*; Shane Ross, *Mary Lou McDonald*; and Deaglán de Bréadún, *Power Play*. I drew upon news reports in the *Independent*, the *Guardian*, *The Nationalist*, the *Daily Mail*, *Time*, the BBC, the *Irish Times* and the *Belfast Telegraph*.

8. The New Leaders

The section about Mary Lou McDonald's rise is based on interviews with people who were members of the Cabra cumann of Sinn Féin at the time and with a current TD. The section about Michelle O'Neill is informed by interviews with staff in Stormont and MLAs. The section on the Renewable Heat Incentive draws on interviews with MLAs.

I drew upon Shane Ross, *Mary Lou McDonald*, and Sam McBride, *Burned: The Inside Story of the 'Cash-for-Ash' Scandal and Northern Ireland's Secretive New Elite* (Merrion Press, 2019); and on news reports from the *Irish Examiner*, the BBC, the *Daily Mail*, the *Irish Times*, the *Belfast Telegraph*, the *Pink News*, the *Irish Independent*, the *Guardian*, the *Irish News*, *Dublin Live*, *An Phoblacht* and RTÉ.

9. The Trials of Mairia Cahill

For my account of Sinn Féin's response to the allegations of Mairia Cahill, I interviewed former MLAs, staff and other republicans with knowledge of Sinn Féin at the time. I did original reporting of Cahill's reaction to her meeting with Mary Lou McDonald while working for the Press Association.

Cahill's allegations were extensively covered by Suzanne Breen in the *Sunday Tribune* and in BBC *Spotlight*'s programme, *A Woman Alone with the IRA*. This chapter also draws on news reports from the *Irish Times*, the *Irish Independent*, the *Guardian* and the *Irish News*.

10. The Abortion Puzzle

This chapter is informed by interviews with a number of pro-choice activists in Northern Ireland as well as human rights solicitors, officials and a close confidant of Sarah Ewart. My special thanks to Alliance For Choice Derry for their assistance.

A friend of Martin McGuinness detailed his feelings on the abortion issue, and I spoke to MLAs from the time about the party's operations and position changes.

I made use of news reporting from the BBC, the *Irish Independent*, the *Irish Times*, TheJournal.ie, the *Guardian*, the *Belfast Telegraph* and the *News Letter*.

11. 'When you're out, you're out'

This chapter is based largely on interviews with former and current staff and representatives of Sinn Féin in Stormont and Leinster House, and with current and former councillors and senators. Party members in Derry were consulted about the story of Dodie McGuinness.

The chapter also draws upon news reporting from *An Phoblacht*, the *Guardian*, *The Advertiser*, the BBC, the *Irish Examiner*, the *Irish Times*, TheJournal.ie, the *Connacht Tribune*, the *Belfast Telegraph* and the *Irish Independent*.

12. Dark Days in Derry

For this chapter I interviewed current Sinn Féin councillors, former members of the Comhairle Ceantair and community workers in Derry, as well as sitting TDs. I also spoke to a party figure who was close to Martina Anderson around the time she stepped down as an MLA.

I made use of news reporting from: the *Irish Examiner*, the *News Letter*, *The Times*, the *Derry Journal*, the *Belfast Telegraph*, the *Guardian*, the *Irish Independent*, the *Donegal News*, *An Phoblacht* and RTÉ.

13. Structure and Chaos

For my account of the 'City of Equals on an Island of Equals' conference, I interviewed senior Sinn Féin staff in Stormont, including McGuinness's speechwriter, and checked facts with Brian Rowan.

Former and current Sinn Féin representatives, including MLAs and MPs, provided information on party structure and operations. The Sinn Féin press office supplied a list of the most recent Ard Comhairle and national officer board memberships.

For my account of the fallout from the 2019 local elections, I interviewed party staff, TDs, councillors and MLAs.

The account of the meeting between the widow and her husband's killer draws on the recollections of two former IRA volunteers and a former member of the security services.

I drew upon news reporting from the *Belfast Telegraph* and the *Irish Examiner*.

14. 'Something is going on'

The section on candidate selection for the 2020 election draws upon interviews with Sinn Féin staff, Eoin Ó Broin and Violet-Anne Wynne. The section on Brexit was informed by an interview with Stephen McGlade. My account of Bobby Storey's funeral and its fallout is informed by interviews with current staff, members of Sinn Féin and elected representatives who were present at the funeral. For the section on the party's preparations for the future, I spoke to party staff and TDs.

The chapter draws upon news reports in the *Irish News*, the *Irish Examiner*, the *Belfast Telegraph*, the *Irish Times*, the *Extra*, the *Daily Mail* and the *Guardian*.

15. Next, Nigh, Near

For my account of Jonathan Dowdall's career in Sinn Féin, I drew upon interviews with members of the Sinn Féin Cabra cumann and residents of the inner city. I also interviewed two members of Jonathan Dowdall's campaign team, a former IRA volunteer in Dublin and a member of An Garda Síochána. For my account of Janice Boylan's abortive resignation from Sinn Féin, I spoke to members of the Cabra cumann and to a close associate of Janice Boylan.

The chapter is also informed by news reports from TheJournal.ie, the *Irish Independent*, the *Irish Mirror*, the *Irish Times* and the *Belfast Telegraph*.

Acknowledgements

This book would not have been possible without the love and support of my friends and family. It was written through some of the hardest times in my life, and I am sure it would not have been completed without their arms around me.

I would like to thank Peter Coyle, for all the love and support he gave me in the early days of this book and in my career. I won't forget it.

Thanks to Paul Hosford and Richard Chambers, who offered listening ears and critical eyes and talked me down off many metaphorical ledges.

To Cate McCurry, who boosted my confidence at every turn.

To Brianna Parkins, who held my hand and made me laugh as we both attempted to write our books and have a hot girl summer, autumn, winter and spring.

To Maria Lyttle and Regan Young, who have always been my biggest supporters and my true soulmates, who offered their homes in Belfast, their shoulders to cry on and baby Connlá for cuddles.

To the friend who took me to London and shouted at airport staff when we missed our flight home.

I would especially like to thank Brian Rowan for his sage advice, and Susan McKay for being a mentor. And thanks to David Young, who brought me home and has looked out for me ever since.

A thank you to the staff in the Linen Hall Library, and to the people of Ennistymon and Lahinch, who offered the shelter and the solace needed to write this book.

ACKNOWLEDGEMENTS

To Michael McLoughlin at Penguin for taking a risk on a mad Derry woman, and to Brendan Barrington for his editing, his support and his patience at my insane voice notes. If he hadn't been bald before this book, he'd have been bald after.

To everyone who gave an interview for this book, many of whom were wary and afraid, risked a lot and trusted me with their stories: thank you. Most such people cannot be named, but I want them to know that I am eternally grateful.

Finally, to the people of Derry, thank you for everything, from your proudest daughter.

Index